Wives, Widows, and Concubines

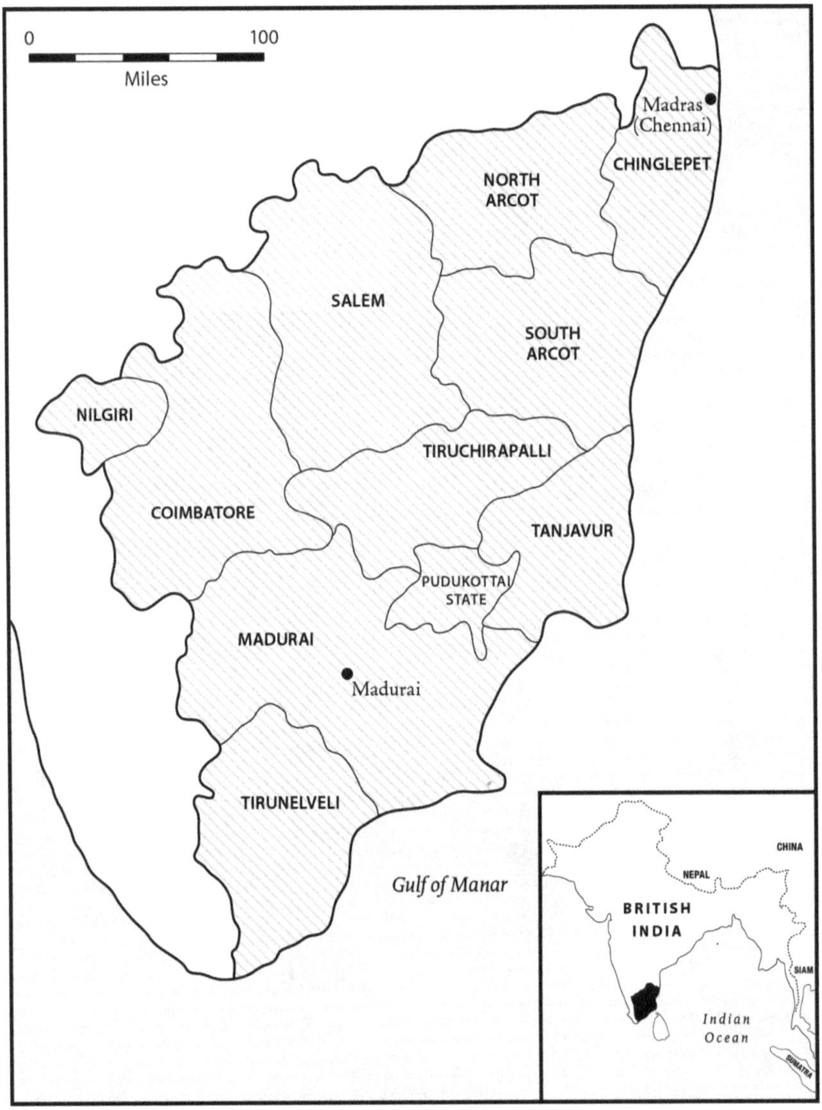

Tamil Districts of the Madras Presidency, 1900

Contemporary Indian Studies

Published in association with the American Institute of Indian Studies

Susan S. Wadley, Chair, Publications Committee/general editor

AIIS Publications Committee/series advisory board
Susan S. Wadley
John Echeverri-Gent
Brian Hatcher
David Lelyveld
Priti Ramamurthy
Martha Selby

Books in this series are recipients of the
Edward Cameron Dimock, Jr. Prize in the Indian Humanities
and the
Joseph W. Elder Prize in the Indian Social Sciences
awarded by the American Institute of Indian Studies and are published with the Institute's generous support.

A list of titles in this series appears at the back of the book.

Wives, Widows, and Concubines

The Conjugal Family Ideal in Colonial India

Mytheli Sreenivas

Indiana University Press
Bloomington and Indianapolis

This book is a publication of

Indiana University Press
601 North Morton Street
Bloomington, IN 47404-3797 USA

http://iupress.indiana.edu

Telephone orders 800-842-6796
Fax orders 812-855-7931
Orders by e-mail iuporder@indiana.edu

The paper used in this publication meets the minimum requirements of American National Standard for Information Sciences—Permanence of Paper for Printed Library Materials, ANSI Z39.48-1984.

Manufactured in the United States of America

Library of Congress Cataloging-in-Publication Data

Sreenivas, Mytheli.
Wives, widows, and concubines : the conjugal family ideal in colonial India / Mytheli Sreenivas.
p. cm. — (Contemporary Indian studies)
Includes bibliographical references and index.
ISBN-13: 978-0-253-35118-0 (cloth : alk. paper)
ISBN-13: 978-0-253-21972-5 (pbk. : alk. paper) 1. Family—India—Tamil Nadu.
2. Marriage—India—Tamil Nadu. 3. Kinship—India—Tamil Nadu.
4. Women—India—Tamil Nadu. I. Title.
HQ670.S64 2008
306.850954'82—dc22
2007042258

1 2 3 4 5 13 12 11 10 09 08

To my family, conjugal and joint, with love

Contents

Acknowledgments

This book has been written with the support of colleagues and friends, and it is my great privilege to thank them, at last. David Ludden and Sumathi Ramaswamy were generous intellectual mentors from the very outset of this project. Their questions always prompted me to think further, and their encouragement at critical stages of my initial research helped to make this book possible. I am deeply grateful.

During various stages of my writing, many scholars shared their comments and suggestions. Sanjam Ahluwalia, Indrani Chatterjee, Barbara Ramusack, and Claire Robertson offered immensely useful advice when the book was still in its planning stages, and their comments helped me to move forward. Alice Conklin, Donna Guy, Kate Haulman, Pranav Jani, Christine Keating, K. Molly O'Donnell, Wendy Smooth, and Mary Thomas have been insightful and encouraging readers. Special thanks to Donna for reading the entire manuscript, in record time, and encouraging me to think more broadly about its implications. Two anonymous reviewers for the Elder Prize Committee also offered valuable suggestions. I am especially grateful to David Lelyveld, whose confidence in this project inspired me to continue writing at a difficult time. His intellectual generosity has been invaluable.

I am thankful for good food, great fun, and perceptive critiques from fellow members of my writing group, Georgina Dodge, Jill Galvan, Christine Keating, and Rebecca Wanzo. Thanks especially to Rebecca for organizing the group and keeping us all on track. I also acknowledge fellow members of the Faculty of Color Caucus in the History Department at The Ohio State University for their commitments to our shared intellectual projects. My deep thanks also go to Judy Wu for helping to make Ohio State such a hospitable scholarly home.

Research for this book was funded by a U.S. Department of Education Fulbright-Hays DDRA Fellowship and a University of Connecticut Faculty Small Grant. The American Institute for Indian Studies, through its Joseph W. Elder Prize in the Indian Social Sciences, has provided support for the book's publication. I am especially grateful to Susan Wadley and the members of the Elder Prize Committee. I also acknowledge the financial assistance of the College of Humanities at The Ohio State University.

Librarians and archivists across three continents have made my research possible. I wish to acknowledge Mr. Sivakumar and Dr. M. Sundara Raj at the Tamil Nadu Archives and Mr. G. Sundar at the Roja Muthiah Research Library in Chennai. At the British Library, Dr. Antonia Moon has gone well beyond the call of duty in making possible my research on *zamindari* estates, and I am thankful for her assistance. The Interlibrary Loan staff at The Ohio State University has been instrumental in locating sources during the final stages of this project.

Several chapters are revised versions of the following articles: "Emotion, Identity, and the Female Subject: Tamil Women's Magazines in Colonial India," *Journal of Women's History* 14, no. 4 (Winter 2003): 59–82, and "Conjugality and Capital: Gender, Families, and Property under Colonial Law in India," *Journal of Asian Studies* 63, no. 4 (November 2004): 937–960. I acknowledge the publishers for allowing parts of these articles to appear here in modified form.

When putting together the final manuscript, I was fortunate to have the support of two wonderful research assistants, Arcenia Harmon and Kathryn Linder. It has also been a pleasure to work with the editorial staff at Indiana University Press, and special thanks are due to Rebecca Tolen and Laura MacLeod.

My research in India was made possible through the hospitality of friends, including Dr. Krishnamohan in Chennai and Mr. Ram Gupta and his family in New Delhi. I am also grateful to Kasturi for her invaluable assistance. My deep thanks go to Sharada and M. Ganeshan, who generously invited me into their home and their hearts. I would not have been able to write this book without you.

Writing a book about families has encouraged me to reflect on my own, which has expanded over the years I have been working on this project. Many thanks are due to Vandana and Mahendra Jani, whose generosity of spirit is always an inspiration. Thanks also to Dipti Prasad, fellow traveler over these many years. My deepest gratitude is for my parents, Venkatachala and Nagarathna Sreenivas. My parents were the ones who first encouraged me to ask questions for which there are no easy answers. For their nurturing of this spirit of intellectual inquiry, and for their constant encouragement and support, I am immensely grateful.

My partner, Pranav, has shared in the many journeys, both familial and scholarly, that have made this book possible. Thank you, in more ways than I can name. Meenakshi, who has accompanied this book from its early stages, and Savita, whose impending arrival hastened its conclusion, have been my greatest joy. In your bright eyes, I see the future.

Note on Transliteration

In transliterating Tamil words, I have generally followed the University of Madras Tamil Lexicon scheme. I make occasional exceptions for reasons of readability; for example, *Grihalakshmi* rather than *Kirakalakshmi*. When a Sanskrit equivalent may make the term accessible to a wider readership, I include it in parentheses, for instance, *tēcam* (Skt. *deṣam*). When authors offer their own transliteration of Tamil words, I retain them. I do not transliterate the names of persons or places. Unless otherwise noted, all translations from Tamil are mine.

For reasons of consistency and clarity, I have used the contemporary spellings of place names but include the colonial-era spelling at first mention, for example, Tirunelveli (Tinnevelly). However, following nineteenth- and twentieth-century usage, I retain the name Madras; the city is now called Chennai.

Tamil naming conventions differ from English, and many of the people who appear in the book do not have identifiable surnames. Therefore, although I include the entire name when first mentioned, I subsequently refer to individuals by the most identifiable part of their name.

Wives, Widows, and Concubines

INTRODUCTION

Situating Families

On 14 July 1934, one R.M.Al.Ct. Chidambaram Chettiar, a merchant owning considerable property who resided in the Madurai (Madura) district of Madras Presidency in southern India, contracted a marriage with one Rangammal. Chidambaram was a widower, having lost two previous wives, Nachiammai and Valliammai; the former had left her husband with one son, Alagu Chettiar. In seeking to marry for a third time, Chidambaram reported that he had first sought a wife from within his own caste community of Nattukottai Chettiars, or Nagarattars. However, when "the girl's parents demanded large sums of money" before agreeing to an engagement, he rejected this alliance and instead joined the Purohit Maruppu Sangam (anti-*purohit* association) in Madurai, which had been conducting weddings at relatively little expense in the absence of Hindu ritual officiants, or *purohits*. Four months later, under the auspices of the Sangam, he married Rangammal, a widow who identified herself as belonging to the Reddiar caste. In subsequent years, Rangammal gave birth to four children, two sons and two daughters.[1]

The family's substantial estate, governed according to the principles of colonial Hindu law, was owned jointly by Chidambaram and all his male patrilineal descendants: his adult son, Alagu; Rangammal's two minor sons, S. Chandran and S. Jayam; and Alagu's minor son, A. Chidambaram. But after Alagu's death in 1942, Chidambaram sought to partition the property into separate shares. Claiming three-fourths of the estate for himself and his two young sons, Chidambaram accorded the remaining one-fourth to his fatherless grandson, A. Chidambaram. However, the boy's mother, Deivanai Achi, contested this allowance, arguing that her son was entitled to one-half of the total estate. The legal basis for her claims was that Chidambaram's marriage to Rangammal was invalid, thus rendering Rangammal not a "wife" but a "concubine," which would disinherit her "illegitimate" sons from any portion of their father's property. Wending its way through the tortuous legal system, the dispute between Chidambaram and his daughter-in-law, Deivanai Achi, appeared before the Madras High Court in the early 1950s.

Abstracted from the personal undertakings of Chidambaram and his family into the universalizing language of the law, the High Court judgment in this case focused upon the legality of the wedding ceremony conducted by the Purohit Maruppu Sangam in 1934. Asserting that marriage was a *samskāra* (sacrament) followed by all Hindus regardless of caste, the judges acknowledged that the law could recognize modifications in sacramental form based upon the specific "custom or usage" of a particular community. They added, however, that "the essential requisite for recognition of such a custom is that it must be sufficiently ancient and definite and the members of the caste or sub-caste or family must recognise it as obligatory."[2] But in the case of the Purohit Maruppu Sangam, no custom could possibly be sufficiently "ancient," since the association had only been started in 1929; nor, given its iconoclastic and anti-caste aspirations, could the association's wedding ceremonies be considered obligatory for a specified population. Furthermore, the judges contended, the Purohit Maruppu Sangam did not represent a particular caste or sub-caste but instead was a group that married "persons of different sub-sects" of a caste. Such an association, grounded in the civil society of a colonial public sphere rather than in "immemorial" caste usage, found no authority within the framework of the law. On this basis, the Madras High Court ruled that Rangammal and Chidambaram were not legally married, that the former occupied the status of a "permanent concubine," and that S. Chandran and S. Jayam were "illegitimate." Nevertheless, the judges added that a father could choose to provide even his "illegitimate" sons with shares of joint property. On these grounds, the two young boys could each accept one-fourth of the family estate.[3]

We thus encounter a striking disjuncture between the state's unflinching insistence on ancient caste custom, on the one hand, and, on the other, the Purohit Maruppu Sangam's introduction of a novel wedding ceremony to unite an inter-caste couple. This book, in some sense, attempts to account for this disjuncture by investigating debates about the family as they proliferated in the Tamil region of India from the late nineteenth to the mid-twentieth century. Throughout this period, claims about the family—

its appropriate membership, its role in buttressing "culture" and "tradition," and the affective and property relations of its members—became critical to the formulation and contestation of Tamil social relations. The family thus emerged as an arena within which Tamil men and women could either maintain or challenge the status quo of caste, gender, and class hierarchies. Yet, at the same time, families were targets for state regulation and sites for the exercise of colonial authority. Within this context, reformers and activists called attention to intimate aspects of family life as a highly public ground from which to defend Tamil society from colonial intervention, as well as to develop novel claims about nation and national identity. Therefore, despite its absence from most Tamil historiography, I suggest that the family—conceptualized both as a set of lived social relations and as a normative ideal—was far from incidental to the development of Tamil politics and society during the colonial period.

This book's focus on the Tamil region refers specifically to the Tamil-speaking areas in the southeast of the subcontinent that constitute the contemporary province of Tamil Nadu in India. The colonial state governed this region as part of the Madras Presidency, a sprawling administrative unit encompassing much of peninsular India. Although Tamil-speaking populations were never isolated from other linguistic groups, the Tamil districts of the Presidency maintained a degree of cultural coherence—rooted both in language and political traditions—from precolonial centuries. The centralizing impetus of British rule helped to strengthen this coherence, and the city of Madras (Chennai) developed into a nodal point of Tamil politics, commerce, Western education, and culture during the nineteenth century. By the twentieth century, Madras also became home to a developing Dravidian movement, in which the Purohit Maruppu Sangam was involved. In explicit contradistinction to Indian nationalist politics, activists in the Dravidian movement envisioned a community and polity composed not of "Indians" but of speakers of Dravidian languages in southern India, especially Tamil.[4] Expanding the term "Dravidian" beyond its original linguistic connotations, they infused it with ethnic, cultural, and caste-based meanings. The movement played an important role in shaping Tamil national identity in the late colonial era and, alongside Indian nationalism, helped to develop the political language within which Tamil families were redefined. Chidambaram and Rangammal seem to have adopted this language, and their wedding in Madurai district likely exemplified Dravidian notions of Tamil identity, community, and politics.

The specific case of Chidambaram and Rangammal suggests several broader themes for investigation into the history of Tamil families.[5] First, there is the question of the state, which occupied a central place in the Madras High Court's treatment of the couple's wedding ceremony. In rendering its decision, the court sought to defend the state's position as the highest authority over marriage and "the Hindu family." The Purohit Maruppu Sangam, the judges argued, had usurped that position, since "an association of persons of different sub-sects [cannot] legislate themselves to lay down a procedure which results in a valid union between two spouses."[6] Marriage was deemed too important to remain outside the purview of state control, subject solely to the vagaries of individual decision, family sanction, or civil society. Instead, it provided an arena for a bureaucratic, centralized state to intervene in the intimate lives of its subjects. This relationship of family with the state—mediated in part by claims about "caste"—was distinct in both form and content from the ruling ideologies and practices that had characterized precolonial Tamil regimes.

There is the further question of the relationship between this regulatory state and the politics of the nation. Both during the colonial period and in the early postcolonial years, the relationship between the state and a nationalist imaginary remained fraught with tension. For example, Chidambaram and Rangammal's wedding in 1934 occurred at the height of the spread of Dravidian nationalism and its unique marriage reforms. Indian independence in 1947 did not resolve the concerns of the Dravidian movement, which continued to reject the authoritative claims of Indian nationalism even after the victory over colonial rule. These political tensions lay behind the substantial public outcry in response to the court's decision invalidating Chidambaram and Rangammal's marriage in 1954. Following the High Court's judgment, the Madras legislature and the Tamil press debated the necessity for legalizing all weddings that were "solemnized among Hindus without the performance of religious or customary rites."[7] The ruling Indian National Congress party viewed legislation primarily as a measure to legitimize previous wedding ceremonies and was opposed to sanctioning "a new form of marriage in addition to the forms prescribed by religion or custom."[8] By contrast, members of the Dravidian movement demanded legislation on explicitly nationalist grounds. Arguing that most "non-Brahman" Tamils now married without the presence either of Brahman priests or Sanskritic rituals, they asked that the law be made commensurate with the politics, and family practice, of the nation.[9] Linking the legal validation of such marriages to broader struggles against caste oppression, legislators from Dravidian political parties made the state's recognition of these wedding ceremonies a political—and not merely pragmatic—demand.

Significantly, these battles about nation, state, and ruling authority were fought over the grounds of property—and, in particular, over the relatively liquid forms of mercantile capital that Chidambaram could partition into separate shares. Having developed property relations that were distinct from those of landholding classes, merchants like Chidambaram, alongside professional elites, were important to twentieth-century struggles to rearticulate both property and the family around an idealized norm of conjugality.[10] Critical of—though never entirely rejecting—the joint family relations of an extended, multigenerational kin group, these propertied men fashioned a new logic of conjugality that gave greater priority to a husband's relationship to his wife and children. Although we cannot surmise Chidambaram's specific motivations, his rearrangement of family and property occurred along these lines. Separating his grandson's share of the family estate from his own and his young sons', Chidambaram created a family-property unit that de-linked the multigenerational patriline from the conjugal family.

Creating this conjugal family depended, in part, upon the successful rearticulation of women's status. In the case discussed here, the widow Rangammal had to be defined, in law and social practice, as Chidambaram's "wife" and not his "concubine." More generally, the state, in order to regulate its female subjects, categorized women according to their conjugal relationships; women's position as wives, widows, or concubines determined their legal status. However, in the process of delineating these conjugal categories, the legal system also produced them. For instance, when judging that Rangammal's wedding was invalid, the Madras High Court assigned specific meanings to both "wifehood" and "concubinage" by suggesting that the couple's own intentions were less important than ritual procedure. The public furor following the legal decision added new connotations to these terms. The Dravidian movement contended that the court's refusal to acknowledge Rangammal's wifehood symbolized a larger Brahmanical contempt for non-Brahman social practice. Indian nationalists suggested, by contrast, that the court's reference to concubinage represented a colonial holdover that needed to be overcome via legal reform. As these debates suggest, the terms "wife," "widow," and "concubine" represented fluid and permeable categories whose meanings were embedded within a wider cultural politics.

Chidambaram and Rangammal's case raises a further question about the agency of women represented as wives, widows, or concubines. Already widowed before her marriage to Chidambaram, and entering into an unconventional cross-caste alliance, Rangammal's actions pushed at the boundaries of conjugal practices among Tamils in the early twentieth century. However, the legal evidence leaves us with no record of her own subjectivity in forming a new kind of family with her husband; we know little about the motivations behind her unusual actions. Rangammal's absence from the court records stands in some contrast to her husband, whose testimony was quoted in the Madras High Court's final judgment. We know similarly little about the actions of Deivanai Achi, the other important female actor in this case. By taking her father-in-law to court, Deivanai Achi contested patriarchal family norms that made Chidambaram the head of the household and the manager of its property. As a widow and mother, she asserted her rights to speak on behalf of her son, A. Chidambaram. Yet, as in Rangammal's case, there is little record of her motivations—or her potential allies—in taking this course of action. Thus, these women emerged as central players in the transformation of their family even as other forces (ranging from the state to male family members) sometimes marginalized their voices. This book investigates these tensions, considering how the gendering of family discourse empowered, and disempowered, women in diverse ways. Taken together, the form of Chidambaram and Rangammal's wedding ceremony, its connection to nation and state, its reconstitution of familial and property relations, and its relationship to women as historical actors all point to critical themes and questions arising from the modern history of Tamil families.

Families in Colonial India

The debates examined here, which concerned the family but did not occur within familial boundaries, produced new normative visions of family life. In particular, we find a growing emphasis on the conjugal relationship that challenged, but did not fully replace, a "joint family" composed of several generations of patrilineal kin. This emphasis developed into what I term a "conjugal family ideal," where the relationship between husband and wife was figured as the central axis of affect and property ownership within families. Though de-centering other family members, a conjugal family ideal did not necessarily remove them from its normative framework or assume that a "nuclear" family (composed of husband, wife, and minor children) provided the only viable family form. Rather, advocates of a conjugal family ideal looked to the husband-wife relationship as foundational to the quality of all other family relations; they maintained that the reform of conjugality was essential to the family and to Tamil society as a whole. Thus, my use of the term "conjugality" carries a dual meaning, referring both to the husband-wife relationship and to the growing centrality of this relationship in representations of family life.

The production of a conjugal family ideal was embedded in varied discourses concerning caste, individual marriage choice, and gendered sexuality. However, across these variations, advocates of conjugality both assumed a clear demarcation between the "domestic" sphere and the "outer" world and re-valued the domestic in shaping the public politics of both nation and state. Thus, in common with other colonial contexts, the conjugal family was privatized even as it became critical to the "public" task of nation building.[11] Further, although the conjugal family ideal offered a language within which women and men could challenge existing patriarchal relations and structures, the "new" conjugal family was, in most cases, also a site for the production of "new" patriarchies. While empowering men differently—typically by rearranging intergenerational power and authority—the emphasis on conjugality did not overthrow the power of men within their families. Instead, in some cases the new norms even solidified their control.[12]

However, "the family" was not solely an ideal or normative vision; it was also an institution and a mode of legitimizing social relations. Indeed, given the latter meanings, there was no such thing as "the family" at all but rather a multiplicity of family forms that varied according to class, caste, region, and individual circumstances. This multiplicity of families both conditioned lived experience and provided frameworks of meaning within which people understood that experience.[13] Women and men who were engaged in the family debates of the colonial period at once produced ideologies and discourses about families and lived familial lives—sometimes bemoaning the lack of consistency between the two. Evidence certainly suggests that conjugal family ideals were not manifest everywhere or completely, even within the families of those who most strongly demanded reform. At times, this disjuncture was so striking that it became the target for public comment; consider, for instance, the numerous male social reformers who championed novel family forms but failed to put these into practice in their own marriages, or in the marriages of their children and dependents.[14] This book calls attention to these tensions and displacements between the family as an ideal, as an embodied institution, and as a site of lived experience, suggesting that such gaps themselves become a target of historical investigation. What produced these clashes between normative visions and familial practice? To what extent did conjugal family ideals actually shape family life, and, indeed, was that the primary goal of the Tamil family debates?

Addressing these questions requires an understanding of key developments in the history of South Asian families, but existing scholarship is inadequate to this task. Indeed, the family has been largely neglected within the historiography of colonial India in favor of a more prominent scholarly emphasis on caste. The recent publication of an important volume of historical essays on South Asian families, edited by Indrani Chatterjee, has only just begun to address this absence.[15] Moreover, although the construction of caste is clearly linked to the family via norms of kinship and endogamy, most studies of caste history have not viewed it in dynamic relationship with the constitution of family life.[16] Scholarship that focused on modern South Asian politics has also neglected families. Perhaps in unwitting echo of modern political discourses themselves, such work has tended to view "the family" as outside the realms of power and ruling authority that developed in the colonial and postcolonial eras. This neglect produces a curious divide within South Asian historiography;

whereas precolonial histories have amply demonstrated the intimate connections between kinship and kingship across much of South Asia, the family has virtually disappeared from nineteenth- and twentieth-century political histories.[17] Further, the impetus from developments in historical demography and social history that were critical to studies of Western families from the 1960s on has provoked little comparative scholarship in South Asian contexts.[18] Finally, although recent contributions to feminist and women's history have noted the importance of families, they have rarely made the family a sustained focus of investigation.[19]

In contrast to the scholarly paradigms of the historical discipline, studies of the family have played a critical role in the development of South Asian anthropology and sociology. Indeed, the majority of South Asian studies of family life have been produced within these disciplinary contexts rather than in history per se. The investigation of household composition, especially the relationship between conjugal family forms and the "Hindu joint family" (composed of multiple generations of patrilineal kin), has been one prolific area of inquiry and has important implications for this volume. Empirical studies of family membership have complicated conventional assumptions about the prevalence of joint families in the historical past and have rejected impressionistic claims about their demise in postcolonial India.[20] However, as Patricia Uberoi argues, in addition to quantitative studies of family size, scholarship must also address the importance of the "joint family" to historical and contemporary claims about "national identity and civilizational self-esteem."[21] In other words, the very production of "the joint family"—as a target of colonial intervention, an incubus of national identity, and a site for colonial and postcolonial scholarly inquiry—has not been adequately examined. Therefore, although a handful of studies in historical ethnography have begun to address such issues,[22] a great need remains for historical research that is attuned to social scientific questions of kinship and family composition but that also examines the production of the categories that frame our analysis.

The contribution of historical research to South Asian studies of families, therefore, cannot be limited to documenting changes in family ideologies and structures over time—history's typical rejoinder to anthropological and sociological investigation. Equally necessary is attention to how families were both shaped by, and helped to construct, wider transformations in South Asian culture, politics, and economy during the nineteenth and twentieth centuries. With an analysis of debates about "joint families" and individual rights, about conjugality and claims of capitalist development, about family life and the politics of nationalism, this book seeks to demonstrate the importance of the family for our understanding of the modern history of South Asia.

Historians of nationalist cultural politics offer a useful starting point for this kind of inquiry. For example, in an influential series of meditations, Partha Chatterjee has argued that the origins of Indian nationalist thought cannot be located exclusively in the explicitly political organizations and agitations of the late nineteenth century; rather, these origins must be seen in an earlier discursive formulation that separated the "outer" material world, in which the West had to be accommodated, from an "inner" spiritual core, which represented the essence of the Indian nation. He suggests that "anticolonial nationalism creates its own domain of sovereignty within colonial society well before it begins its political battle with the imperial power."[23] The family was central to constructing this sovereign inner domain. Excluded from the avenues of political power within the "outer" world of colonial domination, the nationalist middle class figured the home/family/domestic as a national space distinct from both previous "tradition" and Western forms of "modernity." As a result, control over the family—far from being marginal to the development of Indian nationalism—actually became central to nationalist political practice.

Although his work brought innovative and much needed attention to the politics of the family in the nineteenth century, Chatterjee has also been criticized for an exclusive emphasis on the discursive contests between colonialism and nationalism that neglects the political economy of colonial rule. Offering another reading of the intersection between nationalism and the family, for instance, Tanika Sarkar argues that a dichotomous split between "inner" and "outer" domains was not the motivating factor behind the shift of the Bengali middle class from liberal reformism in the mid-nineteenth century to a more aggressive Hindu cultural nationalism during the 1880s and 1890s. Rather, Sarkar demonstrates that middle-class men felt increasingly threatened by lower social classes and castes, the colonial state, European racism, and Bengali women questioning the established social order. Their retreat into cultural nationalism was a product of these insecurities, with the result that "the home . . . had to be a substitute for the world outside and for all the work and relations there that lay beyond personal comprehension and control." Thus, within the cultural politics of nationalism, the home was "not merely an escape from this world but [was] its critique and an alternative order in itself."[24] In Sarkar's analysis, then, the political meanings of the family under nationalism were not simply responses to colonial discourses propagating the superiority of Western culture but instead were grounded more specifically in the shifting fortunes of the Bengali middle class under nineteenth-century colonial rule.

Chatterjee and Sarkar, despite their significant differences, have one aspect in common: both neglect the dynamics of family history in the production of the "family" as a ground for nationalist debate.[25] Although they show convincingly that some conception of the family was critical to articulations of national identity in the nineteenth century, their analyses do not suggest why and how this conception became available for nationalist incorporation during this period. As historians of the family have argued, however, the family was not simply a blank slate onto which any and all meanings could be written; it was not an empty cultural category waiting to be filled with nationalist politics.[26] Instead, the intersection between "family" and "nation"—far from being a one-way transmission of nationalist ideals onto a domestic sphere—was, in fact, dynamic and multifaceted. Viewing the history of nationalism from this perspective, questions arise not only about the motivations for nationalist thought and action regarding "the family" but also about the specific transformations in families that contributed to reshaping nationalist political culture in colonial India. Taking these processes as a starting point, this book investigates a history of nationalist familial politics that historicizes "the family" alongside "the nation" itself.

The book builds on the insights of a developing body of innovative research on the regional histories of families[27] but also bridges a gap between questions of region, nation, and empire that have been inadequately theorized in much of this scholarship. For example, although existing work illuminates the particularities of localized change—for instance, the demise of matriliny among Nayars in Malabar or the construction of family honor among Rajputs in northern India—it does not address the connections between the regional politics of families and the cultural politics of nation and empire that have produced debates about the family during the nineteenth and twentieth centuries. In the absence of such connections, it becomes impossible to consider how and why recurrent themes—the "conjugalization" of the family, the challenge to multigenerational patrilineal kinship, the invocation of companionate marriage—resonate, sometimes variably, across historically and regionally distinct family regimes.

Historicizing Families

In developing a history of Tamil families, the book links "family changes to transformations in the mode of production and 'social reproduction.'"[28] But defining such modes broadly, I maintain that changes in "the family"—as both normative ideal and institution—are linked not only to shifting economic relations but also to struggles over the language of politics, competing claims about religion and tradition, the construction of gendered ideologies of production and reproduction, and the articulation of identities and communities. In other words, what shifts in political economy and society helped to make claims about the primacy of conjugality "sayable" or convincing in late-nineteenth century Tamil Nadu? What constructions of political and social relations made the affective relationship between husbands and wives appear critical to building a national community? Within what shifting cultural contexts could the inter-caste marriage of Chidambaram to the widow Rangammal become the target of legal dispute and political agitation? Or, from another perspective, how might the conjugal family ideal have transformed the ways in which politics, national identity, or individual subjectivity were conceptualized?

In examining these issues, I focus on local Tamil developments but also engage with the wider Indian, colonial, and global contexts in which they occurred. I suggest, for example, that Tamil norms about conjugal families resonated with representations of conjugality that accompanied the development of modern states in many parts of the world from the eighteenth century on. In both the Tamil region and elsewhere, the conjugal family ideal represented a rejection of the patriarchal household, composed of multiple generations, which included kin and non-kin within its permeable boundaries. Modern states, distinguishing themselves from their predecessors, severed their connections with the ruling authority of such households. Whether invoking democratic ideals as in the postrevolutionary United States, or claiming to overthrow "oriental despotism" via a "rule of law" as in British India during roughly the same period, these modernizing regimes sought their legitimacy outside the patriarchal family.[29] Within this context—normatively, if not always in practice—the conjugal nexus of husband and wife emerged as a more suitable unit of governance and target of regulation.

Historical research suggests, further, that new family ideals were intimately tied to the emergence of new market relations in mercantile and industrial capitalism globally. These links have been most thoroughly investigated in Western contexts, where scholars argue that changing forms of property, combined with the uncertainties and depredations of market economies, helped produce a model of bourgeois domesticity. Premised on a gendered separation of spheres, bourgeois domestic ideals emphasized women's roles as mothers and companionate wives; they constructed the "domestic" as an alternative arena of moral order that both countered, and depended on, the "public" world of marketplace and state. Especially in the analysis of capitalism and families in England and the United States, historians tend to view such familial transformations as occurring in organic and dynamic interaction with political economies. In these studies of Western families, the development of "classic" bourgeoisies—as owners of the means of production—thus seems to produce a "classic" bourgeois domestic form.[30]

This book asks what happens to this narrative about the intersecting rise of novel domestic ideals and novel market economies in colonial contexts. Are these seemingly organic developments in family and economy in the West simply inorganic or artificial impositions upon the colonized world, where the bourgeoisie was economically and politically weaker? Or, put differently, what exactly is "bourgeois" about the structures and discourses of bourgeois domesticity? How do we account for the rise of bourgeois domestic ideals even where the "classic" bourgeoisie seems marginal, or even absent? In other words, scholars are left to ponder, as in one study of late imperial Russia, the "'bourgeois' culture" of individual men and women who could lay little claim to bourgeois economic status.[31] Consequently, we encounter contradiction and seeming paradox at every turn. For instance, according to Leonore Davidoff and Catherine Hall's important study of the nineteenth century, middle classes in England reshaped their families in a bid to align their cultural and political power with their growing economic dominance. Their turn to the "privacy" of domestic arenas was a rejection of market-driven values within the home even as they embraced these values in the "public" world over which they exerted increasing power.[32] By contrast, the Bengali middling classes (*bhadralok*) could not lay claim to any such dominance in the marketplace, and their debates about family life were saturated with despair about the loss of power under colonial rule.[33] Their embrace of domestic "privacy" was, in part, a compensation for the heavy losses of the public realm.

Given these apparent contradictions, situating family history within a transnational field requires that we complicate our analysis of both colony and metropole, thus disturbing our certainties about the intersections between families, market economies, and modern states. On one level, following John and Jean Comaroff, I suggest that domesticity was always also a colonial project. A bourgeois domestic ideal did not emerge, fully formed, from the English cities and countryside, prepared to reshape the colonies in its own image. Rather, making "domestic" spaces in the colonies was always linked to "domesticating that part of the metropolis that had previously eluded bourgeois control."[34] Thus, the bourgeois domestic endeavor, in cultural and economic terms, was also a colonial one.

On another level, centering the colonial world within our field of vision highlights the fissures and contradictions that attended the rise of bourgeois domesticity globally. As Frederick Cooper and Ann Stoler argue, neither in the West nor in colonial contexts did there exist any "such entity as a pure bourgeoisie" whose economic power was completely independent of state power or cultural production.[35] Even in England and the United States, which witnessed the rise of powerful bourgeoisies, domesticity did not flow seamlessly from the economic rearrangements of the middle classes. Instead, the development of new familial norms was a contested and tension-filled process, frequently mediated by religious revivalism, women's activism, racialized discourses, or colonial imperatives. Indeed, far from being a mere manifestation of bourgeois economic dominance, novel family forms helped to constitute the structures, ideologies, and boundaries of the "middle class" in the eighteenth and nineteenth centuries in the West.[36] This was equally the case in colonial situations. As the wealth of scholarship on "provincializing Europe" within the historical discipline suggests, Indian and other colonial domestic ideals were not simply latecomers, offering a pale shadow to the supposedly more robust English domestic models. Rather, research on ideologies of domesticity in Africa and Asia demonstrates that colonized populations adopted and transformed bourgeois domestic ideals to suit their own purposes.[37]

Situating family history in this way does not imply that we simply read off family forms from shifts in modes of production. Conversely, we cannot reductively claim that particular family forms allowed the development of specific productive modes.[38] Instead, this book considers how the "logic" of the conjugal family ideal was linked to, and further developed, the "logic" of other political, economic, and kinship relations among various social groups.[39] In other words, for instance, I ask how merchants' dissatisfaction with familial property relations became conjoined to a critique of affective ties among kindred. Similarly, I question how middle-class women's assertions about the primacy of national communities spoke the language of familial intimacy. The goal here is not only to consider how a particular shift in the family debates may be linked to other historical developments but also to suggest how family and political economy constituted each other during the late colonial period.

The complexity of these interactions becomes even more apparent when we consider that debates about Tamil families also addressed other aspects of society and politics. Indeed, sometimes family discourses seemed primarily concerned with other forms of social critique, and the family has historically provided "a rich source of symbols that can be displaced onto the public sphere to make sense of it and change it."[40] A recent collection of essays, edited by Lynne Haney and Lisa Pollard, theorizes these connections through reference to "familialism" as a mode of analyzing the co-development of families, states, and societies. Offering "familialism as sets of symbols, narratives, and metaphors that center on ideal relations within and among familial bodies," Haney and Pollard suggest that, in colonial contexts, familial imagery was especially important to asserting, and resisting, state authority.[41] Perhaps it is unsurprising, then, that especially in moments of upheaval and revolutionary change the family has consistently figured in political debate. Whether for revolutionaries in France and the United States in the eighteenth century, or for Chinese and Indian nationalists in the nineteenth and twentieth, familial relationships offered a language with which to challenge conventional notions of citizenship, ruling authority, and national belonging.[42] Yet, such appropriation of the family was rife with contradiction, particularly around naturalized inequalities between men and women. Across various regional contexts there existed a profound tension between the use of familial language to contest political hierarchies, on the one hand, and the ongoing assertion of gender hierarchies within the family, on the other.

One might then legitimately ask about women's voices within these debates about the family. Although not initially a feminist demand, the rearticulation of families around the conjugal relationship brought new prominence to the place of women in both the family and the polity; that is, an emphasis on conjugality necessarily foregrounded women's roles as wives. Similarly, the intense political attention to domestic spaces perforce directed attention toward women's lives and labors within their families. Yet, all this attention did not necessarily allow women to emerge as subjects of debate; instead, the figure of "woman" became a site for the rearticulation of various other issues. In other words, many of the family debates that I investigate here appeared to be about women but gave little attention or space to women's own voices. This was especially the case in the nineteenth century. However, by the 1920s, the situation changed somewhat with the rise of an organized women's movement that claimed to represent Indian women to the nation and the colonial state. Although the movement was limited by class and exclusivity, the organized activism and agitation of a minority of women made newly visible the absence of most women's voices from the public record. Therefore, to the extent possible, this book pays close attention to women's public interventions in Tamil debates about the family.

However, the historical emergence of some women's voices in the public record cannot resolve the problem of the structural and theoretical exclusion of women's subjectivity from the production of public archives.[43] In some sense, perhaps the creation of these archives as sources of historical knowledge hinged upon this gendered exclusion; the delineation of "public" knowledge depended on the removal of a whole host of "private" knowledges typically associated with women. In addressing this problem, some feminist historians have sought alternative archives. Thus, for instance, in her study of three women writers in colonial and postcolonial India, Antoinette Burton excavates memories of home as "an archive from which a variety of counterhistories of colonial modernity can be discerned." Suggesting that such memories are not merely supplemental to the accounts of historical change available in official archives, Burton maintains that the primacy of home within "the resources that women have used to imagine the past" mandates that we, as historians, give critical weight to the home as a source for historical understanding.[44] As such, Burton crafts a history of "house, home and nation" that does not automatically privilege the official colonial archive.

Drawing from these insights, I contend that not only home but also the imagination of "family"—of its affective as well as social relations—may provide a rich source from which we may excavate women's subjectivities. In particular, as I argue in a subsequent chapter, women writers developed a new emotional language in and through their participation in the Tamil family debates. On the one hand, women writing about marriage invoked particular emotions, especially love, affection, and pleasure, to ground their critique of Tamil families. On the other hand, and perhaps more important, women's language of emotion produced a rich archive of women's historical agency. Thus, I examine these texts not only to "go where the women are" in the public debates about marriage but also to consider how women writers' crafting of emotional subjectivity may transform the frameworks in which we understand the intersections of "family" with "history" in the Tamil region.

Plan of the Book

The book is organized chronologically and thematically around questions attending the reconstruction of families and family ideologies from the late nineteenth to the mid-twentieth centuries. Each chapter highlights a particular moment of tension in the redefinition of Tamil family ideals and situates these tensions in relation to shifts in gender ideologies, political economies, and discourses of community, nation, and state. In each case, I assert that "the family" was not simply acted upon by other historical forces. Rather, shifts in family ideologies and experiences both motivated, and were motivated by, other historical changes in the Tamil region.

My attention to this complex relationship of family with historical change gives prominent attention to "Hindu" social practice. This is partly because, despite substantial Muslim and Christian populations, the majority of Tamils identified as Hindu. Further, upper-caste Hindus, vastly overrepresented in the mercantile and professional classes, began to rearticulate family identities and ideologies in the late nineteenth century. This is not to suggest, however, that only Hindu families were under contention during this period, or that constructions of Hindu family life were isolated from shifts in Muslim or Christian contexts. For instance, Christian missionaries played an important role in translating Western norms of domesticity into Indian contexts; much "Hindu" reform occurred in relation to perceived Western and Christian, as well as Muslim, practice. Moreover, given the possibilities of religious conversion and the fact that "Hindu" identity was partly a colonial production, the boundaries between Hindu and other families was not always clear.[45] Therefore, although my focus remains the nexus of culture and economy within which "Hindu" families were embedded, I situate them in relation to other developments when pertinent.

Families in South Asia—Hindus as well as others—suffered political dislocations under colonial rule. As I discuss in the first chapter, when the bureaucratic colonial regime severed kinship, lineage, and household from state authority, it disrupted the politics of families. In a process akin to the establishment of modern states elsewhere, the colonial administration thus removed kinship from the process of establishing kingship. Once denied access to ruling authority, the de-politicized households of erstwhile ruling classes became newly available for colonial intervention, typically via laws and legal regulation, into "native" society. Women, in particular, bore the brunt of these changes as legal assumptions about caste and ritual distinguished the rights and privileges of "wifehood" from the lower status of "concubine." Yet, despite their importance to the state's regulation of family life, women were typically situated as objects within, rather than subjects of, legal discourses. Reading women's testimonial narratives against the grain, chapter 1 begins discussion of how women may have reconstructed wifehood under changing familial circumstances.

Ultimately, the households of precolonial ruling families did not provide a model of either domesticity or politics for the new elite classes that developed under colonial rule. Instead, as I demonstrate in chapter 2, merchants and Western-educated professionals began to delineate new models of "family" and "economy" beginning in the late nineteenth century. Maintaining that the affective ties between husbands and wives superseded those of a multigenerational unit of male kin, these men (and they were almost exclusively men) constructed a novel discursive framework that linked claims about conjugality to an emphasis on capitalist development. However, landed classes tended to reject these links; these men typically invoked forms of joint property ownership in the name of Hindu tradition and patriarchal privilege. Once again, women bore the brunt of these contradictions and were ultimately figured as the representatives of "tradition" within the "modern" conjugal family-property unit. As such, even as wives became discursively central to the assertion of male individual ownership rights, women themselves (as either wives, widows, or daughters) were excluded from individual rights to property and rendered dependent upon the "joint family."

This vision of the conjugal family, with its contradictions of both gender and property, became the ground for debates about nation and national identity that began in the 1920s. Nationalist interventions, as I argue in chapter 3, harnessed the conjugal family ideal both to specific claims about national culture and to global discourses and ideologies of domesticity. Nationalists built their claims upon the premise that the conjugal family—imagined though not everywhere implemented—would be the incubus of the nation. However, Tamil nationalist politics in this period produced at least two, often competing visions of both the family and the nation: Indian nationalist claims about marriage via its campaigns for the Child Marriage Restraint Act, and Dravidian nationalist reforms that hinged upon a thorough reevaluation of caste, ritual, and familial authority in the production of conjugality. Both these movements to reform marriage held in common the sustained participation and leadership of women activists who were newly emergent as an organized political force in the twentieth century. In both cases, however, nationalist movements subsumed the transformation of families (including the critique of patriarchy) to the goals of nation building.

Much remained "unsayable" within these multiple and competing claims about conjugality in the late colonial period. In an effort to explore the boundaries of these conjugal norms, chapter 4 analyzes a developing culture of print produced by, or directed toward, Tamil women. From the emergence of such texts in the 1890s, and through their proliferation in the context of mass nationalism from the 1920s to the 1940s, I argue that women's print culture developed a novel paradigm of conjugal emotion that challenged existing patriarchal norms of family life. On the one hand, women writers politicized emotions; that is, references to love, affection, and pleasure became the grounds for explicitly political critiques of caste, gender, and class hierarchies that supposedly hampered the development of conjugal relationships. On the other hand, as I demonstrate, these texts also interiorized emotion so that affective experience became the hallmark of an individualized (female) subjectivity. Reading women's emotional language as an alternative archive for developing a history of families, this chapter suggests that issues and themes virtually absent from other sites of debate, particularly the invocation of female sexuality and desire, found a partial and circumscribed presence in women's culture of print.

All these debates about the family—which sought to reform family relations while rearticulating broader social, political, and economic relationships—produced what I term a "Tamil familial imaginary." The familial imaginary provided a rich language through which Tamils could make sense of, and transform, their society during the latter decades of colonial rule. However, even while debates about the family opened up some radical possibilities for challenging colonial inequalities, the ongoing naturalization of gender hierarchies within marriage also foreclosed other alternatives. As I argue in the conclusion to the book, these tensions in the familial imaginary extended into the postcolonial era as well. In the aftermath of independence and partition, debates about the family continued to mediate between community and nation; discourses about family life shaped the very possibilities for (women's) citizenship within the postcolonial state. Focusing on the reform of Hindu law in the first decade after Indian independence, I suggest that family history provides a critical framework for deconstructing the implied identification of "family" with religious community and nation, and, in the process, challenges the subordinate position of women within each.

ONE

Colonizing the Family: Kinship, Household, and State

The Zemindar [*sic*] used to take his meals with me. The Zemindar used to sleep during nights in the upstairs of the new palace. I and he used to sleep in the same bed.

Menakshi Sundra Nachiar, Annapurni Nachiar v. Menakshi Sundra Nachiar and G. S. Forbes, 1893

Whenever my husband felt amorous, he would occasionally cohabit with any woman and pay her occasionally. This is all. They were concubines.

Muthuverammal, Sundaralingasawmi Kamaya Naik v. Ramasawmi Kamaya Naik, 1885

The history of the establishment of colonial rule in India is also a history of families. As the colonial state developed from its origins among soldiers and traders of the East India Company into a centralized bureaucracy under the British Crown, the intimate connections between household and polity characteristic of precolonial regimes were disrupted. Indigenous elite families, whose political status had been expressed through the language of lineage and kinship, found themselves excluded from ruling authority. State power, in other words, was no longer constituted in and through relations among households.

In the Tamil region, precolonial ruling elites—called *pāḷaiyakkārars* in Tamil and "poligars" in British parlance—bore the brunt of these changes. These warrior rulers offered stiff resistance to European conquest during the late eighteenth and early nineteenth centuries. Subduing them and acquiring a degree of control over their resources became essential for the fiscal and military viability of the Company state. The administration of Madras Presidency sought to achieve this by means of a Permanent Settlement (1803–1805) that granted titles in land to *pāḷaiyakkārar* kin. These newly titled *zamindars* controlled land subject to their payment of fixed sums of revenue to the state. In Nicholas Dirks's terms, the zamindari Permanent Settlement thus sought to render the former "little kings" of the old regime into "landlords" answerable to the colonial state.[1] By the end of the nineteenth century, 804 zamindars held approximately 40 percent of the land in Madras Presidency; the remaining land was controlled by about 3 million peasant proprietors under the ryotwari (*raiyatwari*) system of land tenure.[2]

Although zamindars and their households represented a small minority of the Tamil population, their significance for understanding the intersection of family and polity in colonial India far outweighs their limited numbers. Forced to contend with the radically transformed political system of the colonial state, the former "little kings" turned landlords did not lose all claims to ruling authority. Instead, as Pamela Price argues, the development of a "modern" centralized politics during the nineteenth and twentieth centuries occurred "contemporaneously with the fragmentation—not destruction—of precolonial political visions" represented by the zamindari household.[3] In Price's estimation, nationalist politics cannot be understood without reference to the fate of precolonial political culture, and the "little kings" cast a long shadow over the mobilization of ruling authority in colonial Tamil Nadu.

I maintain, further, that this political culture was as concerned with the household/family as it was with the polity. Prior to the advent of colonial rule, the political activities of *pāḷaiyakkārar* kin were virtually inseparable from the mobilization of affect and alliance within and among households. By seeking to de-politicize these household relationships, colonial ideologies fostered the emergence of new models of familial domesticity that were disconnected from the state and (ostensibly) apolitical. Nationalist appropriations of family life, dating from the late nineteenth century, occurred over this emptying out of political content from indigenous ruling households. The removal of households from state power thus set the terms by which not only "politics" but also the "family" could be conceptualized within colonial society. Therefore, although their substantial wealth and patterns of landholding meant that zamindari kin were not representative of Tamil families in a sociological sense, the reordering of their household relationships produced the discursive and ideological parameters within which Tamils debated publicly about family identity and belonging.

This chapter examines how Tamil families were redefined when zamindari households confronted the politics and institutions of the colonial regime during the nineteenth and early twentieth centuries. The focus is on the colonial legal system, which, in the absence of other sites of political competition, became an important venue where conflicts within and among households were played out. On one level, zamindari kin used the colonial law to establish their claims to resources and ruling authority. Although the title of zamindar was typically granted to men, women were also deeply involved in this household politics. On another level, when adjudicating disputes, judges made decisions about the constitution of zamindari households and the status of various "family" members within them. As a result, the legal process made household relations available for state regulation and contributed to the development of colonial discourses about "native" families and family life.

As the epigraphs to the chapter suggest, these intersections between households and the state were frequently expressed in gendered terms. The relationship between men and women operated as an axis along which household members staked their claims to familial authority and belonging, established their legitimacy, and sutured together their identity in the face of political ruptures engendered by the colonial regime. Conjugality became an especially important point of contention. Although insisting upon women's monogamy and sexual fidelity, the legal system accepted various non-monogamous conjugal relationships for men. Within this context, many women sought to escape the stigmatizing label of "concubine" by asserting their wifely intimacy with their husbands. For Menakshi Sundra Nachiar, in the first epigraph, establishing "wifehood" offered a path toward control of the Uttumalai zamindari estate. For Muthuverammal, in the second epigraph, discrediting other women as "concubines" became critical for demonstrating her own wifehood and, implicitly, her authority over the Saptur zamindari. These women thus used the evidence of their bodies and domestic practices to secure access to the substantial economic and political resources of zamindari estates. Actively engaged with legal institutions, they both invoked the language of the colonial law and developed models of wifehood, concubinage, and familial belonging that challenged legal constraints. Thus, the colonial state's ideologies of the family were not a one-way imposition upon indigenous elite households but instead developed out of a multifaceted negotiation between legal institutions and household members in which women played a prominent role.

Ultimately, the domestic politics of zamindari households proved difficult to sustain within the colonial legal system. Court disputes extended for lengthy periods, sometimes decades, at vast expense to the litigants. Moreover, in the process of asserting their status, household members engaged in a politics of exposure and shaming that helped to make zamindars a target of criticism by colonial officials, European missionaries, and Indian social reformers.[4] The "hollow crown" of zamindari rulership, to use Nicholas Dirks's apt metaphor, thus also had serious implications for zamindari households;[5] separated from the politics of rule, the zamindari politics of the family was transformed and curtailed. Consequently, zamindari kin remained distinct from the new elite groups who would take charge of family debates beginning in the last decades of the nineteenth century. To examine these processes of change—from the politicized household of precolonial regimes to a depoliticized family of nationalist aspiration—I turn first to the history of South Asian polities prior to colonial rule.

Families and Polities in Early Modern South Asia

Analyzing the history of families in early modern South Asia requires, first of all, a specification of the category itself. Without collapsing the early modern "family" into the unit of affective kinship first imagined in the nationalist era, historians have emphasized that no firm boundaries separated the "family" from the "household" in the several centuries preceding colonial rule.[6] Indeed, in South Asia, the early modern period (roughly from the sixteenth to eighteenth centuries) witnessed a continuation of medieval-era practices that did not limit the "family" to a narrowly defined group of biologically related kin. Instead, as in medieval and early modern societies in the West, blood ties were one—but certainly not the only—method of incorporation into households.[7] Other methods included adoption, strategic marriage alliance, fictive or imagined kinship, and outright purchase. As a result of these different practices, families could include members of varying status who were not all related by blood or marriage; family membership potentially crossed boundaries of class, caste, and slave/free status.[8] Considering families this way means that we must reject any assumption of a blood-related family "core," surrounded by "peripheral" groups of servants, slaves, or other dependents; it requires, instead, that we rethink the boundaries and the modalities of family relationships in the early modern period.

Research on the household of the *Nazim* of Murshidabad in Bengal during the eighteenth century provides one example of the differences between early modern families/households and contemporary imaginings of the affective family. Within this household, as Indrani Chatterjee demonstrates, slaves and concubines could become critical to the political and social status of lineages even while blood-related kin were marginalized.[9] Similarly, as Pamela Price illustrates for Tamil and Telugu "little kings" and Ramya Sreenivasan notes for elite lineages in precolonial Rajasthan, servants/slaves and concubines proved critical to the maintenance and manipulation of kinship networks.[10] Such examples make visible the intersection of families with their various political, economic, and social contexts. Put another way, rather than being a haven from inequity, oppression, or hierarchy (as in nationalist imaginings), the family represented one site where the dynamics of power, privilege, and status were played out within early modern regimes.

Historians of South Asia are familiar by now with the imbrication of early modern households/families with state power and political authority. Analyses of state formation from the sixteenth to the eighteenth centuries have demonstrated that across a diverse array of South Asian regions, and within both "Hindu" and "Muslim" regimes, families played a constitutive role in the establishment and continuing success of precolonial states. Investigating the intersection of familial and state power over the *longue durée* of South Asian history, David Ludden suggests that the early modern period witnessed an intensification of family-state relations and a concomitant increase in the power of families (and of male family leaders) within society and politics.[11] In particular, families—variously defined—became critical to systems of alliances that bound overlords to local leaders.

The precise ways in which families were important to state authority varied depending upon the particular circumstances of early modern states and their ideologies of ruling. These connections have perhaps been best theorized for the Maratha polity, which, as André Wink has argued, was substantially shaped by institutionalized conflict (*fitna*) which often included families and lineages. Rather than reading the Maratha state as negatively characterized by disorder as a result of these conflicts, Wink claims that "sovereignty was primarily a matter of allegiances; the state organized itself around conflict and remained essentially open-ended instead of becoming territorially circumscribed."[12] Elaborating on this concept, Sumit Guha demonstrates that the family feud emerged as a particularly important site at which the Maratha polity could manage tensions and conflicts while extending its own political power. Intervention on one side or the other of particular family feuds offered the state opportunities for "political aggrandizement." Through its involvement in disputes about the legitimacy of heirs, or supporting one side among rival claimants within a family to local political power, the Maratha regime was able to leverage its own authority. Indeed, according to Guha, the "entry of Maratha power into the political structure of Central India was predicated upon the successful exploitation of family broils in the erstwhile ruling houses."[13] Taken together, Guha's and Wink's arguments suggest that the "family" was therefore neither discrete from, nor outside of, the polity; rather, successful intervention in family disputes was essential for the political activity of the state.

Although these intersections between familial and state politics preoccupied ruling families—or those aspiring to ruling status—attention to their activities does not necessarily imply a narrow focus on elites. As Indrani Chatterjee has argued, wealthier and poorer households in early modern India were closely linked; for instance, marital alliances could unite a wealthy ruling family with a subordinate lineage, often through the marriage of daughters into the higher-status family. Examining patterns of marriage alliance between ruling families and their poorer vassals outside the political center, she emphasized the "significance of . . . lordly households for understanding commoner households too."[14] Further, the incorporation of slaves and servants, brought into the household for various sorts of labor including reproduction, points to the significant connections between ruling elites and lower social classes. Thus, elite lineages were not permanently closed off from commoner families.[15] Of course, emphasizing these connections does not occlude the forms of exploitation that occurred within and between families and households. Quite the opposite: to understand the political intersections of family and state, it is necessary to debunk the notion that the "family" was a sphere of (apolitical, non-exploitative) affect and instead locate it firmly within the cultural and economic processes that led to the formation of early modern states.

Historians of state formation in southern India, most notably Burton Stein, have proposed a model of segmentary statehood that offers a useful starting point for thinking through the relationship between families and political authority in the early modern Tamil country. According to Stein, a segmentary state consisted of "differentiated elements [segments] of a single, universal moral system." Each segment was a localized group defined by kinship, occupational group, or territory, but segments could come together to form supralocal combinations. Segments were further connected "in their recognition of a sacred ruler whose overlordship [was] of a moral sort and [was] expressed in an essentially ritual idiom." In other words, the ruler in a segmentary state exercised effective political power only within a narrow core area of the capital but held ritual sovereignty over a wider realm. The resulting "sacral and incorporative kingship" offered a model of ruling authority emulated by all smaller rulers within the domain.[16] A segmentary state was thus characterized by de-centralization rather than centralization, and had fluid rather than absolute territorial boundaries. Although Stein developed this model in the context of his research on the Chola and Vijayanagara polities, he suggests that segmentary organization remained an important feature of Tamil statehood over time.

This theory of segmentary statehood raises an important question for historians of the family: What modes of integration linked the segment (variously constituted) to the overlordship of the domain? How, in other words, did an "incorporative kingship" actually incorporate its constitutive elements? Among several potential ties (including religious authority) that bound together a local ruler with his titular sovereign, kinship played a crucial role. As Pamela Price argues, Tamil models of incorporative kingship involved creating "an identity of shared kinship with subordinate chiefs." Such shared kinship could be manifest in the ceremonial sharing of food, in the sharing of lineage names with subordinate "little kings," or in forging strategic alliances across various levels of political authority. Kin-based connections within a sub-caste or clan could form a crucial basis of support for aspirant "little kings," and could solidify the political claims of more established rulers.[17] Therefore, although kinship was certainly not the only glue holding together the segments of a Tamil polity, it was one available factor that could be manipulated at multiple levels for crafting the segmentary state in southern India.

Although segmentary models of statehood have apparently existed over many centuries in the Tamil region, the specific contours of segmentary states changed in the context of ideological, political-economic, and technological shifts. For the early modern centuries, in particular, these changes may be broadly characterized as an intensification of state formation, an increasing authority vested in the person of the king, a changing balance between temples and warrior forts in expressions of political power, and a shift in some areas (from the seventeenth century on) toward a more commercialized cash economy less exclusively rooted in the land. These shifts also implied changes in notions of ruling authority, and a paradigm of "heroic kingship" based in constant warfare gave way to more complex and diffuse royal images that incorporated diverse layers of society into the polity.[18]

Unfortunately, existing historical studies do not allow us to chart how each of these developments may have reshaped the Tamil politics of kinship or shifted the terms by which kin-based connections could manipulate state authority. However, studies of northern Tamil Nadu in the seventeenth century suggest that, in situations of great change and tension, the politics of kinship—and especially marriage—acquired increasing salience in the arrangement of segments within an overarching political framework.[19] The fluid conditions of the eighteenth century, which witnessed the increasing commercialization of the economy and the arrival of European contenders for power, likely also lent themselves to kin-based modes of politics. In this sense, the importance of kinship does not imply a static polity that was closed to new claimants—indeed, just the opposite. "Making" kin, through marriage or other means, was also to make one's claims to ruling authority by successfully incorporating into the domain a higher-level political figure. As we shall see, however, the language and structures of politics changed significantly with the establishment of colonial rule, as "family" and "state" were disconnected—and reconnected—in fundamentally different ways.

Colonial Conquest and the De-Politicization of Families

Although some European men in India, usually mercenaries and other military adventurers, successfully inserted themselves into the indigenous kinship networks that shaped political power in the early eighteenth century, the East India Company eventually built a state according to different principles.[20] Concerned with maximizing the profits of its shareholders, the Company attempted to craft an administrative system that could reliably secure a transfer of revenues from its various Indian territories to its board of directors in London. Over time, this goal motivated an increasingly complex administrative machinery that developed by the latter nineteenth century into the modern, bureaucratic state of British India.

This transition between precolonial polities and the developing colonial state, as David Ludden notes, was marked by the severance of the politics of kinship from the politics of rule. Since European men did not marry into the political system as their predecessors had, the family lost its centrality in creating political institutions. In its place, the East India Company developed a new state in which novel ideologies of citizenship, law, markets, and private property became central to ruling authority.[21] To institute this shift, European administrators dismissed the manipulation of kin relations as a form of "corrupt intrigue" that was contrary to supposedly "rational" forms of colonial governance. They challenged all vestiges of family and communitarian authority, seeing these as threats to colonial power and revenue.[22] Significantly, this attack on kinship had gendered consequences because it "domesticated and trivialized" a critical source of women's political power.[23]

Therefore, the colonial state, which stood atop a subjected society but was not linked to it via ties of kinship or community, was quite different in form and structure than the segmentary polities it replaced. On one level, as a centralized, bureaucratic regime, the colonial state did not share its ruling authority with indigenous political institutions. The "little kings" of south India and their families, whose political power had both buttressed and been based on the overarching sovereignty of greater lords, experienced this as a loss of kingly authority within indigenous society.[24] On another level, because the colonial state redirected political power and resources toward a more clearly defined center, revenue collection and ruling authority were less dispersed and segmented than they had been in precolonial times.[25] Consequently, new urban centers of power—most notably Madras city—became critical to the emergence of new modes of politics that replaced the earlier kin- and caste-based forms.

Severed from their political meanings, kinship ideologies and structures were then rendered into artifacts for colonial study and preservation. While assiduously de-linking kin connections from access to ruling authority, the colonial administration nevertheless claimed to preserve its outward forms. In other words, the colonial state "put itself above family but also made family traditions inviolable."[26] This is not to imply that kinship ceased to have meaning within Tamil society—quite the contrary. Rather, analogous to shifts in caste during the same period, a newly de-politicized kinship became available for new sorts of recuperation by colonial ethnography, missionary enterprises, and, eventually, by nationalist movements.[27] Therefore, despite the state's claims to leave "native tradition" untouched, the advent of colonialism changed how families were organized and imagined throughout the nineteenth and twentieth centuries.

Some of these changes arose from the state's attempts to define the "family" itself. On the one hand, the stabilization of territorial boundaries under colonial rule fostered the notion that households—and, by implication, families—were characterized by a fixed residence.[28] On the other hand, in enumerating populations in early census attempts, colonial officials struggled with various definitions of what exactly constituted a family within indigenous society. Sometimes membership in a "family" implied a co-sharing of property and resources; alternatively, it was defined as "those who live together or who cook their food at the same hearth."[29] These varied definitions existed in relationship and tension throughout the colonial period, but neither could fully capture the complexity of household and family relations. Moreover, as recent research on nineteenth-century Malabar suggests, colonial definitions of the family consistently deemphasized the relationship of households with their non-kin dependents, such as servants, slaves, or service providers. Encouraging the severance of ritual ties linking these groups to particular households, colonial laws and revenue policies instead enforced contractual obligations based exclusively in economic relations.[30] State policies thus began to characterize the household/family as a group of blood-related kindred who, occupying a fixed residence, lived together.

In addition to these changes in the boundaries of inclusion and exclusion, families and households were also shaped by their interaction with colonial capitalism and its often devastating effects on the agrarian economy. Many scholars now agree that colonial conquest did not introduce capitalism into India but that forms of mercantile capital had been developing during the preceding two centuries. However, the advent of colonial rule did direct the economy in new ways. Detailed historical work on the concomitant transformation of households and families is still needed, and the following account of how the colonial agrarian economy set the stage for shifts in families necessarily remains schematic. First, the colonial regime established some forms of private, alienable property in land. In some cases an intensification of precolonial trends, the result was never a "free" market in land; rather, as David Washbrook has argued, colonial constraints meant that land ownership was limited, partial, and circumscribed in numerous ways.[31] Further, the newly minted property in land ownership was subject to the colonial state's revenue assessment, which put a very heavy burden on agrarian society. The monetization of revenue increased this burden; in combination with an inflexibility of collection dates, the revenue demand resulted in a huge expansion in rural indebtedness and land alienations.[32] This situation led to frequent agrarian crises of varying magnitude, including devastating famines. In response, the colonial state attempted different revenue schemes. However, given the financial pressures of imperial expansion, which demanded an ever increasing stream of resources, administrators were hard-pressed to develop a sustainable revenue policy.

Within this context, the state's attempts to collect land revenues also fostered subtle changes in relationships among kin groups. Seeking intermediaries who could ensure a dependable flow of payments, the administration buttressed the power of landowners—like zamindars in the Tamil region—by supporting their powers of coercion over cultivators.[33] Because they could secure greater returns from lower-class cultivators than from their kinsmen, and confronted with the pressures of revenue demands and the world market, these landowners sought to expel their kin from privileged land tenures. This process fractured the unity of kin-based land control across the subcontinent.[34] Studying this process in detail in Malabar, for instance, G. Arunima shows that the empowerment of the male "head" of the Nayar *tharavadu* (household) eventually resulted in a backlash by junior members of the family and lower castes who, by the late nineteenth century, challenged both kinship and landowning structures.[35]

Feminist scholars have demonstrated that this rise of a particular class of landlords also represented the empowerment of upper caste men vis-à-vis upper caste women as well as lower castes of both genders. As the state assigned land titles across the subcontinent—even in matrilineal Malabar—almost exclusively to men, colonial laws supported these male rights over land. The colonial revenue administration also devalued rights of usufruct, which were important for women's and lower castes' access to land, in favor of outright male ownership. Describing this process as an overall "masculinization" of the economy, Veena Oldenburg has argued that, when combined with the agrarian crises of colonial capitalism, the result was a severe imbalance of power between men and women within households and families. Women's devaluation within the colonial economy echoed, and further exacerbated, their marginalization within their families. Sometimes, as in cases of female infanticide which Oldenburg examined in Punjab, women's very lives were at risk.[36] The point here is not that patriarchy coincided with colonialism; clearly patriarchal forms of kinship, family, and land control predated the advent of colonial rule.[37] Rather, most significant is the extent to which the greatly elevated power of certain men within indigenous society could change the balance of authority within families and within society as a whole.

These structural changes in household and kinship organization developed in relation to colonial discourses and ideologies about family life. More than the state—whose official policies often disclaimed any "interference" in indigenous cultural practice even while these policies engendered change—European missionaries were vocal in their attacks on Indian domestic arrangements. Directing their attention to indigenous elite families during the nineteenth century, many missionaries identified the *zenana,* or women's quarters within elite households, as a primary site of Indian civilizational backwardness. Targeting women's quarters as a locus for proselytization and social reform, missionary organizations inaugurated a number of "*zenana* missions" throughout the nineteenth century whose purpose was to transform indigenous domesticities along European and Christian lines.[38] Questions of conjugality, especially of monogamy, were important to missionary discourses. Viewing the diversity of conjugal relationships among Hindus as a "moral opposite" of Christian conjugality, missionaries in the Tamil region, for example, sought to mold indigenous households in accordance with the hierarchies, property relationships, and affective norms of Victorian separate spheres.[39] Although Hindu and Muslim women within the *zenana* often resisted missionary attempts, and the *zenana* missions produced few converts, missionary interventions helped to propagate new colonial ideals of domestic life that overlay—and sometimes justified—ongoing transformations in household and family under the colonial regime.

Occasionally missionaries lobbied the colonial state on issues of domestic reform; in combination with pressure from Indian social reformers, these efforts spurred administrators to intervene in family life and kinship relations via legislation. Many of these interventions concerned women and girls, and are well known to historians of social reform and nationalism. They ranged from legislation on *sati* (the immolation of widows), child marriage, widow remarriage, and infanticide to the intimate regulation of female sexuality among laborers and prisoners.[40] However, these more visible activities of the colonial state—activities that have typically received the greatest share of scholarly interrogation—were merely one aspect of the much broader history of families and households under colonial rule. The de-politicization of the family, the disavowal of non–blood-related kin as household members, the shifting power and authority of propertied families within agrarian society, the transformation of gendered power dynamics within families, and the development of novel colonial discourses on domestic life all formed the basis upon which the "family" became a target of state regulation under colonial rule. In the Tamil region, specifically, the households of zamindars became one important locus of these state interventions.

Zamindari Households and the Reconstruction of Families

In the decades following the Madras Permanent Settlement of 1803–1805, zamindari households developed into large establishments that incorporated numerous kin and non-kin dependents. Household members competed for access to resources and authority within zamindari estates that could encompass thousands of tenants who were settled in dozens of villages and spread over hundreds of square miles. Whereas, in the precolonial era, competition among ruling elites had occurred through diverse means including warfare or the collection of tribute, under colonial rule the legal system became a prime site for a household-based politics. Since the colonial law maintained that zamindari inheritance was patrilineal and, unlike in the case of other Hindus, followed the principles of primogeniture, colonial litigation often hinged on identifying a legitimate heir of the zamindari estate.

Zamindari disputes began to enter the colonial courts in the early nineteenth century, but, from the outset, the bureaucratic procedures of the colonial legal system were at odds with the political goals of zamindari kin. As Pamela Price notes, the colonial law, with its claims of universality and uniformity, did not view itself as an arbiter of locally specific political disputes, but as establishing precedents in the regulation of Hindu families and their property. Zamindari litigants, on the other hand, turned to the courts to engage in battles over honor, status, and power. They did not limit their conflicts to legal procedures over land inheritance but used the courts as one venue for a broader assertion of royal authority. As a result, zamindari kin employed the legal system but often showed little interest in, or respect for, legal procedure. Further, their use of the colonial courts occurred at some financial risk to litigants. The most prolonged cases, which lasted for several decades, required the mobilization of substantial ideological and financial resources by each side, and sometimes bankrupted the estate itself.[41]

Through its investigations into disputes, the colonial state's legal bureaucracy generated a massive documentation of zamindari litigation. Legal records, numbering in the hundreds or even thousands of pages of printed text for each case, are both revealing and strangely elusive. Primarily depositions and testimony from dozens of witnesses, these texts were originally produced in Tamil or, more rarely, in Telugu; to my knowledge, however, they have been preserved only in English translation. Further, the depositions were taken in the form of questions and answers between lawyers and witnesses, but only the responses have typically remained on record. Finally, some of the female witnesses lived in *gosha*, or seclusion, within the women's quarters (*zenana*) of the zamindari palace; sometimes these women did not speak directly to their lawyers but gave their testimony through a curtain or through intermediaries.[42]

Given the vast sums of money involved, and the acknowledged prevalence of bribery and perjury in these cases, it would be extremely problematic to assert that the "evidence" of depositions represents an unfiltered insight into any witness's or litigant's construction of family or ruling authority. Indeed, the obvious legal intervention in the collection of testimony and depositions serves to underscore the constructed nature of these documents as artifacts of the colonial law rather than as more spontaneous creations of the witnesses themselves. Nevertheless, even though they were produced within the heavy-handed constraints of legal procedure, these texts were not purely inventions of the colonial state but were constructed with some reference to the claims of litigants and their allies. I read them, then, as a joint discursive project—albeit one in which power and authority were severely imbalanced in favor of lawyers and judges.

Wending its way from a local district court to the Madras High Court of Judicature and, occasionally, to the Privy Council in London, zamindari litigation mapped the dense network of intersections between household and state power in colonial Tamil Nadu. I examine these networks at the site of three zamindari estates: Saptur and Bodinayakanur in Madurai district, and Uttumalai in Tirunelveli (Tinnevelly) district. During the late nineteenth century, when these disputes originated, the colonial legal system was well established, and some judicial precedent existed in the regulation of zamindari households. These particular cases, whose content made them important for setting further precedents in the colonial law, hinged on the status of women and, in particular, on the distinction between "wifehood" and "concubinage" in defining family membership and property ownership among zamindari kin. Some women in the Saptur, Bodinayakanur, and Uttumalai households made their claims as wives and mothers to secure resources for their sons; others claimed zamindari lands, and the accompanying (feminized) title of *zamindarni* in their own right.

These three estates and their ruling families were not necessarily typical of all zamindari households; indeed, recourse to the courts to resolve household/family disputes was not the norm. However, although the specific circumstances prompting the disputes may have been unusual, their legal resolution calls attention to an intersection of state and households that characterized the colonial regime overall. In particular, these cases reveal the gendered terms by which the colonial law removed the "family" from "politics." In Saptur, Bodinayakanur, and Uttumalai, female litigants mobilized familial resources; they effectually called into question the boundaries separating the domestic/familial from the public/political that underlay the foundations of the colonial regime. However, in rendering its judgments, the legal system reasserted this separation, and, in the process, marked new boundaries around the content of "domestic" life among zamindari kin. These three cases thus bring to light a broader reconfiguration of gender, power, and ruling authority that developed when indigenous elite households confronted the colonial state.

In their attention to the status of women, the disputes over Saptur, Bodinayakanur, and Uttumalai were not alone or unique in the colonial law; several other legal cases during the nineteenth and early twentieth centuries called attention to similar questions involving wifehood and concubinage, and included testimony from women.[43] The cases discussed here, however, were unusual in offering an especially rich archive of women's voices, albeit densely mediated by legal procedure. Rather than assuming that this archive reveals the "truth" of wifehood as experienced within zamindari households, I ask how legal categories and requirements shaped the ways in which various women laid claim to wifely status as part of asserting their ruling authority. Which aspects of women's testimony were given validity by the courts, and which were disregarded? To what extent could women disrupt legal categories, and to what degree could judges reassert their own interpretations and meanings of "wife" in the nineteenth century? What aspects of wifely behavior were within the purview of legal discussion, and which remained outside legal investigation? In examining how testimony from individual women factored into legal decisions about the ownership/rulership of zamindari estates, a genealogy of concepts of conjugality and family emerges at the points where colonial law and indigenous elite households intersect.

Wifehood and Concubinage in the Saptur Zamindari

First, let us consider a dispute concerning the Saptur estate, the largest zamindari in the Tirumangalam *taluk* (subdivision) of Madurai district. Initially taken to the courts in 1889, the litigation concerned succession to the estate, which was claimed by the two younger sons of the previous zamindar, Nagayasawmi Kamaya Naik.[44] After the zamindar's death in 1885, Saptur had been passed on to his eldest son, who died while still a minor in 1887. Following this son's death, two other minor sons came forward—each represented by his mother—to claim the estate. The younger of the two was Ramasawmi Kamaya Naik, whose mother, Muthuverammal, was also the mother of the former heir. The older of the two boys, Sundaralingasawmi Kamaya Naik, was the son of another of the zamindar's wives, Nagammal. On an immediate level, the litigation concerned the rights and status of two women, Muthuverammal and Nagammal, both claiming to be wives of a zamindar; their status determined their sons' rights to the estate. More broadly, the case concerned the incorporation of women into a household/

family and, as will become apparent, raised questions about the role of caste, ritual, and (non-monogamous) conjugality in that incorporation.

The court's investigation began with legal knowledge produced by one T. Ranga Rao, the Deputy Collector of the district. Immediately after Nagayasawmi's death, the last adult zamindar, Ranga Rao filed information with the government of Madras regarding the extent of the estate, the operations of the household, and the claims of its members. He maintained that Nagayasawmi left four widows, including Muthuverammal, all of whom the zamindar had married according to "the usual marital rites." Each of these women came from other important zamindari families in the district. The zamindar also left two other widows, including Nagammal, who had been married via a "dagger" form of marriage; in this type of wedding, a dagger (*kaṭṭāri*) sent by the groom substituted for his presence at the ceremony. Ranga Rao suggested that, although this was an "inferior" form of marriage, it was acceptable to the zamindar's caste of "Kambala Tottiyan" and provided Nagammal with the status of "wife." However, as a mark of her lower ranking, he granted Nagammal a smaller monthly maintenance than Muthuverammal and her other co-widows. Ranga Rao also noted the presence of "five illegitimate sons by two concubines named Sadayammai and Pachiammal" to whom he gave maintenance from the zamindari estate; five other women claiming the status of concubines were denied any funds.[45] At this point, in November 1885, the succession to the Saptur zamindari appeared clear, as the zamindar's eldest "legitimate" son was also the son of the senior wife, Muthuverammal, who was married according to the "usual marital rites."

However, after the death of this eldest son two years later, Nagammal—the so-called "dagger-married" wife—sought to wrest control of the estate from Muthuverammal, who held it on behalf of her son. Financed by a Nagarattar merchant, and supported by members of her natal family who were connected to the neighboring Paraiyur zamindari, Nagammal asserted that her son's greater rights to the estate were vested in the fact that he was the eldest, legitimate, surviving son of the zamindar.[46] Thus, from the outset, Nagammal's case was framed within the language of the colonial Hindu law, which characterized zamindari landholdings as inheritable estates that would devolve according to biological, patrilineal kinship. Within this legal logic, litigants sought to prove not that they were the most effective rulers (as they might have under precolonial regimes) but that they held legal "ownership" of the estate in question. Indeed, given that Nagammal's son, Sundaralingasawmi, was younger than ten, his claims could hardly be linked to his ruling abilities but instead were tied to his qualifications within legal categories of inheritance. Similarly, Muthuverammal defended the rights of her son, Ramasawmi, according to legal criteria, arguing that he was the sole legitimate son of the Saptur zamindar. Sundaralingasawmi could not inherit the estate, she claimed, because his mother, Nagammal, was merely a lower caste "concubine." The legal investigation thus put Nagammal's claims to wifehood on trial.

Although lawyers questioned Nagammal about her natal family's status and her alleged wedding ceremony, she emphasized her behavior and status after arriving in the Saptur palace. Describing her daily life in great detail, she focused on her position in the women's quarters, or *zenana,* of the zamindar's household. Nagammal provided an especially detailed description of the zamindar's meals, which he took in the presence of his wives. Noting that food was prepared in a separate building, she stated:

> From there meals would be brought for the Zemindar [*sic*] and placed in the Court-yard. Thavasi Ammal would come and serve food to the Zemindar; another wife would bring water to wash the feet; another woman would bring water to wash hands; one woman would fan; another woman would cool water for drinking. After meals were over, I would bring him the plate containing betel leaf. Kumarammal would fan . . . [After the zamindar's meal] all the eight of us [wives] will [*sic*] arrange ourselves in a row and spread leaves, and I would bring the leaf which my husband used when eating and thus we would all take meals. I would bring one day the said leaf and take meals in it; another wife would do the same on another day.[47]

This image of service to her husband during meals, which she claimed to have performed twice daily throughout her marriage, played a critical role in Nagammal's claim to wifehood. Noting that only wives were allowed such close proximity to their husband during meals, Nagammal maintained that the zamindar's concubines resided outside the palace compound and did not join, or even witness, his mealtimes. Further, her claim about eating the leavings off the zamindar's leaf, which Nagammal includes as a sign of her high status, constructs a vision of wifehood rooted in the intimate, yet socially acknowledged, display of service and subordination. Upon these grounds, Nagammal staked her claim to "legitimate" wifehood and, by implication, to her son Sundaralingasawmi's control over the Saptur estate. Interestingly, Nagammal's assertion of her daily physical proximity to the zamindar was largely limited to these claims about meals. Although she mentioned her son's birth, she never alluded to (and was presumably not questioned about) her sexual relations with her husband.

The other wives of the Saptur zamindar, all of whom supported Muthuverammal against Nagammal's claims, also emphasized the physical arrangement of meals within the women's quarters—rather than a sexual relationship—as important to wifely identity. For example, in the words of Muthukrishnammal, one of the "regularly married" wives, "When our husband takes meals we would be doing services to him. Kumarammal and Nagammal did not do any service. They would remain quiet in a secluded place."[48] Building on this point, Muthuverammal herself argued that the social recognition of wifely status—exhibited via service at mealtimes—was far more significant than a sexual relationship with the zamindar. Indeed, sexual partnership with the zamindar, even when it produced children, in no way elevated a woman's status. Thus, as noted in the epigraph, she claimed: "Whenever my husband felt amorous, he would occasionally cohabit with any woman and pay her occasionally. This is all. They were concubines."[49] More meaningful markers of wifehood, according to Muthuverammal, were the form of marriage ceremony, the place of a woman's residence (within or outside the palace compound), and her caste identity. On all these grounds, Muthuverammal asserted her superior status compared to Nagammal.

Muthuverammal's testimony, together with that of other higher-status wives, dovetailed well with the concerns of the colonial courts; she was successful in linking her claims to status with the mandates of the developing colonial law. Therefore, although both the lower district court and the Madras High Court found that Nagammal was legally married in the dagger ceremony and therefore was not a "concubine," they agreed with Muthuverammal's argument that Nagammal was a wife of lower status. This inferior status was shown, according to the district court, "by her marriage in dagger form . . . It is shewn [*sic*] by the way in which she and other dagger wives were treated . . . They messed separately."[50] The Privy Council agreed that Nagammal's "status and rank was inferior to that of the Respondent's mother [Muthuverammal], the latter being the daughter of a zemindar [*sic*] while the former was the daughter of an ordinary *ryot* [peasant proprietor.]"[51] The Council confirmed that Muthuverammal's status as the senior wife further buttressed her son's claims to Saptur.

Therefore, in parceling out the estate as a piece of inherited property, the colonial law fostered conflicts among zamindari kin that were expressed as debates over female conjugality and sexuality. Rather than seeing this conflict as a fluid and fundamentally political process for access to power and resources, the colonial law sought the "truth" of Nagammal's conjugality within two critical linchpins of this case: caste and ritual practice. Through this process, the courts sought to fix Nagammal's status as determined from the moment of her entrance into the Saptur household. As a result, her wifehood was not a malleable category that shifted according to her activities subsequent to her wedding. Instead, these activities, including the arrangement of meals, only reinforced a status distinction based in the ritual of "dagger marriage." Therefore, even though the non-monogamous relationships of the Saptur zamindar created the conditions for conflict and competition among wives and their supporters, these conflicts, from the court's perspective, were fundamentally irrelevant to the issues of ritual and property upon which it adjudicated. Concerned with setting legal precedent, the judgment in the Saptur case provided guidelines for several subsequent cases regarding dagger marriage and the rights of illegitimate and lower-status sons among the "Kambala Tottiyans." These principles also appeared in colonial ethnography, including in Edgar Thurston and K. Rangachari's massive documentation, *Castes and Tribes of Southern India,* further overwriting the specificity of the Saptur household with the generality of caste and ritual.[52]

"A Virgin of Another Sect": Caste and Sexuality in Bodinayakanur

Questions of caste and ritual were writ equally large in a dispute over the Bodinayakanur zamindari located in the Periyakulam *taluk* (subdivision) of Madurai district. The first zamindar of Bodinayakanur was Kamaraja Pandya, who was granted his *sanad* (title) in 1880.[53] Like his Saptur neighbors, Kamaraja was identified as belonging to the "Kambala Tottiyan" caste, and the two zamindari households maintained close kinship relations during the late nineteenth century. For instance, Muthuverammal, the successful claimant to wifehood in the Saptur case, was the daughter of the Bodinayakanur zamindar by his wife Kamulammal. Upon the zamindar's death in 1888, the colonial administration granted Kamulammal, who had no sons, control over the zamindari estate.

In 1904, however, sixteen years after her husband's death, an adult son of the zamindar, one T. B. K. Visvanathaswami Naicker, challenged Kamulammal's title. Visvanathaswami claimed that his mother, Karuppaye, was a wife of the zamindar, and, in the absence of other "legitimate" sons, he was the rightful heir of the Bodinayakanur estate.[54] Karuppaye appeared as a witness on her son's behalf, and, after his death, the case was taken to the Privy Council in her name. For her part, Kamulammal rejected Visvanathaswami's claims on the grounds that Karuppaye was the zamindar's "concubine," and therefore her son was "illegitimate." Thus, as in the Saptur litigation, the legal dispute hinged on interpretations of wifehood and concubinage among women in the zamindari household. To assert their claims to control over Bodinayakanur, both Kamulammal and Karuppaye offered the evidence of their relationship with the zamindar. Further intensifying trends in the Saptur case, the legal judgment about Bodinayakanur ignored women's activities and behavior within the household, in this instance dismissing claims of affect and conjugal companionship between Karuppaye and Kamaraja. Instead, linking conjugality to caste and ritual incorporation within the household, the court ultimately maintained that Karuppaye—who entered Bodinayakanur as a "virgin of another sect"—had no right to the zamindari estate.

Karuppaye's testimony about her status went beyond the caste and ritual categories that were central to colonial law. She began by describing her sexual respectability in relations with the zamindar. As in the Saptur case, the specific questions prompting Karuppaye's responses were not included in the record:

> I have no husband now. I had one. He died 10 or 15 years back. I won't tell his name. He was the Zemindar [*sic*] of Bodinaickenur [*sic*]. He married me after I attained puberty. He never married me. That is, there was no "Kalyanam." He took me a month or a month and a half after I attained puberty. I was about 15 years when the Zemindar took me. I was the wife of the Zemindar. I used to go to the well on the west near the Zemindar's palace to get water. He saw me there. There is one Ponnammal. The Zemindar told Ponnammal to bring me to him. Ponnammal came to me and gave me the message. I said to her, that was not proper and I scolded her.

Karuppaye added that another intermediary, one Mahamoye, again conveyed the zamindar's request, to which she responded that she "would go to him if he would take me as a wife and not otherwise." After Mahamoye indicated the zamindar's consent to this stipulation, Karuppaye approached her parents, whom she described as tenants of the zamindar. Following their approval, she went to the zamindar's palace, where she met Kamaraja and his mother:

> The Zemindar spoke to me then. He asked me thus:—I sent word to you, calling you, why did you get angry. I said I was not angry. I could not be coming and going irregularly; that would not make the family [*sic*]. Then, the Zemindar said he would take me as wife. I consented thereto.[55]

Karuppaye concludes this narrative with a description of a cloth and jewel which she then received from the zamindar.

Beginning with an initial ambiguity about whether a marriage had occurred—due perhaps to the use of multiple Tamil terms, including "*kalyāṇam,*" to denote wedding or marriage—Karuppaye's testimony held fast to the claim that she had refused to engage in sexual activity without the status of "wife." On this basis, she forcefully rejected any suggestions that she was a concubine:

> How can anybody call me the concubine of the Zemindar. That would be degrading to me. That would anger me. I would never call myself as the concubine (*vaippāṭṭi*) of the Zemindar. It would be improper to call me who is a wife as concubine.

Karuppaye buttressed her argument about her wifely status with evidence about the quality of her relationship with the zamindar. Thus, like Nagammal in the Saptur case, Karuppaye claimed that her behavior and relationships after marriage, and not her social status or ritual incorporation into the palace household, marked her as a "wife." Unlike Nagammal, however, who focused on ritual proximity during mealtimes, Karuppaye spoke of her affective ties: "The Zemindar is [*sic*] much attached to Plaintiff [Visvanathaswami] as also to me. He was more attached to me than to the first Defendant [Kamulammal]." The closeness of her relationship was also sexual, but not exclusive, as Karuppaye acknowledges: "he used to bed with me sometimes and with first Defendant [Kamulammal] sometimes."[56] Therefore, although Karuppaye was not the zamindar's only wife, her testimony suggests that her sexual respectability when entering the household, combined with her emotional-sexual companionship after marriage, marked her wifely status.

Despite Karuppaye's claims, Kamulammal's testimony was ultimately more effective in mobilizing the legal categories of "wifehood" and "concubinage." For instance, she asserted that Karuppaye's mode of joining the zamindar's household clearly marked her as a concubine; "my husband brought her into the palace one night and I heard of it the next day." No wedding ceremony or ritual marked this entrance. Noting further that the zamindar had installed Karuppaye in a separate residence where he never joined her for meals, Kamulammal attributed this separation to caste: "Marava people cannot get food in the same row as Kambalas." Further, Karuppaye and her son ate separately because they "belonged to an inferior caste." Indeed, in Kamulammal's terms, Karuppaye's caste status put her beyond the pale of zamindari wifehood: "She was not treated as a wife by my husband or by relations, and Plaintiff [Visvanathaswami] was not treated as a legitimate child by anybody."[57]

Although she emphasized the exclusiveness of her own status as wife based on caste and ritual, Kamulammal did not entirely ignore the issues of affection, sexuality, and conjugal companionship so central to Karuppaye's claims. Rather, Kamulammal represented herself as an appropriately subordinate and forbearing wife, one who was even willing to acknowledge Karuppaye's relationship with the zamindar:

> I never remonstrated with my husband for bringing 4th Defendant (Karuppaye) into the palace compound. I left him to follow his own inclinations. "What matters it to me," I thought.

Indeed, Kamulammal asserted that Karuppaye's arrival did not change her relationship with her husband: "The Zemindar used to sleep in my bed-room mostly even after taking Karuppaye. He used to sleep with me even down to his death." Her intimacy with the zamindar extended into a detailed knowledge of his body, a knowledge that Kamulammal shared in testimony supporting her claim that he was physically able to write a will shortly before his death: "He required the help of nobody to support him when he moved about then . . . Even after his bowels moved on the two days before his death, he did not complain of exhaustion except during the moments of chest pain, which was only intermittent." Notably, in this part of her testimony—in contrast to her claims about Karuppaye's caste status—Kamulammal did not draw a firm distinction between herself and Karuppaye. Acknowledging that prior to the zamindar's death Karuppaye was "generally by his side and even shampooing [*sic*] his legs when there was nobody else," she suggests that this proximity was not a sign of Karuppaye's wifely status.[58] In other words, in the face of Karuppaye's "inferior" caste and her mode of entrance into the zamindari household, her emotional and sexual relationship with the zamindar was irrelevant to determining her wifehood/concubinage.

In its judgment, the district court agreed with Kamulammal's claim that Karuppaye was not a "lawful wife" but rather a "permanent concubine." On this basis, the judges determined that her son, Visvanathaswami, could not inherit the estate.[59] Upon appeal, the Madras High Court based its judgment on whether there existed "a custom among the Kambala caste which would create the relationship of husband and wife without any marriage ceremony by the mere fact of a Kambala taking a virgin of another sect into his family as his wife and treating her as his wife."[60] Described solely as "a virgin of another sect," we see that Karuppaye's caste status was rendered inseparable from her gendered and sexual identities, such that her access to wifehood hinged on the customary practices governing Kambalas and Maravars. Indeed, in the very framing of this question, Karuppaye's extensive testimony about her closeness—physical, emotional, and sexual—with the zamindar was swept away, as were her claims about her propriety in insisting on marriage prior to sexual relations. The court, based on numerous Kambala witnesses testifying about caste practices, that any such custom was "neither a definite nor an ancient one, is not proved to be regarded as a proper one by the community, and is not plural or uniform," labeled Karuppaye a concubine and Visvanathaswami her illegitimate son.[61]

Therefore, as in the Saptur case, a woman's own behavior subsequent to entering the zamindari household was rendered marginal to determining her status; instead, her identity as a wife/concubine was marked at the moment of her entrance. In this sense, the boundaries of the household were fixed in new ways. The permeability that allowed Karuppaye to enter the Bodinayakanur palace did not reshape the legal contours of the zamindar's marriage or family relations. Kamaraja's family was now defined as a fixed entity whose unchanging borders were mapped by caste, and severed from its kinship and ritual connections to lower-status households. In other words, Karuppaye's parents entered the legal record as "tenants" of the zamindar whose daughter could only become a "concubine" and not a "wife" within the landlord's household/family. Within this legal context, successful competitors for zamindari resources like Kamulammal spoke a language of reified caste and blood kinship.

Reconstructing *Dharmic* Conjugality in Uttumalai

Women contested legal interpretations of the family and its attendant implications for access to resources within the zamindari estate. Here let us turn our attention to one female litigant, Menakshi Sundra Nachiar, who produced such a critique of colonial legal norms. In staking her claims for control over the Uttumalai estate in Tirunelveli district, her testimony developed a model of what I term "*dharmic* conjugality." As in Pamela Price's formulation of "*dharmic* kingship," Menakshi's conjugal models referenced the "moral order of the cosmos and correct relations among human beings in a domain" that characterized precolonial relations of ruling; in particular, she invoked the notion of a ruler as a redistributor of largess within the domain of Uttumalai.[62] At the same time, with its attention to wifely status, Menakshi's *dharmic* model adopted colonial-era discourses of conjugality. Intertwining her position as a wife with her claims to ruling authority, Menakshi maintained that conjugality was both a political relationship and a domestic one; she combined the two to argue for the title of *zamindarni* (female zamindar) of Uttumalai.

The Uttumalai estate was part of the original Permanent Settlement in 1803, but the colonial state frequently took control of the estate's management throughout the early nineteenth century. This situation changed somewhat with the death of a zamindar in 1850, whose title passed to his son, Irudalaya Marudappa Taver. Because the new zamindar was still a minor, his mother, Peryanayaki Nachiar managed the estate for a number of years, during which time it was not retaken under direct colonial control.[63]

After reaching adulthood sometime in the 1860s, Irudalaya married Annapurni Nachiar and Menakshi Sundra Nachiar. His choice of Annapurni, who was only five or six years of age at the time, helped to cement an alliance with her natal kin, who resided in the village of Kurukulpatti. It appears that the Kurukulpatti family supported him in his ongoing conflicts with his uncle, a titled landholder in the village of Chokkampatti.[64] Because of her young age, however, Annapurni did not immediately join her husband, and only Menakshi (an adult at the time of her wedding) entered the palace at Verakeralampudur. Upon Irudalaya's death in 1891, the Uttumalai estate passed to the zamindar's adopted son, Navanithakrishna Marudappa Taver. Because the heir was still a minor, the Court of Wards administered the estate. However, Navanithakrishna died just a few months after his adoptive father, and succession to Uttumalai became the subject of litigation between Annapurni and Menakshi.[65] The case hinged on the question of each wife's relationship to the zamindar and to his adopted son, Navanithakrishna.

Menakshi claimed that Annapurni had never lived with the zamindar but had been divorced by her husband just a few years after their marriage because her family had converted to Christianity. She added that about twenty or twenty-five years after the divorce, in 1889, Annapurni had forcefully entered the palace at Verakeralampudur and refused to leave it.[66] Annapurni and her lawyers, on the other hand, argued that the zamindar had never legally married Menakshi and that she was simply "taken under his protection" several years after Annapurni's own marriage. Further, Annapurni alleged that, because of his severe illness, the zamindar was physically and mentally incapable of adopting Navanithakrishna in the months before his death. And, finally, in perhaps one of the most extreme examples of the centrality of ritual procedure within the logic of colonial law, Annapurni suggested that Menakshi had been incapable of participating in any adoption ceremonies, as "she was then in a state of pollution in consequence of her monthly courses."[67] This ritual incapacity, Annapurni argued, meant that Menakshi was not the true adoptive mother of Navanithakrishna, and therefore was not entitled to inherit the zamindari as the boy's closest relative.

In responding to these allegations, Menakshi's testimony developed a model of zamindari wifehood that wove together the norms of *dharmic* morality, claims of wifely companionship, and the legal requirements of caste and ritual into a relatively seamless whole. Her construction of this model of *dharmic* conjugality began with the caste-class status of her natal family. Noting that, like the zamindar, she belonged to the Maravar caste, Menakshi asserted that she was blood-kin to the Uttumalai household even prior to her marriage. Beyond her natal family, Menakshi also ascribed her status to her position as a wife of the zamindar, noting that her husband had gifted her considerable lands. Menakshi emphasized that she used this wealth for "charitable purposes, such as giving to temples, building temples and making jewels to God. I have been spending in such charitable purposes for twenty years." When asked, Menakshi also produced detailed lists of the recipients of her charitable giving:

> I had the front Mantapam [hall] of the temple in my village built fifteen years ago. I had jewels made for the said temple. I had jewels made with the inscription of my name for Menakshi's temple at Madura. I did so eleven years ago. I had a curtain made for the bedroom of Minakshi's [*sic*] temple with my name on. Ten years ago I had jewels made for the use of Thirupparamkuntram temple with my name inscribed therein and presented the same.[68]

Her list includes other major temples in southern India, such as at Tiruppati and Tiruchendur, as well as smaller temples within Tirunelveli district. Returning to this charitable giving more than once over the course of her testimony, Menakshi represented this activity as central to her claims of zamindari wifehood. It was not simply the extent of her wealth that proved her ruling status; rather, it was the *dharmic* uses of such wealth—via charitable giving—both within Uttumalai and beyond it, that marked her claims to the estate. Menakshi's construction of her authority hearkened back to earlier ideologies about the redistributive responsibilities of south Indian rulers. However, this emphasis on sociopolitical behavior, by directing attention away from blood kinship and domestic conduct, cut against the grain of legal assumptions about women's roles within zamindari households.

Menakshi's proof of her wifely status also hinged on her companionate relationship with the zamindar; she consistently emphasized that her husband had no such relationship with Annapurni. Echoing the key themes of the Saptur and Bodinayakanur cases, Menakshi maintained that "the Zemindar [*sic*] used to take his meals with me. The Zemindar used to sleep during nights in the upstairs of the new palace. I and he used to sleep in the same bed." More unusually, and perhaps to highlight modes of emotional intimacy, she noted that she could read, and that the zamindar was her regular correspondent when he traveled. As part of these descriptions of marital companionship, Menakshi also noted her willing subordination to the zamindar's dictates. For instance, she emphasized that she did not question the zamindar about his marriage to Annapurni in the village of Kurukkalpatti for two or three days after his return: "I did not see him and ask anything. He was Zemindar [*sic*]. I was the bride. I did not ask him what his thought and intention [*sic*] were." Acknowledging that she did speak to him later about this, Menakshi made no further statements about her feelings toward a co-wife. Her testimony concludes with information about the ceremonies surrounding the adoption of her brother's son, Navanithakrishna.[69]

From this broad-ranging evidence, Menakshi staked her claims to wifehood both in terms of her activities as a *dharmic* ruler in her own right, and in her (subordinate) companionship with her husband. This model of conjugality refused to separate a "private" sphere of domestic intimacy from a "public" sphere of ruling authority; Menakshi represented her marital relationship as simultaneously political and familial, such that her claims to wifely status were buttressed by her demonstration of effective rulership. However, setting aside most of her testimony, the colonial courts focused narrowly on two legal issues: the question of the zamindar allegedly "divorcing" Annapurni, and Menakshi's ritual ability to adopt Navanithakrishna. Although the district judge in Tirunelveli disallowed the divorce on the grounds of custom, he did allow that Navanithakrishna had been legally adopted by the zamindar and Menakshi; he also dismissed, because of insufficient evidence, Annapurni's claims of Menakshi's ritual "pollution." On this basis, the district court awarded the Uttumalai estate in full to Menakshi, as the "sole adopted mother and nearest heir of the last holder of the estate," the child Navanithakrishna.[70] The Madras High Court dismissed an appeal from Annapurni, and the Privy Council also upheld the district court's decision to give the title of *zamindarni* to Menakshi. However, Menakshi did not gain this title on her own terms, and her model of *dharmic* conjugality was ignored in all judicial opinions. Despite her own claims to the contrary, Menakshi's success—like that of Muthuverammal and Kamulammal in the other cases—was based in the court's interpretation of caste-based ritual practice.

Defining the Domestic

The colonial legal system's intervention in zamindari households resulted in several changes in family ideologies. The Saptur, Bodinayakanur, and Uttumalai cases all suggest that, although kinship remained important to the maintenance of honor and status under colonial rule, the meaning of "kin" had changed during the course of the nineteenth century. The legal separation of wifehood from concubinage contributed to this transformation. By distinguishing "wives" from "concubines"—and by fixing these identities permanently upon particular women—the colonial judiciary marked the boundaries of zamindari households in more rigid, less permeable ways than before. Specifically, judges investigated the status of household members based upon their birth, caste, and blood relations, producing, in the process, a "core" of biologically related kin surrounded by a "periphery" of servants and service providers who labored to support a "family" of which they were not a part.

Women did not regard these developments passively but were actively engaged with legal institutions. The public nature of the legal process, which included the collection of testimony and appearances in court, offered women a new arena for asserting their rights to zamindari estates. As we have seen, women, often with the support of their kin, took advantage of their access to this public space by instituting court cases and defending their rights to property and ruling authority. In this regard, as Pamela Price correctly notes, historians must read zamindari litigation not as corrupt household intrigue but as a deeply gendered mode of politics.[71] However, women's political activity occurred over a narrowly circumscribed terrain, in which their ascriptive identities were inseparable from women's marital status. In other words, the appellation of "wife" had embedded within it a rigid, ritualized form of caste identity.

Within this circumscribed context, women like Menakshi Sundra Nachiar of Uttumalai developed new models of wifehood; however, the colonial legal system typically disregarded these alternatives. For instance, judges tended to dismiss women's patronage as "extravagant" or "corrupt" mismanagement of zamindari estates. Similarly, they disregarded women's varied labors within the household—ranging from service in meals to the bearing of children—as less relevant than caste or ritual in establishing status.[72] While rejecting these older models of female behavior, the law was equally dismissive of women's assertions of marital companionship, typically ignoring claims about affective and sexual relations between men and women. Instead, in seeking to regulate zamindari households, legal institutions produced patriarchal family forms that disregarded women's political authority while emphasizing their socio-sexual status as "wives" or "concubines" under the control of male zamindari kin.

Methods of legal procedure magnified the impact of these interventions. Once taken to the colonial courts, disputes within zamindari households were no longer contained in the boundaries of the locality but became newly publicized in the district or presidency center. As a result, the political manipulations of zamindari household members were now rendered available for critique by men and women who were not part of these households.[73] Under these conditions, the non-monogamous conjugal practices of zamindari kin—and particularly the activities of women within the *zenana* (women's quarters)—emerged as a target of public debate and reform.

Several factors converged to make the question of conjugality so important to debates about zamindari households. Within precolonial polities, the presence of multiple royal women within a ruling household lent legitimacy and political effectiveness to south Indian "little kings."[74] However, this situation changed under the colonial regime. Within a legal system that classified royal women either as wives of zamindars and mothers of legitimate heirs, or as concubines whose offspring were denied property rights, one female litigant's success in the courts could mean the simultaneous exclusion of other women from the status of wife. Thus, women seeking property and political authority could best assert their claims before the courts by questioning the propriety, sexual respectability, and claims of wifehood made by other zamindari women. For instance, as we saw in Bodinayakanur, Kamulammal's authority over the estate depended on her ability to degrade Karuppaye's relationship to the zamindar as one of concubinage.

European missionaries and Indian social reformers seized upon these public disputes among women to figure the *zenana* as a pathological space in need of either Christianizing or Indian nationalizing reform.[75] In stark contrast to precolonial representations of royal women, reformers argued that zamindari women were victims of a corrupt *zenana* culture that epitomized the failures of Indian conjugality. For example, European missionary discourses of domesticity, which centered on the heterosexual monogamous couple, represented the polygamous sexuality of zamindars as an anathema that highlighted the moral degradation of Hindu civilization.[76] Indian nationalists and social reformers found the diverse conjugal practices of zamindari households to be equally problematic. Selectively appropriating Brahmanical norms to recuperate an Indian "tradition" of monogamy, nationalist discourses dismissed zamindari conjugality as a corrupt practice that misrepresented Indian ideals. As they did with other alternative conjugalities, nationalists tended to stigmatize zamindari non-monogamy as lower caste and morally degenerate. Thus, the zamindari household, with its multiplicity of "wives" and "concubines," found little place either in the nationalist rewriting of the Indian past or in its visions for a national future.

Ultimately, therefore, when the emergent middle classes of Madras city sought to reconstruct the "family" as the incubus of nation and national identity, they did not look to zamindari households as repositories of either political or domestic traditions. In the political realm, they rejected many elements of zamindari ruling authority, turning instead to an urban-centered public sphere and print culture developed under colonial rule.[77] In the domestic realm, the *zenana* became "an archive of what was . . . a repository of the past that nationalists, imperialists, and feminists agreed should be confined to history."[78] The discrediting and disintegration of the zamindari household under colonial relations of rule thus produced the context in which Tamil middle classes rearticulated the family as a private, inviolable, and apolitical space of cultural regeneration. In other words, I suggest, a nationalist family ideal developed over the rejection of the gendered ideologies and politics of the households of former ruling elites.

In this way, the ideological intersection of the colonial state with former ruling households opened up some new modes of political activity while foreclosing others. The law's removal of the household from formal sites of politics set the stage for the prominence of a new domesticity around which Indians organized their political aspirations. In this regard, the "home" was not simply available for nationalist recuperation in the twentieth century. Rather, nationalism adopted a separation of domestic and political spheres that was a product of colonial rule. In other words, nationalists assigned meanings to domestic arenas under terms and conditions created by the colonial history of household spaces. Therefore, although the particulars of zamindari experience were limited to a minority of Tamils, the fate of these vast households was critical to shaping future ideological developments in Tamil family history.

TWO

Conjugality and Capital: Defining Women's Rights to Family Property

The very principle of the joint family is against giving equal rights to females.

P. C. Tyagaraja Iyer, 1935

Writing to the government of Madras, P. C. Tyagaraja Iyer, a judge in the southern Indian town of Chittoor, argued against legislation granting women rights to property owned by their families.[1] Rejecting the notion that daughters and sons could possess an equal stake in familial property, the judge defended the family as a site of male patrilineal privilege. Although such sentiments were not unusual—Tyagaraja Iyer's letter is just one among a voluminous correspondence opposed to legal reform—the epigraph makes starkly explicit a gendering of property and family that was often left implicit in colonial discourse; that is, property relations among family members, including the constitution of the "joint family" itself, depended upon women's inequality. In its mid-1930s context, Tyagaraja Iyer's emphatic assertion of such inequality was occasioned by a developing legal and political challenge to his vision of the patrilineal joint family. Whereas the judge maintained that property must be held jointly by fathers and sons, other legislators and activists invoked discourses of conjugality and capital to articulate a novel model of family and economy.

This discursive alignment of conjugality and capital, which emerged in Tamil urban centers beginning in the late nineteenth century, rejected the sprawling households of zamindars and other landholding elites. Men who were engaged in a developing mercantile and professional economy in the

Tamil region advocated a smaller family, centered on the property and affective relations of a monogamous husband and wife, which they claimed would foster capitalist development and economic prosperity. To create such families, however, these men were forced to contend with the property laws of the colonial state. Although allowing some individual rights to property, the colonial legal system maintained that property ownership was primarily a joint obligation or trust.[2] In the case of the zamindari settlement, as we have seen, this system implied that a wide range of kin and household members were entitled to share in the resources of an estate, even though the land was nominally under the control of an individual zamindar. In the case of the majority of Hindus, who were not governed under the zamindari settlement, the law assumed that property was held jointly; it mandated that ownership be shared by groups of male agnatic kin. However, mercantile and professional classes claimed that joint ownership—and the broader legal conception of property as trust—did not correspond either to the changing political economy or to the "natural" bonds of affection within families. Instead, they demanded legal reforms that would diminish the claims of family members, loosen the obligations of joint ownership, and strengthen the ability of individual men to control their property within a market economy.

When propertied men began to question the colonial law in the 1890s, women did not initially figure as agents in the debate. Instead, men challenged colonial property relations largely through reference to women as wives, widows, and daughters. Within this gendered discourse, they represented male individual rights to property as benefiting women. Invoking the bonds of affection within a conjugal family, proponents of legal reform suggested that husbands and fathers—rather than an extended group of male kin—would be the best providers for women. But although not originating in response to women's demands, this reconceptualization of men's individual ownership in the late nineteenth century did become crucial to raising the question of women's property in subsequent decades. By the 1930s, in the context of feminist and nationalist challenges to family hierarchies, some women began to debate the issue of women's rights to property. However, as we shall see, the assertion of women's property rights was severely restricted by both colonial and nationalist interpretations of the "tradition" of joint ownership within families.

The challenge to joint ownership, and its vociferous defense by men like P. C. Tyagaraja Iyer, was not solely about property relations. Through questioning the model of property as a joint trust, the men and women who challenged the colonial law rearticulated individual subjectivity and family identity. However, given that "the colonial economy, subordinated to the needs of the imperial centre, did not produce conditions under which a full and unrestrained flowering of individualism could occur,"[3] the discourse of conjugality and capital did not completely reject colonially inspired traditions about the joint family. Instead, women came to represent "tradition" even within claims about a modernizing family/nation and their rights were defined in extremely narrow terms.

Women's changing legal relationship to property can thus illuminate broader contradictions in the Tamil conjugal family ideal. In making this claim, I do not imply sociological changes in women's property ownership, although such changes most likely occurred. Rather, drawing from feminist scholarship on the social history of the law,[4] I consider, on the one hand, how concepts of the family determined the legal possibilities for women's ownership, and, on the other, how the dynamics of property relations transformed normative ideals of the family. The Tamil family debates negotiated the resulting tensions between individual ownership and joint control, between men's rights and women's "dependency," and between the putative "traditions" of a joint family and the modernizing aspirations of a conjugal family ideal.

Women, Families, and the Colonial Property Laws

The discourse of conjugality and capital made visible an ongoing tension between a developing mercantile economy and the property relations of landed classes. These tensions did not originate with colonial rule but may be traced to at least the early eighteenth century.[5] Under precolonial regimes of "military fiscalism," scribal and merchant groups became prominent as administrators, revenue collectors, and bankers. These new classes increased their power vis-à-vis landed groups by expanding the realms of personal (though not necessarily individual) property rights at the expense of communitarian usage. However, as David Washbrook has demonstrated, the colonial state reversed these mercantile trends through its gradual replacement of indigenous capital with European capital. In processes of "peasantization" and "traditionalization"—both buttressed by colonial law—the state expanded the realm of joint obligation at the expense of individual property rights and market economies.[6] Therefore, insofar as scribal and mercantile groups were concerned, early colonial rule actually restricted the development of new property relationships.

Nevertheless, even within the agrarian-dominated economy of British India, mercantile activity continued and depended on the fluidity of forms of capital. Unlike agrarian groups, and despite colonial constraints, Tamil mercantile castes organized their kinship and property relations to maximize this fluidity.[7] Like mercantile activities, the economic relations of professional elites could also be distinguished from the agrarian economy. From the early nineteenth century on, scribal castes had entered colonial educational institutions and transformed the professional landscape.[8] These lawyers, doctors, and other professionals and administrators acquired wealth independent of their family property. For the most successful of these men, such wealth, which they claimed was the result of individual effort rather than familial collaboration, far exceeded income derived from the land.[9] Therefore, like their mercantile counterparts, professional elites had distinct economic interests that did not necessarily coincide with the colonial state's conception of property as a joint obligation. I emphasize, however, that these analytical distinctions were fluid in practice. Although mercantile or professional activity was sometimes linked to particular castes, it was not always—or completely—separate from the agrarian economy. Merchants and professionals sometimes invested their profits in agricultural land, and, similarly, agrarian groups sometimes engaged in mercantile and industrial activity.[10] Therefore, my analysis refers to agrarian, mercantile, and professional interests, recognizing that these interests mapped imperfectly onto social groups in the Tamil region.

Developing its property regime in relation to these competing interests, the colonial state typically supported the economic and household relationships of landholding classes. Concerned with securing collaborators who could ensure a reliable stream of revenue, the British administration forged alliances with agrarian patriarchies, effectually buttressing control of resources within agrarian society by particular men (as heads of families).[11] The form of these alliances varied over time and by region. For instance, we have seen that the Madras Permanent Settlement created a class of zamindars whom it represented as the "native aristocracy" of the region. In other parts of Madras Presidency, colonial administrators supported family-based forms of land control not vested in an individual owner. Indeed, throughout the colonial period, the Indian subcontinent was crisscrossed with diverse forms of land ownership, and no uniform system of property relations was applicable to all inhabitants. Yet, across these differences, colonial administrators in the nineteenth century retained the notion that property was a joint obligation, and they limited individual property rights.

The colonial legal system played a critical role in enforcing this interpretation of property ownership. From the late eighteenth century on, the colonial state developed a network of laws and courts that combined British legal procedures with a selective interpretation of indigenous "legal" texts. In governing the property relations of most of its Hindu subjects in Madras Presidency, colonial law drew its principles from the Mitakshara legal doctrine of Vijnaneshwara (ca. twelfth century CE). The Mitakshara doctrine was a prescriptive text rather than a body of law in the modern sense. Its ideological impact was largely limited to upper castes, but colonial law took the Mitakshara and other Hindu *sastras* as relevant for governing property relations among all Hindus.[12] Although the courts occasionally accepted customs and practices that differed from these principles, in practice litigants found it difficult to prove the authenticity of custom.[13]

Consequently, colonial property law diminished the diversity of indigenous property relations in favor of an upper-caste–inspired uniformity of "tradition." In terms of the family, as Janaki Nair argues, the law instituted a "Brahmanical patriarchal family form with its reproductive sexual economy at the centre."[14]

The Mitakshara system differentiated between property belonging jointly to male agnatic kin, on the one hand, and separate individually owned property, on the other. According to its colonial interpretation, joint—or coparcenary—property referred to any property "coming into a person's hands, by inheritance or survivorship, on the death of his father, father's father, or father's father's father." Separate property was either self-acquired or inherited from other family members.[15] Coparceners could also agree to partition their joint property, creating separate shares that were individually owned.[16] The colonial interpretation of the Mitakshara excluded women from ownership of joint property.[17] As daughters, they were entitled to maintenance and marriage expenses from the men in their natal coparcenary. As wives or widows, they were entitled to maintenance from the joint property of their husbands. When a woman inherited property—rather than simply being maintained by it—the inheritance was termed a "woman's estate." Distinct from men's inheritance rights, a woman's estate would revert upon her death not to her own heirs but to the heirs of the last male owner. This legal principle became central to disputes in court about the extent of women's control over property. It both curtailed attempts to expand women's property rights and reinscribed women's relationships of dependence upon male-owned property.[18] Women did have greater ownership rights over one kind of property, known, under colonial law, as *stridhana,* which included property a woman had earned, that family members or others had given her as a gift, or that had been granted to her in place of maintenance. Women exercised full, legal control over *stridhana,* except under certain circumstances, when a husband might use the property.[19]

The legal system thus established a normative vision of family and property relations, but this did not translate directly into social practice. In the Tamil region, as elsewhere in British India, a vast diversity of family and property forms continued to exist, many bearing little relationship to legal norms. The universalizing impulse of the law did not eliminate such diversity. For one thing, not all communities turned primarily, or exclusively, to the law to resolve property disputes, as caste- or village-based forms of regulation continued to function throughout the colonial period.[20] For another, the interaction between the law and indigenous practices depended on already existing ideologies and structures of gender, kinship, caste, and economic relations among various social groups. In particular, women's access to property was shaped by various factors outside the law, such as patterns of village exogamy that determined a married woman's proximity or distance from her natal home as well as customary practices regarding divorce and the remarriage of widows. Furthermore, substantial evidence suggests that property holders attempted to circumvent legislation when it did not accord with existing social norms. Women's limited legal rights were frequently ignored or deliberately avoided in actual practice.[21] Therefore, the social impact of colonial property laws cannot be analyzed as a one-way transmission of ideals, for the meaning of the law for women depended heavily on social and economic relations in the societies where the law was imposed.

Even among groups that interacted most directly with the state's legal system, the law was not solely responsible for changes in property and family relations, which depended on broader ideological and economic shifts. For instance, the colonial period witnessed a reduction in common lands over which many people, including women, shared usufructory rights. As part of a "masculinization" of the colonial economy overall, the state replaced usufructory rights with new titles of land ownership, which it largely granted to men. In addition, with the decline of matrilineal patterns that had characterized some communities, women gradually lost access to and control over property and resources.[22] Thus, broader social changes combined with the law to limit women's customary rights over property and to enforce new male forms of ownership and control.[23]

Wives and the Property Rights of Men, 1891–1918

The universalizing language of the law, with its claims of applicability to all colonized subjects, offered a new framework for debate about property relations under colonial rule. Beginning in the late nineteenth century, propertied men used the legal system to express long-standing tensions between agrarian and mercantile interests, and, in the process, they raised questions about the relationship between women's rights and male control over property.[24] In particular, men who were engaged in professional or mercantile activity challenged the colonial laws of the Mitakshara coparcenary, arguing that joint ownership by coparcenary members stifled (male) individual economic initiative. Seeking to remove their property from the bonds of joint obligation, they claimed that individual ownership would usher in capitalist development in the Tamil region. Yet, they also emphasized the primacy of the monogamous conjugal couple, suggesting that property relations between a husband and wife superseded the interests of the male coparcenary. In this way, the property relations of wives became central to the advocacy of male individual rights. This connection of conjugality with capital represented a new legal and economic discourse that, in emphasizing the fluidity of capital forms, reflected mercantile and professional interests as they had developed in this period.

One of the earliest public expressions of this discourse was the Gains of Learning Bill, introduced by Sir Vembakkam Bhashyam Iyengar in 1891. The bill focused on the interests of professionals and sought to separate the individual earnings of professional men from the joint property of families.[25] Under the existing law, if a son's education was funded by coparcenary property, any income he subsequently earned also became part of that property. A nascent, Western-educated professional class became the core of opposition to this notion of joint property. Bhashyam Iyengar himself was a prominent member of this class. After graduating from Presidency College in Madras in 1864, he worked briefly in government service and then joined the bar in 1872. Specializing in the Hindu laws of land tenure and inheritance, Bhashyam Iyengar developed a large clientele of wealthy merchants and zamindars. By the 1880s, he was one of the wealthiest lawyers in Madras Presidency, and in 1900 he was appointed to the Madras High Court.[26]

Bhashyam Iyengar's Gains of Learning Bill would ensure that professional men like himself could keep their earnings separate from joint family property. However, professional interests had little legislative power in late-nineteenth-century Madras Presidency, since the legislative assembly included few elected Indian members and was based in a narrow franchise. Nor did the bill gain a large public following, with opponents condemning it as a law designed for people "who are utterly devoid of sympathy towards their parents and relations."[27] Facing severe opposition inside and outside the legislature, the Gains of Learning Bill failed to become law.

This failure, however, did not signal the end of the legal reinterpretation of property law but rather prompted its continuation in new forms. Between 1891 and the transformation of the Madras Legislature under the Montagu-Chelmsford Reforms in 1919, debates developed about the logic of inheritance and the nature of property rights. Much of this debate coalesced around the Hindu Coparceners' Partition Bill, introduced before the Madras legislature by Ramachandra Rao Pantulu in 1916.[28] This bill, which was not voted into law, sought to simplify the process of partitioning joint families by allowing a coparcener to separate his property through a unilateral declaration. By weakening the legal bonds holding together the coparcenary, the bill sought to expand the individual property rights of men at the expense of joint obligation.

Contemporary observers argued that this expansion of individual rights served the interests of a professional-mercantile elite while disadvantaging landowners. For example, in his comments on the Hindu Coparceners' Partition Bill, A. Subbarayulu Reddi of Cuddalore weighed these competing interests:

> No doubt a small minority of the Hindu community will welcome and even rejoice at the passing of the [Hindu Coparceners' Partition] Bill. The

> minority . . . consisting mostly perhaps of lawyers, merchants, men in higher public service, etc. . . . might feel anxious to appropriate to themselves and their progeny the extraordinary gains they might be making in their respective callings . . . But what about the vast majority, viz., the agricultural community? There the joint family status is the rule . . . Nothing is more noteworthy and charming than the peace and contentment that often prevail in a joint family, or the self sacrifice, self-denial and genuine fellow-feeling that every coparcener often practises and has to practise to secure the well-being and prosperity of the joint family.[29]

Subbarayulu Reddi, who was both a lawyer and a landowner in the South Arcot district, thus maintained that the "agricultural community" needed joint property relations. Eliding the bonds of property with those of affect and residence, he made no distinction between joint property and the joint family. Individual right was operative, in morally ambiguous terms, only for professionals and merchants. Others expressed the importance of joint ownership for agrarian elites even more strongly. According to M. Venkataraghuvulu of Sriperumbudur, "the [j]oint family system preserves and maintains the prestige of the family which has money value in rural areas, where it is this prestige that secures the cheap labour of men and cattle, if not gratuitous [*sic*]."[30] By contrast, he warned that individual ownership would fragment landed estates and thus undermine the economic and social status of landowning families.

Organizational support for, and opposition to, the Hindu Coparceners' Partition Bill bore out these claims about mercantile and professional versus agrarian interests. For instance, the Southern India Chamber of Commerce, an organization grounded in mercantile capital and directed by the most powerful businessmen in Madras, voiced strong support for the bill. In contrast, the Madras Landowners' Association was too rife with dissent to submit a unified opinion to the Madras government. Nevertheless, leading members of the Landowners' Association, including important zamindars, submitted individual memorials to the government in opposition to the bill.[31] Indeed, throughout the debate, supporters of the bill emphasized that individual ownership would facilitate the mobility and flexibility of capital, thus supporting professional and mercantile activities. Proponents of the coparcenary, on the other hand, claimed that the obligation of joint ownership maintained the socioeconomic dominance of landholding families.

To some extent, these debates reflected long-standing conflicts between professional, mercantile, and agrarian economic activities. However, they acquired new meaning when expressed in the language of the colonial law. Landowners characterized their property relations as representing a universalized Hindu "tradition" of joint male ownership and joint family relations.

Professional and mercantile interests, in contrast, invoked a national "modernity" rooted in individual ownership, capitalist development, and the conjugal relationship. The Hindu Coparceners' Partition Bill suggested the terms of these discursive alignments. In his "Statement of Objects and Reasons" offered for the bill, Ramachandra Rao Pantulu argued that the existing laws for partitioning joint property placed unnecessary restrictions on a coparcener who sought individual ownership:

> A coparcener who has no male issue very often desires to separate and obtain his share in the joint family properties and pass it on, either by grant or by inheritance, to his wife, daughter or other relative, but this intention cannot at present be carried out.[32]

In other words, although existing property laws bound a coparcener to the multigenerational unit of male agnatic kin, the Hindu Coparceners' Partition Bill privileged the conjugal relationship by allowing, but not requiring, the transfer of property from a male individual owner to his wife and children.

Opponents of this legislative change criticized male individual ownership and its attendant redefinition of the family. For example, in the words of V. Appanna Sastry: "The tendency now-a-days amongst the people, especially those who receive Western education, is towards individualism"; this tendency, however, led to the "rapid loosening of the grip of Hindu religion and customs upon the minds of the people and the disruption of joint Hindu families." Proponents of joint property emphasized, in particular, the need to exclude women to maintain "Hindu religion and customs." For example, an opponent of legal reform, M. Venkataraghavulu Reddi, questioned the value of women's property rights: "If wholesale grant of the entire share to a wife who will squander it in most cases or to a daughter who stands otherwise provided for by marriage is wholesome at all, is a matter for consideration." Others, such as T. E. Ramanuja Achariyar, focused on wives' supposedly divisive influence on the men of the joint family: "The introduction of outside female members who have no previous relationship is causing inroads into the undivided character of the family. The present Bill only encourages such unsympathetic females to compel their husbands to seek partition."[33] These arguments reject any property relationship that would link husbands and wives, or fathers and daughters; they assert the primacy of male agnatic kin within an agrarian economy.

By contrast, professionals and merchants who supported greater individual property rights challenged the assumption that joint property relations were economically necessary or socially beneficial. In fact, they suggested that joint ownership could have negative consequences for contemporary society: "The age demands this [individual ownership] as a considerable portion of the Hindu population is given to commercial and industrial avocations which require individual freedom and individual capital." They linked individual rights to claims about property relations that were "suited to the present time" in implicit opposition to "traditional" joint ownership. Easing the requirements for partitioning joint property could thus "foster a proper spirit of enterprise and industry" and "conduce to the profitable employment of capital in industrial enterprises"[34] that legal reformers claimed was necessary for the economic development of the Madras Presidency and of the Indian nation as a whole.

These arguments about capitalist development also invoked women's access to property. The prominent lawyer C. P. Ramaswamy Ayyar extolled the economic benefits of partition and argued that supporting male individual rights would "certainly improve the position of the female members of the family by giving them a right to the acquisition of a separate member's property and will raise their position in society."[35] Other proponents of change, including the lawyer and Congress leader C. Rajagopalachari, supported the rights of the conjugal couple and their children over more distant agnatic kin:

> (T)here is no reason whatever to deprive a daughter inheriting to her father, to favour the son of a brother . . . There is equally no justification to deprive one's own widow and prefer the brother when the brother is not worthy of the confidence (which is mostly true) that he would treat the widow of the deceased brother kindly.

Rajagopalachari suggests that the bonds of property (and implicitly those of affection) ought to link husband, wife, and children. He even questions the affective bonds of the larger patrilineal unit: "The perfect mutual kindliness and sympathy which alone would make the joint family a boon is almost totally absent as is clear from the fact that 90 percent of the families do divide."[36] Within this discourse of conjugality and capital, the economic interests of professional and mercantile groups began to coincide with claims about familial affection. Male individual ownership would supplant the joint property relations of male kin—just as the conjugal family would supplant the patrilineage as the site of emotional allegiance.

Mercantile and professional organizations furthered this discourse when they attempted to secure inheritance rights for wives. A year after the failure of the Hindu Coparceners' Partition Bill, the Madras Mahajana Sabha petitioned the Madras government to allow the Married Women's Property Act (1874) to apply to Hindu women.[37] This law set frameworks for husbands to make inheritance provisions for their wives but excluded Hindus from its purview. The Madras Mahajana Sabha argued that Hindu men and their immediate families were entitled to the protection of this act. The advocate-general of Madras supported this claim:

> In the case of Hindus, [this protection] is in fact even more imperatively required than in the case of other communities as *the intention of a Hindu male to benefit his wife and children is not unlikely to be frustrated in half the cases by the law of the joint family* which enables an undivided coparcener to succeed by right of survivorship in preference to a widow or daughter [emphasis added].[38]

This text clearly pleads for the unhindered succession of property from a man to his wife and children, and criticizes the transmission of that property through the man's agnatic kin. The Southern India Chamber of Commerce made the same request. Having been a strong supporter of the Hindu Coparcener's Partition Bill, the Chamber expressed concern to the Madras government about the extent to which property passed outside the immediate family and into the wider group of patrilineal kin.[39] In both cases, these mercantile and professional groups wanted to replace the property relations of the coparcenary with the conjugal family.

Within these debates about property and families, neither proponents nor opponents of legislative reform figured women as agents or subjects. Rather, they renegotiated the property rights of men through reference to women, particularly wives. These challenges to joint property relations did not succeed as legislation, but they did set the terms for further reforms of colonial Hindu law that would develop in new legislative and political contexts. Within these new contexts, the issue of women's ownership would enter the debate about conjugal families, joint ownership, and the nature of individual rights.

Joint Families and the Property Rights of Widows, 1919–1937

After 1919, the institutional context for legal debates about property was transformed. The Montagu-Chelmsford reforms of that year introduced a system of dyarchy, dividing the tasks of governance between provinces and the central government in New Delhi. One result of this shift was the expansion of the provincial government in Madras through an increase in the size of the legislature and a broader franchise. The Government of India Act of 1935 ended dyarchy but continued the process of legislative expansion. Under both administrative reforms, the franchise remained limited to property owners, and the legislature continued to be dominated by elite groups. Nevertheless, by widening the authority and popular base of the legislatures to some extent, the administrative changes of 1919 and 1935 increased the importance of state institutions for the expression of politics.[40] The legislatures became a new terrain to play out conflicts among interests and ideologies, while shaping the terms by which the conflicts were debated. The tensions between agrarian, professional, and mercantile interests over the nature of property ownership were influenced by these institutional changes.

This period also witnessed a new political context for legal discourses on property and families. The development of various nationalisms as mass movements changed the terms of political debate as a whole and particularly the property question. The language of Indian nationalism—nationalist claims about tradition, modernity, and national identity—became implicit in questions about joint property versus individual rights. Nationalist discourses intersected with a nationwide women's movement, represented by the Women's Indian Association (WIA), founded in 1917, and the All-India Women's Conference (AIWC), founded in 1927. These groups, although composed of fairly elite women, transformed the terms of the "woman question" by making women—*qua* women—the subjects and agents of debate. The WIA and AIWC attacked property laws that disadvantaged women, and demanded that women have access to and control over property.

Two successful challenges to the laws of joint ownership developed within these new institutional and political contexts. In 1930, the Madras Legislature passed a Gains of Learning Act. Following the principles of Sir Bhashyam Iyengar's 1891 bill, it rendered professional earnings part of separate individual, rather than coparcenary, property. However, this law cannot be read simply as a triumph of professional interests within the new legislature. Rather, reflecting the colonial state's partial concession to individual ownership in this period, the bill passed into law only with the support of the British administration and against the opposition of a significant number of Indian members.[41] The second change, the Hindu Women's Rights to Property Act, passed by the Indian legislature in 1937, included widows among the heirs to the intestate succession of a husband's separate property and provided them with the same interest as a husband in his joint property. Although widows took this property only in the limited interest known as a woman's estate, this was the first law to introduce women as owners of property within the coparcenary, and thus it represented a fundamental shift in legal conceptions of joint property and family relations.

Historians, quite correctly, have situated women's property rights within the broader context of the "woman question" in colonial India.[42] From this perspective, they place the Hindu Women's Rights to Property Act within a historical narrative about legislative reforms concerning women, such as laws about *sati,* child marriage, and widow remarriage. Although each of these reforms appeared to open the door for change in gender ideologies and women's rights, the extent of change was severely limited because they recast women to serve the interests of a modernized Indian patriarchy. Similarly, while the Hindu Women's Rights to Property Act gave women greater rights of ownership, these rights were extremely narrow and far from equal to men's rights. In further contrast to men, women's access to property hinged not on their natal families but on their marriage. The limitations of the 1937 act become even more apparent when we consider that it was the least comprehensive of several contemporaneous, failed attempts to increase women's rights to property.[43]

To understand this process of recasting women's property rights within a patriarchal system, we must place the 1937 law within the context not only of the "woman question" but also of property and the family as they emerged in late colonial India. The Hindu Women's Rights to Property Act, from this perspective, was part of the broader renegotiation of colonial concepts of joint property and joint families discussed above. Supporters of women's property rights vis-à-vis the joint family drew from similar discourses and interests as the proponents of rights for men as individuals. As in the case of men, claims about the conjugal family underlay attempts to include women as property owners. Yet, women were only partially and problematically conceptualized as property-owning "individuals" within the law.

Because women's rights to joint property challenged the male coparcenary, opponents of this reform attacked notions of individualism in familial and property relations. In the words of one legislator:

> We are accustomed to the joint Hindu family which is so very felicitous to our conditions and very helpful too. But now Western influences have come in to teach us individuality; the wife is allured by individuality to be by herself; the husband does the same thing; the son does not like to be joint with the father, and so on.[44]

The legislator rejects women's property rights by setting individualism, associated with the "West," against the values of joint ownership and living that supposedly characterize Hindu tradition. Such claims had the effect of inseparably linking support for "Hinduism" with support for the existing property laws, leading some defenders of the status quo to appeal to the colonial state as "defenders of their faith" against the inroads of women's individual rights.[45] Tyagaraja Iyer, quoted in the epigraph to this chapter, stated his opinion even more bluntly by claiming that "the very principle of the joint family is against giving equal rights to females."[46]

Some proponents of legal change also employed the language of male individual rights, in this case invoking discourses of conjugality and capitalist development to buttress women's claims to property, albeit with reference to men's economic activity. One colonial administrator, for instance, supported a law mandating women's succession on the grounds that if women had inheritance rights, men would no longer have to devise extralegal methods of supporting their wives and daughters. Under existing law, in a "legitimate but economically unsound method," men made these provisions through "investment of large sums in female ornaments," sacrificing the quality of their houses and other expenditures. It would thus benefit "the woman, the family and public hygiene" if female inheritance rights resulted in more sound investment decisions by men.[47] Thus, like the debates about male individual rights, notions of conjugality and capital entered into the demand for women's rights of ownership.

Unlike the arguments about men, however, the link between women's rights to property and claims about modernity was problematic; indeed, the connection was more deeply embedded in references to tradition. The "tradition" in question rendered women dependent upon, rather than owners of, family property; even the strongest proponents of legislative change assumed women's dependent status. For instance, Harbilas Sarda, a prominent legislative reformer who favored a widow's absolute right to inherit joint property, argued that reform was based on one "principle . . . which is that the lot of a Hindu widow, who at present neither gets a share in her father's property nor in her husband's, should be ameliorated by giving her some rights in the property which belonged to her husband, for her support in her widowed life." These rights did not challenge tradition but were necessary precisely because of the *collapse* of traditions in colonized India: "with the disappearance of moral safe-guards which existed while old Hindu traditions were honoured and acted upon, and owing to their non-possession of legally enforceable rights to property, the position of widows is becoming precarious."[48] Similarly, in the words of P. Kunku Panikkar, "with the unloosening of family ties and disintegration of families everywhere, the Hindu Widow becomes helpless in the present state of the law, and a Bill securing to her independent rights is essential."[49] These men did not represent women's property rights as refiguring women's relationship to family and economy—as in the case of men—but as rebuilding the essence of a tradition in decline.

Women's groups also invoked tradition in their advocacy of greater property rights for women. Beginning in the 1930s, the Women's Indian Association's magazine, *Stri Dharma*, took increasing notice of women's inequality in property relations, criticizing the fact that "three-quarters of India's women have no inheritance rights."[50] Claiming that women's formerly "high place in the Hindu religion" included rights to property, *Stri Dharma*'s writers demanded legislative change. According to Umeshwari Nehru:

> The Hindu law is a system which works primarily for the benefit of families, and takes cognizance of individuals only as constituents of families . . . This system has worked satisfactorily for several centuries but present day conditions are entirely different to those of olden days, and the system is ill suited to them. Besides, certain abuses have crept in which

> have stultified it. A steady tendency towards the lowering of the status of women is the worst and the most serious evil which is greatly responsible for its disintegration.[51]

Turning Sarda's argument on its head, Nehru argues that the joint family's abuse of women is the cause, rather than the consequence, of its decline under "present day conditions." Later in the article, she condemns colonial interpretations of the Hindu law of joint ownership, focusing on women's limited estate and their exclusion from the coparcenary. However, Nehru does not reject joint traditions wholesale but demands reforms that will bring the "Law of Inheritance more into conformity with its progressive interpretations and ancient spirit and the Western ideals of equality with men."[52] Thus, rather than a straightforward association of women's rights with the supposed modernity of conjugality and capital, evocations of Hindu traditions and Western modernity are juxtaposed in this demand for women's rights.

Asserting Widows' Rights: Judicial Interpretation of the Hindu Women's Rights to Property Act

The ambivalence surrounding women's property rights, in which they were the representatives both of the "tradition" of joint families and the "modernity" of conjugality, developed even further within the courts. Indeed, more than through the legislation itself, the workings of the law in practice allow us to see clearly the contradictions underlying the reconceptualization of women's ownership.[53] The Hindu Women's Rights to Property Act produced a considerable case law that began to reach the appellate courts by the mid-1940s and continued into independent India until the 1960s.[54] These cases turned upon the interpretation of the 1937 act but did not typically produce the voluminous documentation characteristic of zamindari litigation. Given the far fewer resources available, litigants did not often appeal the Madras High Court's verdict and the cases rarely reached the Privy Council (or, later, the Indian Supreme Court). As a result, women's voices—even in the mediated forms present in zamindari litigation—are difficult to locate in these legal discourses.[55] In light of these differences, my reading of these cases focuses on judicial interpretation rather than on litigants' own testimony about property ownership or family membership. As I argue, the courts' interpretations of the Hindu Women's Rights to Property Act highlighted the conflict between women's new rights to property ownership and an ongoing assumption about their dependent status within (joint) families.

The central question before the Madras courts was the extent to which a widow acquired coparcenary rights once she assumed the same interest in joint property as her deceased husband. Was she, in other words, a true owner in the same way as a male coparcener? The law stated clearly that a widow acquired one right of ownership: the right to demand partition of joint property into separate shares. But in the absence of other rights, a widow's status as a property owner—rather than as a dependent upon male-owned property—was difficult either for her to sustain or for the courts to enforce. In particular, women's position in their families determined and marked their ability to claim legal ownership of property.

This was the case in *Rathinasabapathy Pillai v. Saraswati Ammal.*[56] Saraswati Ammal had married Kunchitapatham Pillai after the death of his first wife, with whom he had had two sons, Rathinasabapathy Pillai and his brother, unnamed in the suit. Upon Kunchitapatham's death in 1947, Saraswati (according to her rights under the 1937 law) sued to partition the family's joint property between herself and her husband's two sons, asking for a one-third share. The dispute arose over the enumeration of the joint property, with Rathinasabapathy claiming that his father had given a significant portion of it to another relative, and thus it was not subject to partition. In effect, his assertion greatly diminished any claims that Saraswati Ammal could make to joint property by removing much of it from consideration.

The court noted a profound contradiction in the 1937 law, which gave widows some rights of coparceners but not others. In other words, any alienation of joint property—such as Kunchitapatam's "gift"—could be "questioned by the coparceners, but not by the widow, who is not a coparcener." This proved disastrous for Saraswati's property claims; she had the right to partition the property but no right to challenge the alienation of the bulk of this property prior to partition. Her property rights were thus virtually nullified. In a further irony, Saraswati could gain more through a decree of maintenance (which would apply to the whole of the property prior to any alienation) than she could by taking her separate share of joint property that was granted under the 1937 law. The court was critical of this result: "This is one of the anomalies where the Act which was promulgated to give her better rights to property results in practically diminishing her rights, if she is to sue for partition and recover a share."[57] Consequently, the judges decided that Saraswati be given the right to demand maintenance from Rathinasabapathy and his brother; a widow's new rights to own property did not reduce her former rights to maintenance. Thus, Saraswati materially benefited from pursuing her long-standing status of dependence upon male-owned property, and implicitly upon the patriarchal family, rather than from asserting her more recent rights to claim ownership.

Although the Madras court occasionally offered a more expansive view of women's ownership rights, Saraswati's case represented a dominant trend.[58] For instance, the case of *Movva Subba Rao v. Movva Krishna*

Prasadam concerned property owned jointly by Nagiah and his three sons, Subba Rao, Sitaramaiya, and Krishniah.[59] In May 1945 Krishniah died, and a few months later his widow, Ramabanamma, gave birth to a daughter, Krishna Prasadam. Under pre-1937 law, Ramabanamma would have had a right to maintenance for herself and her daughter from her husband's joint estate; if necessary, she could request a court to fix this sum of maintenance and enforce its payment. However, Ramabanamma, like Saraswati in the previous case, demanded her new rights under the 1937 act. In 1950, five years after the death of her husband, she filed a suit demanding partition of the joint family property. Upon partition, she would receive one-fourth of the joint property; the remaining three-fourths would be retained by her husband's father and brothers.

Before her suit could be decided, Ramabanamma died, leaving behind her young daughter. Other relatives (unspecified in the suit) claimed, in 1951, that Krishna Prasadam could become her mother's legal representative. The young girl's uncle and grandmother (her grandfather Nagiah had also passed away by this time) contested this claim, arguing that Ramabanamma could not pass on any property rights to her daughter. The key legal point in dispute here was whether a widow could take her husband's joint property as an heir. If so, Ramabanamma could be considered an heir of her husband, and, upon her death, Krishna Prasadam could be considered the next heir. This mode of transferring property would be analogous to some forms of male inheritance. However, it contradicted how women's rights were configured within the broader corpus of Hindu law.

In order to reconcile the Hindu Women's Rights to Property Act with the Hindu law more broadly, the Madras court asserted that a woman's estate could not be "an estate of inheritance." Justice Venkatarama Ayyar found the legal justification for this limitation not in the 1937 law but in the Hindu *sastras* themselves: "According to Hindu theory," a widow's rights were "founded on the fiction that her husband continues to live in her." Given this fiction of the husband's ongoing life, he concluded, a wife could not become an heir to her husband. Furthermore, Krishna Prasadam—as a daughter—ought not to benefit from the 1937 act, as the purpose of the act was "not to confer rights upon persons other than the widow, but to limit her [the widow's] rights over the estate to which she becomes entitled."[60] The judge added, however, that Krishna Prasadam (age nine by this time) did have the right to maintenance from the joint property of her uncles. Thus, the broader framework of Hindu law—in which women were not full owners of property but depended on support from male family members—set the parameters for women's rights even after 1937.

In ensuing case law, the Madras High Court maintained that the broader structures of Hindu law would not allow widows to become coparceners. The case of *Manicka Gounder v. Arunachala Gounder*, which involved the joint property of two brothers, Nagoji and Krishnamurthi Rao, established this legal principle even more firmly.[61] Nagoji died in 1950, leaving his widow, Kamala; his brother, Krishnamurthi, who was unmarried, died just two days later. Kamala claimed that all the joint property became hers by the principle of survivorship. Like any male coparcener, she had rights to all the property as the last surviving member of the coparcenary. Nagoji and Krishnamurthi's sister, Rukmani, argued, however, that she was the heir of her unmarried brother (since he had neither a wife nor sons) and thus had a right to half the joint property. As a result, granting a widow's right produced conflicts between women—as widows and as sisters. Both Kamala and Rukmani sold their shares to others, and these men, Manicka Gounder and Arunachala Gounder, brought the dispute to court.

The court decided that if Kamala were to take all of the family's joint property, then this "would implicitly make such heir [Kamala] a coparcener on a par with the male coparceners of the family." The court added that because the term "coparcener" in English referred to the Sanskrit *apratibandha daya* (which the court translated as an "unobstructed heritage"), it necessarily excluded women who married into a joint family; in other words, individuals not born into the coparcenary could not legally join it. This fundamental exclusion stood unchanged by the 1937 act, which did not "make her [a widow] a coparcener which she was not prior to the Act."[62] As a result, a widowed woman could only claim partition but not take the full rights of ownership accorded to men. Thus, Kamala was only entitled to her deceased husband's share of the joint property, not the entire amount. Once again, then, we find that the case law of the 1937 act did not fully acknowledge women as owners of property but limited their rights because they were outsiders by birth to the family property they inherited.

Women faced further restrictions regarding questions of sexuality that were irrelevant to men's property rights, individual or joint. For example, in *Ramaiya Konar v. Mottaya Mudaliar,* the court's finding that the widow Alamelu had been "unchaste" prevented her from exercising any rights under the 1937 act.[63] The court's judgment in this case concerned legal issues surrounding the interpretation of statutes, and only in fragments and traces may we find a narrative about Alamelu and her property claims. Nevertheless, the court records suggest that Alamelu had been married to Muthuvelu, who owned property jointly with his brother and resided in a village in the Tiruchirapalli district. During her husband's lifetime, Alamelu "eloped with a paramour, Thangavelu, and lived with him in adultery" in the town of Kumbakonam. The court's narrative adds that Muthuvelu brought Alamelu back to his home, thus "condoning her adultery."[64] After a few days, however, Alamelu again returned to Kumbakonam, where she lived with Thangavelu until Muthuvelu's death in August 1943. Upon his death, Alamelu took possession of a house in which Muthuvelu had lived and sold it to Ramaiya Konar. Alamelu's sale of the house was contested by her husband's brother, Sabapathi Padayachi, who claimed Muthuvelu's house on the basis that Alamelu's "unchastity" excluded her from inheriting her husband's property. As Muthuvelu's brother and coparcener, Sabapathi asserted his rights to ownership of the house, which he sold to Mottaya Mudaliar. These two rival purchasers of Muthuvelu's house, Ramaiya Konar and Mottaya Mudaliar, brought the question before the Madras courts.

The Madras High Court accepted the lower court's findings about Alamelu's sexuality and proceeded from the assumption that Alamelu was an "unchaste" widow who had committed "adultery" prior to her husband's death. The principle that a widow needed to be "chaste" in order to inherit her deceased husband's property was well established within colonial Hindu law long before the 1937 act, and the Madras judges could invoke the authority of the Hindu *sastras* and extensive case law to maintain that Alamelu's relationship with Thangavelu would severely curtail, perhaps even eliminate, her property rights. Alamelu's claims to own and sell Muthuvelu's house, however, did not rest solely upon established precedent but also invoked the 1937 act, which granted new rights to widows. But the new law did not mention chastity as a condition for widows' inheritance, producing, in the words of one commentator, "perhaps an unintended result" of changing the established Hindu law on questions of female sexuality.[65]

To determine whether the Hindu Women's Rights to Property Act invalidated prior requirements of female chastity, the Madras court engaged in a detailed analysis of the relationship between women's property and sexuality within Hindu law. Arguing that the legislators who passed the 1937 act had no intention of changing the legal norms governing women's sexual behavior, the court ultimately decided that chastity remained a precondition of a widow's inheritance. Alamelu, as a result, had no right over her husband's house. To determine otherwise, in the words of Justice Panchapakesa Ayyar, went against "the deep-rooted sentiments of the people" that "for the Hindus chastity in a wife is the first thing required, all other qualities paling into insignificance beside it."[66] Justice Viswanatha Sastri elaborated further upon the point that women's rights to property depended on their sexual behavior:

> The family, a pivotal institution extolled by the *Dharma Sastras*, depended for its unsullied cohesiveness and continuity upon the sanctity of the marital relationship, with its attendant obligation of chastity . . . [I]t could not have been the intention of the Act to give charter of unchastity to married women or to abrogate the inhibitions of a law designed to preserve the purity and sanctity of family life.[67]

Sastri thus insisted that women's sexual behavior—and its underlying implications for the family—was central to the legal regulation of property. Women did not gain access to property as individuals; rather, their "rights" were subject to the reproductive economy of the Hindu (joint) family. The threat of losing property served as an "inhibition" to enforce female chastity, and, within Sastri's reading, the Hindu Women's Rights to Property Act did little to change this fundamental legal principle.

Therefore, judicial interpretation of the Hindu Women's Rights to Property Act did not question the notion that women were dependent upon, rather than owners of, property. When family members challenged the limited new rights that the law granted, the Madras High Court generally rejected the possibility that women's ability to demand partition could fundamentally refashion the relationship between women, joint property, and joint families. Moreover, because of a technicality in the law, the legal reform of 1937 excluded women from inheriting agricultural land, thus preventing women's access to a crucial economic resource.[68] Nevertheless, at least some women did manage to assert their rights within the legal system. My reading of their efforts is necessarily partial, since we have little archival record of women's voices within this legal process. Also, the court's slender evidence of these efforts does not allow us to assume that a woman was a prime actor in the case simply because a case was instituted in a woman's name. The complexities of colonial and postcolonial law, as well as many women's limited economic resources, probably made it difficult for women to institute a case without the support of others, including men. Limitations of the legal archive thus make it difficult to document women's agency in reconfiguring property relations.

Another way we might consider the nature of women's initiatives, however, is by examining the kinds of cases brought under the Hindu Women's Rights to Property Act. In the Madras litigation concerning this act, very few challenged the property relations of a conjugal family composed of monogamous parents and their unmarried children.[69] Instead, the cases appear to challenge the property relations of the coparcenary, as they concerned property belonging to a wider set of kin: a man's second wife and the sons of his first wife, a widow and her husband's parents or brothers, two widows of a polygamous marriage, or a widow and her sisters-in-law. By filing suits under the 1937 act, widows did not maintain such relations with the families of their deceased husbands but asserted their rights to control property separately, a separation that could also be reflected in a widow's residence. But the provisions of the colonial law—even as reformed in 1937—mandated against any consequent centrality of conjugality, either in terms of property or of affect. Because women did not gain property as wives but did so as widows, their new rights did not enable the creation of new conjugal families. Instead, property was meant to support a widow during her lifetime, after which it would return to her husband's coparcenary heirs.

Property and the Conjugal Family Ideal

The discourse of conjugality and capital linked claims about the family to a legal rearrangement of property relations. As I have argued, professional and mercantile interests that favored male individual ownership of property within a market economy also advocated the replacement of a multigenerational unit of agnatic kin with a unit focused on the monogamous conjugal couple. I do not read this invocation of conjugality as obscuring the "real" material interests of emergent capitalism; I suggest, instead, that notions of conjugality and capital shaped each other, together setting the parameters governing individual rights in law. From the 1880s to the 1920s, this individual subject was almost invariably male, and legal reformers sought to expand men's rights by partitioning joint property and severing individual earnings from the obligations of joint ownership. However, their efforts were only partly successful. Landowning interests effectively limited men's individual rights by casting joint ownership as essential to Hindu "tradition."

By the 1930s, discourses of individual ownership together with an emerging women's movement raised the question of women's property rights. However, the logic of conjugality and capital ultimately came up short in producing a female property-owning subject. Advocates of property ownership for women confronted a colonial political economy that both fostered capitalist relations in some sectors and restricted them in others, especially in agriculture.[70] Even more than for men, women's problematic relationship to property highlights the contradictions underlying such combined and uneven development. Landowning interests that rejected men's individual rights also weighed in strongly against women's individual property rights. Judicial interpretations further narrowed women's access to coparcenary property. As a result, the figure of the female property owner contained competing versions of family and economy that sought to reconcile conjugality and capital with agnatic kin groups and noncapitalist relations.

Because questions of property were resolved within the frameworks of colonial and indigenous patriarchies, they were posed not in terms of women's equality but as problems of how to properly negotiate the competing claims of a "tradition" supported by colonial law and agrarian elites versus the demands of a "modernity" emerging from professional and mercantile interests. Thus, even reformers who strongly advocated the modernity of male individual property rights did not reject the tradition of joint ownership in either rhetoric or practice when discussing the rights of women. Within this context, the Hindu Women's Rights to Property Act granted some limited ownership rights to widows, so that the principle of joint property no longer rested upon the complete exclusion of all women from ownership. Judicial resolutions to this legislative change, however, tended to reinforce ideas that women's rights to property followed from their status as dependents rather than as coparceners in their own right.

These contradictory developments set the terms for political appropriations of the family in the twentieth century. On one hand, the conjugal family form imagined by professional and mercantile interests challenged certain patriarchal hierarchies within the joint family—most notably by reducing the power of senior men to control the property of their male descendants. On the other, professional and mercantile visions of the conjugal family retained, at their center, an assumption about women's subordinate position. This view of women as dependents was used to justify individual male ownership while largely excluding women from developing these individual property relations themselves. Indeed, the politics of conjugality and capital depended on this exclusion, which allowed for an unabashed espousal of "modern" economic relations even while retaining the "traditional" status of the Hindu family. As we shall see, the conjugal family of nationalist aspiration was rooted in these tensions.

THREE

Nationalizing Marriage: Indian and Dravidian Politics of Conjugality

There can be no doubt that, now that India is soon to take her rightful place in the comity of nations, it is all the more necessary that we should put her domestic affairs in order.

Government of India, Report of the Age of Consent Committee, 1929

Divinity, custom, and *sastra* [scriptural texts] are all opposed to the progress, rationality, and freedom of the people. That is why Self Respect marriage leaves no room for these regressive and anti-freedom concepts.

E. V. Ramasami, "Respect for Self—Respect for Puranas," 1934

With the rise of mass nationalism in the early twentieth century, Tamil activists—both nationalist and feminist—targeted marriage as a critical site for producing the nation. For these activists, a reformed conjugality offered a metaphor for national freedom and provided a model for national citizenship. Thus, as the Age of Consent Committee asserted in its recommendation to raise the marriage age for girls, the proper ordering of the conjugal relationship was a necessary step in India's transformation from a colonial possession to an equal member of the global "comity of nations." Further, as E. V. Ramasami claimed on behalf of the Dravidian nationalist Self Respect movement, rational marriage practices could exemplify modernizing progress for an emergent Tamil citizenry. In these ways, conjugality became thoroughly embedded in the language of nationalist politics from the 1920s on.

As the epigraphs to this chapter suggest, the imbrication of family and nation occurred in two distinct contexts in the Tamil region: one was an Indian nationalist politics centered on the age of consent and child marriage, and the other a Dravidian nationalist politics of Self Respect marriage. With regard to the former, administrative changes in the colonial state beginning in the mid-1920s provided an opportunity for intense discussion and debate within the legislature about the shape of Indian conjugality. Male nationalists as well as activists in the Indian women's movement played a role in these debates, which culminated in the passage of the Child Marriage Restraint Act in 1929, instituting fourteen as the minimum age of marriage for all girls in British India. The rhetoric of Indian nationalism, in subsequent years, shifted away from questions of conjugality, and, by the 1930s, only the women's movement continued campaigns about marriage reform.

The trajectory of Dravidian nationalist interventions was somewhat different in both chronology and scope. The concept of a distinct Dravidian nation composed of speakers of the Tamil language was articulated at various sites beginning in the 1910s. However, it was the activist-oriented Self Respect movement, founded in 1925 by Ramasami, that developed Dravidian nationalism's conjugal politics. The movement created a novel wedding ceremony that challenged the normative caste and gender hierarchies of Tamil society. Self Respect weddings, called *cuyamariyātait tirumaṇam* in Tamil, were conducted by movement activists rather than Brahman ritual officiants, and in the Tamil language rather than Sanskrit. These weddings also eliminated many conventional ritual practices involving the families of the bride and groom in favor of a brief ceremony centering on the couple's marital vows. Originating with activists and then spreading among other Tamils throughout the late 1920s and 1930s, Self Respect weddings were at once a site for the enactment of a Tamil national community and a tool of movement propaganda. I read these weddings as deeply politicized performances that, more thoroughly than in the Indian nationalist case, situated marriage reform at the center of Dravidian nationalist activity.

As Ramasami's denunciation of "regressive and anti-freedom concepts" suggests, these nationalist contests over conjugality negotiated competing claims about modernity and progress in the Tamil country. For instance, Indian nationalists used child marriage to support their own claims to bring modernizing progress to the nation; rejecting the colonial state's position in this regard, they maintained that only a national government could inaugurate the family reforms that would modernize Indian politics and domesticity.[1] Similarly, through the Self Respect wedding, Dravidian nationalists demonstrated their rejection of what they termed "traditional" caste and gender hierarchies. Their new wedding ceremony would publicly model an antitraditional and progressive vision for the Tamil nation. In this regard, claims about "the modern" functioned as a "claim-making device" in the Tamil politics of marriage.[2] Both Indian and Dravidian nationalisms authorized their visions of conjugal reform through reference to their modernizing content; appropriate forms of marriage would usher in the "progress, rationality, and freedom of the people" that Ramasami demanded. Therefore, in investigating the "modern" content of marriage debates, I am not suggesting that "modernity" was a clearly definable entity that entered the Tamil region by means of the politics of either Dravidian or Indian nationalism. Rather, this chapter investigates how claims about "becoming modern" shaped and limited the scope of Tamil debates about conjugality, ultimately producing divergent Indian and Dravidian constructions of what "modernity" might mean for Tamils.

Across these differences, both Indian and Dravidian politics shared a focus on conjugality as the pivot of family relations and, indeed, of modernity itself. Although the content of conjugal reforms varied, ranging from feminist demands for companionship and equality to eugenicist claims about female sexuality and reproduction, in each case activists maintained that the husband-wife relationship offered the greatest potential for nationalist politics but also required significant change. This emphasis on marriage did not mean that nationalists ignored other axes of affect and alliance within families, for example, that between mothers and sons. However, in common with ongoing debates about the family in colonial India, Indian and Dravidian nationalisms consistently directed attention to conjugality as a site for the production of a new polity. Indeed, the professional and mercantile interests that advocated a conjugal family in relation to property forms also tended to support these nationalist redefinitions of conjugality.

By analyzing Indian and Dravidian politics in relation to each other, I suggest that the process of nationalizing marriage—and of nationalist cultural politics overall—cannot be understood solely as a contest between the forces of Indian nationalism and the coercive powers of the colonial state. Therefore, although following Partha Chatterjee's insight that culture was a critical site upon which nationalism developed its claims to hegemony and political authority in colonial India,[3] I emphasize that these cultural contests were not conducted exclusively in relation to the discourses and policies of the colonial administration. Rather, within a multifaceted cultural terrain, competing ideologies—in some cases more radical and progressive than those of Indian nationalism—jostled for power within the authoritarian constraints of colonial rule.

As a result, and despite its own claims to the contrary, Indian nationalism did not define the entire content of indigenous discourse about modernizing the family in colonial India. Instead, when Indian nationalists and their allies in the women's movement sought to propagate their own claims about nationalizing marriage, they actively marginalized and removed alternative national visions from the sites of public debate. Consequently, in a historical process often overlooked in scholarship, Indian nationalism figured its hegemonies over national culture through a process of displacement and erasure of alternative national visions. Yet, this process was neither complete nor absolute; from the 1920s on, Dravidian conjugal politics offered a significant alternative that challenged the limitations of an Indian nationalist politics rooted in child marriage. By foregrounding Dravidian practices of *cuyamariyātait tirumaṇam,* I call attention to these displacements and tensions, and thus offer a more complex reading of the nationalist politics of marriage and modernity.

Finally, although Indian and Dravidian marriage reforms each emphasized their uniquely "national" character, their conjugal politics was also deeply implicated in a discourse of bourgeois domesticity that was transnational in scope. As the Age of Consent Committee maintained, for instance, the reconstruction of Indian domestic life necessarily occurred with an eye toward a global domestic order. This globalizing domesticity helped to consolidate the boundaries of emerging middle classes in the metropole as well as in the colonies.[4] In the Tamil region, where professional and mercantile interests sought greater power even while they were constrained by colonial capital, the development of a conjugal family ideal invoked and reshaped middle-class marriage practices. At the same time, however, given the hegemonic aspirations of bourgeois culture within capitalism globally, discourses of domesticity also extended beyond the middle class to encompass the entire society. Within a colonial context, in particular, these universalizing aspirations were often expressed in (anticolonial) national terms. Indeed, as Ranajit Guha notes, under colonial conditions, bourgeois ideologies and politics perforce took on a national form.[5] Along these lines, advocates of new domestic ideals in the Tamil region did not limit their claims to middle classes alone but maintained that their reforms were necessary for the entire "nation." The process of nationalizing marriage in Tamil Nadu operated within these intersecting contexts—both national and trans-national, Indian and Dravidian—to shape the cultural politics of nationalisms during the critical decades of the 1920s and 1930s.

The Politics of Child Marriage

In the late nineteenth century, two events brought the question of child marriage to the forefront of public debate in colonial India. The first concerned Rakhmabai, the nineteen-year-old daughter of an elite non-Brahman family in Bombay. At the age of eleven, following customs widespread (but not universal) among caste Hindus, Rakhmabai was married to one Dadaji

Bhikaji; after the wedding, she continued to live with her mother and stepfather while pursuing an education. Several years later, Bhikaji requested that his wife live with him. When Rakhmabai refused, Bhikaji, in 1884, filed a suit for the restitution of conjugal rights. Defending her refusal to join her husband on the grounds of socioeconomic and personal incompatibility, Rakhmabai argued that she had been married at an age when informed consent was impossible. At one stage of the proceedings, she even faced the threat of a prison sentence rather than live in her husband's home. The case dragged on until 1888, when, in an out-of-court settlement, Bhikaji relinquished all claims for the restitution of conjugal rights in exchange for a share of Rakhmabai's property.[6]

Widely publicized in a developing Indian print culture, the Rakhmabai case raised a number of questions about the role of consent and compatibility in marriage, about the concept of restitution of conjugal rights in Hindu law, and, at its very base, about the validity of any child marriage. Championed by social reformers and eloquent in her own defense, Rakhmabai exposed the degradation of women within a marital relationship which they neither chose nor desired.[7] However, among orthodox defenders of pre-puberty marriage for Hindu girls, Rakhmabai represented the very antithesis of true womanhood, and they saw in her case evidence that the education and "Westernization" of Indian women could only destroy the Hindu family.

The second event, involving the painful death of a ten-year-old Bengali girl named Phulmoni, was perhaps even more shocking to contemporary sensibilities. In 1890, the young Phulmoni died after being raped by her thirty-year-old husband, Hari Mohan Maiti. Although testimony from Phulmoni's mother confirmed the brutality of Maiti's assault and Phulmoni's excruciating suffering, he could not be charged with rape. Instead, because Phulmoni was ten years old—the legal age of consent—and married to Maiti, he was tried for manslaughter and sentenced to twelve months of hard labor.[8]

The details of Phulmoni's death were reported by the contemporary press in Bengal and in other parts of India, thus bringing questions about child marriage into stark public view. In response to the controversy, reformers demanded that the colonial state introduce legislation raising the legal age of consent. The British government, although reluctant to undertake initiatives that would threaten its alliance with dominant classes, ultimately acceded to reformist pressure and raised the age of consent to twelve years. This change resulted in a massive negative outcry on the grounds that, according to Hindu *sastras* (scriptures), girls must be married before puberty and consummation must take place soon after the first menstruation. If consummation were delayed—as by a higher legal age of consent—then the *pinda*, or ancestral offerings made by the sons of such marriages, would be impure. On this basis, opponents of the bill argued that, in the case of a girl attaining puberty before age twelve, her husband would be forced to choose between disobeying the law of the state or the law of his religion.

The opposition to the government's Age of Consent Bill ultimately situated "ideas about Hindu conjugality at the very heart of militant nationalism."[9] Developing a rhetorical connection between "home" and "nation," defenders of pre-puberty marriage questioned the ruling authority of the colonial state. In the words of the fiery nationalist Bal Gangadhar Tilak: "If our 'home' is attacked, how can we afford to quietly submit? If national aspirations are blighted, how can we allow our enemies to enjoy themselves at our expense?"[10] Although this imbrication of conjugality and nationhood produced a politics that exceeded the limitations of the more staid Indian National Congress (founded in 1885), it could not serve nationalism for long. As Tanika Sarkar shows, the coercive core of child marriage ideologies—which demanded the bodily pain, perhaps even death, of the child wife—clashed impossibly with the hegemonic aspirations of revivalist nationalism. The "grounding of an imagined nation upon sheer pain" had come "far too close to [nationalism's] own description of the prescriptive, loveless, disciplinary regime that is colonialism."[11] The centrality of this Hindu conjugal norm became a discursive dead end for nationalists, who, after the 1890s, looked to other relationships (notably that of mother and son) for expressions of national community that opposed the colonial state.

Events during the 1920s, however, helped to renew the connections between marriage and nationalist politics. Significantly, Indian nationalism itself underwent important changes. Under the leadership of Mohandas Gandhi and others, the Indian National Congress began to organize mass struggle in opposition to colonial rule. As nationalist agitation occupied an increasingly prominent place in the colonial public sphere, nationalist rhetoric suffused a range of social reform efforts, including around the family. Occasionally nationalist aspirations were expressed in legislative arenas, and the Montagu-Chelmsford Reforms of 1919 took incremental steps toward making this expression possible. Inaugurating larger legislative assemblies that included some elected Indian members, and widening the franchise to a slightly larger fraction (though still a minority) of the Indian population, the reforms increased the number of Indians in the legislative process. Beginning in the mid-1920s, several Indian members of the legislative assemblies supported bills to raise the age of consent and to introduce a minimum age of marriage.[12]

These legislative efforts acquired an increasingly nationalist cast following the publication of the book *Mother India* in 1927. Written by Katherine Mayo, an American journalist and self-styled "impartial observer" of Indian life and culture, the book claimed that "the whole pyramid of the

Indian's woes" was based in "his manner of getting into the world and his sex-life thenceforward."[13] The title of the book—at once a reference to the condition of Indian mothers and a critique of nationalist invocations of *Bharat Mata* (Mother India)—placed child marriage at the very heart of its argument. Mayo's graphic account of her visits to hospital maternity wards, alongside her lurid descriptions of childbirths attended by a traditional *dai* (midwife), formed the polemical core of her text. Mayo invoked a necessary connection between the broken body of the child wife/mother, on the one hand, and the weakened, ineffectual state of the Indian body politic, on the other. She argued that the "weak" race reproduced by child marriage and emasculated by sexual practices like masturbation would be unable to "seize or to hold the reins of Government" and required the supervision of an Anglo-Saxon race "coming into full glory of manhood."[14] Through *Mother India,* therefore, Indian conjugality and sexuality became powerfully intertwined with claims about British imperialism and Indian *swaraj,* or self-rule.

Mayo's book was immensely popular both in Britain and the United States, and Indian reformers found themselves in the difficult, sometimes painful situation of countering her allegations while advocating social change. Women, especially, struggled to negotiate this terrain. For instance, Muthulakshmi Reddi, a medical doctor from Madras Presidency who became the first woman appointed to the Madras Legislative Council, reflected upon her reaction to seeing copies of *Mother India* onboard ship sailing from India to Britain: "In the P&O steamer in which I traveled I found two such books (by Miss Mayo) kept in one library and the passengers were reading the book with great interest. Of course, the Indians who travel with them cannot certainly feel comfortable in the company of the passengers who hold us in such contempt." Although a staunch advocate of child marriage legislation in the Indian context, Muthulakshmi, when speaking to Europeans, attempted to minimize the book's impact upon the public imagination by asserting that it "was only a description of the sick people in hospitals."[15] Similarly, Gandhi, an opponent of child marriage himself, famously dismissed *Mother India* as "the drain inspector's report." Indeed, across the entire subcontinent, Indian nationalists called public meetings to denounce Mayo's text.[16]

In the wake of this controversy, the Indian women's movement harnessed the cause of child marriage to the powerful engine of Indian nationalism; activists argued that legislating an appropriate marriage age offered the most effective nationalist response to Mayo's imperialism. Two major all-India women's organizations with an overlapping membership, the Women's Indian Association (WIA) and the All-India Women's Conference (AIWC), organized campaigns to enact age of marriage legislation. In seeking support for legislative changes, these groups petitioned legislators, organized public meetings, and developed alliances with British women's organizations. In one blistering attack on an attempt to make age twelve, rather than the medically recommended age of sixteen, the minimum age of marriage for girls, the WIA and AIWC argued:

> At this psychological moment when Miss Mayo has focused the attention of the world on the sex life of India . . . you men think yourselves reformers when you fix the age of 12 as the proper age for girls. To make this age legal against the wishes of the organized, vocal, and progressive women will do more to retard Home Rule than you have at all realised. You will give the impression that Indian manhood approves of what other races in the world consider the sex standard of the degenerate.[17]

The women's movement thus posited a connection between Indian nationalism and conjugality that differed fundamentally from the militant revivalism of the 1890s. Rather than championing child marriage as a sign of national cultural superiority, as did the defenders of Dadaji Bhikaji and Hari Mohan Maiti in the late nineteenth century, Indian feminists demanded the rejection of child marriage to signify national respectability and progress. The path toward home rule necessarily required the transformation of an Indian domestic order.

Thus, the WIA and the AIWC invoked the rhetoric both of nationalism and women's rights when making their claims to Indian legislators and the colonial state. They maintained, alongside other Indian nationalist reformers, that only a national government, not a colonial one, could solve the underlying problems of poverty and lack of education that supposedly perpetuated child marriage. Activists maintained, moreover, that conjugal reform was a prerequisite for the modernizing progress of the Indian nation. In the words of WIA member Muthulakshmi Reddi: "If we want to grow into a strong, robust and self-respecting nation, if we want to reach our full physical and mental height, the system of child marriage must go."[18] Similarly, for Harbilas Sarda, the author of the Child Marriage Restraint Act, marriage reform was necessary for the nation to come into its own. With the elimination of child marriage, "every man, woman, and child in this country [could] grow to his or her full growth and be able to work without shackles for the good of the country till we reach the goal we have set for ourselves."[19]

This consistent advocacy of marriage reform in the name of national progress stood in stark contrast with the ambivalent position of the colonial state, which claimed to be India's preeminent modernizing force but at the same time remained dependent on alliances with social groups whose traditionalized forms of patriarchy mandated against reform. Caught within this contradiction, colonial ideologies were unable to offer an alternative to Indian nationalism's championing of marriage reform in the service of its own political goals. Therefore, largely through the efforts of the women's movement, Indian nationalism successfully wrested the mantle of modernizing progress away from the colonial regime. Further, as Mrinalini Sinha perceptively notes, women's activism around child marriage opened up possibilities for the "mobilization of a gender identity as women"—unsubordinated to the religious "community"—that could universalize claims about rights and press its demands upon the state.[20]

Facing these nationalist and feminist pressures, the colonial administration established an Age of Consent Committee in 1928. Including among its members Rameshwari Nehru, the Delhi representative of the AIWC, the committee's mandate was to investigate the operations of existing age of consent legislation and to suggest modifications.[21] After traveling across British India to solicit public opinion, the committee published its report in 1929. Having determined that a legal age of marriage (hitherto unknown in colonial Indian law) would be more effective and enforceable than a higher age of consent, the committee recommended a marriage age of fourteen for girls. A bill then pending in the Legislative Assembly, sponsored by Harbilas Sarda, adopted the committee's recommendations.

The Child Marriage Restraint Act (also known as the Sarda Act) was fiercely debated across the country, especially in Madras Presidency, where a group of Tamil Brahman men formed the core of opposition to legislating any minimum age of marriage. Voicing their opinions in newspapers and public meetings, as well as in the Indian Legislative Assembly, these men created a storm of protest that—as contemporaries noted—shook Madras out of the relative quietude of its reaction to the 1890s Age of Consent debates. Brahman opponents of legislation, who claimed to put forward Hindu "orthodox" opinion on the question of marriage, rejected legal reform on grounds similar to their counterparts in 1891. Pre-puberty marriage, they argued, was an essential component of Hindu, and specifically Brahman, *dharma*. For instance, according to M. S. Sesha Ayyangar, any attempt to legislate a minimum marriage age was "a case of directly flouting the *Shastric* injunctions upon which we take our stand."[22] Obedience to the *sastras* required women's coercion, if necessary. As T. R. Ramachandra Iyer argued before the Age of Consent Committee, securing a Hindu girl's or woman's consent to marriage was irrelevant, because "as far as women are concerned they are expected to marry and they must marry."[23] Similarly, for M. K. Acharya, legislation on marriage age was "based on the fundamentally wrong notion that a female after a certain age can consent to sexual intercourse with any man of her choice. This is purely a western notion. The Hindu idea is that no woman of any age can consent to sexual intercourse with any man other than her lawful husband."[24]

To some extent, such claims referenced the specific marriage practices that characterized many families in the Tamil Brahman community. Tamil

Brahmans, like their caste counterparts across India, had a lower age of marriage than the population as a whole. This distinction between Brahmans and other Hindus was further sharpened in the Tamil region, because most non-Brahman caste Hindus—as well as so-called untouchable castes—had a relatively high average age of marriage, the second highest in all of British India.[25] Therefore, compared to other parts of the country, where Brahman practices may not have diverged so sharply from that of other upper castes, Brahman marriages in the Tamil region were visibly different from the broader community. However, the distinct contours of Tamil Brahman marriage practice cannot fully explain the strength of the controversy. On the one hand, not all castes who practiced child marriage came to its defense within a legislative or public arena; Brahmans stood virtually alone among Hindus in their opposition to legislation.[26] On the other hand, despite a comparably young marriage age among Tamil Brahmans in the 1890s, they made no similar outcry against raising the age of consent during that decade.

In order to explain the strong opposition to child marriage legislation in Madras, we must look beyond the specifics of Tamil Brahman marriage practices and toward the broader framework of caste politics in this period. During the 1920s, a strong critique of Brahman dominance initiated by the Dravidian movement resonated across the entire Tamil political landscape. Dravidian ideologies first took an organized political form through the Justice Party, founded in 1916 by a group of upper-caste Hindu men—defining themselves as "non-Brahman"—who challenged Brahman overrepresentation in colonial educational and administrative institutions. These ideologies assumed a broader scope in the context of E. V. Ramasami's Self Respect movement, which developed a critique of Brahman -+socio-ritual dominance in Tamil society. By the time of the child marriage controversies, Dravidian rhetoric suffused Tamil politics and, I argue, shaped the terrains of conjugal debate in Tamil Nadu.

The criticism of child marriage as a specifically Brahman family form resonated with a broader attack on Brahman patriarchal privilege. Thus, according to Ramasami, Brahman advocacy of child marriage was simply a way that Brahman men could "exploit the people . . . in the name of the *sastras*."[27] For Brahmans who opposed reformist legislation, the defense of child marriage was equally a defense of Brahman dominance and ritual status. Practicing child marriage, in T. R. Ramachandra Iyer's terms, allowed a girl-bride's father to "become a complete Brahmin [*sic*] in divine and spiritual superiority."[28] As such, the child marriage question, I maintain, generated more controversy in the Tamil region than in any other province in British India, not only because of the specific content of legislation or its impact on marriage practices but also because of its connection to ongoing tensions about the place of Brahmans within Tamil society.

Thus, beginning in about 1925 and continuing until legislation was passed in 1929, organized opposition to marriage reform was especially strong in Madras Presidency, and Brahman legislators from the Tamil districts spearheaded efforts to derail the Child Marriage Restraint Bill in the Indian Legislative Assembly. To validate their case for pre-puberty marriage, these men both referenced Hindu-Brahman tradition as represented in the Hindu *sastras* and invoked a dystopian specter of Western modernity run amuck. For example, assembly member M. K. Acharya, a Tamil Brahman who represented South Arcot and Chinglepet districts, spoke out forcefully urging his colleagues to vote down reform. According to Acharya, Hindu—and especially Brahman—tradition exacted women's subservience in a manner unparalleled globally: "No other community either in the past or present has or can put forth an ideal which . . . teaches the girl to think and say, 'Prince or beggar, he, that is my wedded lord, is my god.'" The Child Marriage Restraint Act threatened to undermine this subservience by introducing "social conditions in India very much like those obtaining in very many 'civilised' countries. Parental authority will be disregarded. Girls will begin to make their own choice in their own way. Such cases must come of indiscreet love episodes."[29]

By the 1920s, unlike in the 1890s, this rather desperate defense of pre-puberty marriage had lost its claims to nationalist authority. In the course of Legislative Assembly debates, Brahman opponents of reform acknowledged that they did not speak for the nation as a whole. Instead, maintaining that "the minority [not] be in any way trampled under foot, or subjected to any tyranny of the majority," several legislators supported an amendment to exempt Brahmans from the purview of the Child Marriage Restraint Act.[30] However, as passed by the legislature on October 1, 1929, the final form of the act allowed no such exemptions on the basis of caste or religion, bringing all girls in British India under its authority. No longer could pre-puberty marriage represent a nation resistant to the colonial state. Just as important, no longer could the caste or religious "community" stand as a bulwark against the nation's authority over matters of social reform. This refusal to make community exemptions stands unparalleled in the subsequent legal history of marriage and family reform in twentieth-century India.

Representing Consent

Indian nationalism, in developing its conjugal politics, claimed to achieve two goals: to protect Hindu "tradition" and also lead India into a "modern" era. Nationalists argued that child marriage was nowhere sanctioned in the Hindu *sastras,* and that post-puberty marriage represented a return to "traditional" Hindu marriage practices. Yet, they also maintained that outlawing child marriage would bring India on an equal plane with other nations of the world. Through conjugality, then, the demands of Indian tradition could be realigned to suit the needs of a modernizing nation-state. S. Srinivasa Iyengar made precisely these points when addressing the Indian Legislative Assembly in support of child marriage legislation:

> Let us realise that we who stand up for Hinduism have also a duty to see that Hinduism promotes the growth of a virile race of men and efficient race of girls who will become the mothers of a greater India. I do believe, Sir, that the time has come for race improvement, and I honestly feel that this Bill does not interfere with Hindu religion.[31]

In Srinivasa Iyengar's framework, the authority of medicine and eugenics surpasses that of scriptural sanction, and his call to improve the Hindu "race" draws upon discourses that were gaining authority not only in India but also internationally.[32] Implicit in his rhetoric is an attention to modernizing change; he emphasizes that the "time has come" to develop a physically powerful "greater India." However, he does not openly reject the Hindu *sastras,* concluding, instead, that raising the age of marriage will not "interfere" with Hindu religious practice.

This complex negotiation of tradition and modernity hinged upon representations of a girl's or woman's consent to marriage. Many nationalist reformers defined consent exclusively in terms of a female body's biological ability to tolerate sexual intercourse and produce healthy children. This notion of bodily consent foreclosed a potentially radicalizing discussion of women's subjective agency in the conjugal relationship. The Age of Consent Committee's *Report,* which recommended fourteen years as the minimum age of marriage, is exemplary in this regard. Seeking to explain the choice of fourteen, which contravened medical opinion, the *Report* offered the following: "We expect that some time will be taken in arranging matches after fourteen and some further period may elapse before actual consummation takes place. Maternity will thus be nearer sixteen, *viz.,* the safe age according to medical opinion."[33] Operating virtually unchanged from the 1890s, this representation of consent focused not on a girl's or woman's decision to marry nor on her choice of a husband or her agency in sexual activity.[34] Instead, under the assumption that a girl's family would arrange her marriage, and that consummation would immediately follow the wedding, the committee concerned itself solely with delaying pregnancy until the age of sixteen. Therefore, in a mirror image of child marriage advocates who insisted that the Hindu-Indian community could be properly reproduced only through the body of the child wife, most nationalist proponents of reform insisted that the Indian "race" could be properly reproduced only through the bodies of girls who were more than fourteen or sixteen years old.

The Indian women's movement challenged this limited notion of consent, opening nationalist closures by rendering visible women's subjective experiences of marriage and, implicitly, sexuality. In her message to the Third International Conference on Planned Parenthood, Muthulakshmi argued that the "choice of marriage should be left to each individual a girl or a boy, as it is in the West," and that not all men and women needed to marry.[35] Her statement rejected the assumption, common in male nationalists' arguments, that "choice" in marriage was solely a male prerogative and introduced the possibility of not marrying, a theme virtually unheard of even in progressive attacks on child marriage.

Other activists argued that women's bodily and emotional experiences superseded any scriptural authority on questions of marriage. Bhagirathi Ammal, for example, discounted claims that the Hindu *sastras* mandated severe punishments for parents of unmarried girls: "While the hell to which the parents go [by not marrying daughters before puberty] is an imaginary one, what about the *karma* of the sending of their girls now to a living hell by selling them to old widowers?"[36] Changing the emphasis from pain to pleasure, Gomathiammal Gomathinathan (secretary of the Tirunelveli branch of the WIA) maintained that delaying marriage would allow consummation and marriage "to take place together" so that "the enjoyment of marriage happiness should not be postponed on any account."[37] This emphasis on women's individual choice and (sexual) pleasure invoked a different notion of consent than the claims of bodily coercion and capacity that characterized the nationalist debate on the marriage question.

Despite developing this more expansive vision of consent, the women's movement rarely attacked the core patriarchal premises underlying Indian nationalist interventions in marriage. Although activists sometimes criticized the nationalists' appeal to tradition, they more often stepped back from rejecting scriptural authority outright. Muthulakshmi was a case in point. On one level, she offered a thoroughgoing rejection of Hindu orthodoxy from the perspective of an empiricist rationality:

> If the orthodox should still persist in quoting their out of date and antiquated authorities written by somebody at some unknown date without facing the actual matters of fact existing today in our midst, in the interest of the suffering womanhood of the Brahman community, and in the interest of the future race, I will be put to the necessity of publishing a list of cases, many of which are even to be found at Madras in the well-to-do and educated families to support Miss Mayo, on the evils of early marriage and the incontinence of the Brahmin youth.[38]

Within Muthulakshmi's framework, the "out of date" scriptural authorities could not refute the empirical evidence of her own medical practice. Her threatened list of cases—an enumeration of the bodily harm caused by pre-puberty marriage—invoked the authoritative status of science (and implicitly modernity) in the service of legislative reform. However, Muthulakshmi stopped short of rejecting the *sastras* completely, adopting instead the nationalist line that a proper interpretation of Hindu tradition could motivate reform: "Why should [the] marriage of every boy and girl be made compulsory and considered necessary in a land that once advocated lifelong *brahmacharya* [celibacy] and continence for the attainment of intellectual and spiritual greatness?"[39]

While Reddi's claims about tradition were typically a perfunctory addition to her medical arguments, others in the women's movement outlined their position on the *sastras* in greater depth. Consider, for instance, this argument from the WIA in favor of child marriage legislation:

> No cultured or civilised nation can tolerate the idea of motherhood being thrust upon a child of 12 whether she will or not. But we do not ask you to accept Western standards of culture or morality, however good, but to just go back to the pure Hindu teaching of the Shruti . . . We have discussed this question with learned Pandits and Shastris and are informed that the ancient Vedic teaching clearly visualised marriage as between a mature young man and woman. We cannot find that Hinduism in its original purity teaches that the mothers of the race are to be uneducated children, but rather thinking, educated, grown women.[40]

The resonance with Indian nationalist claims about tradition is apparent. From an emphasis on a "pure" past rooted in the Vedas, to the assertion that traditional forms of marriage were in accord with modern racial theory, to the telescoping of tradition to include only a particular interpretation of Hindu scripture—the women's movement operated within the same frameworks as did Indian nationalism.[41] Ultimately, subsuming their own potentially radical claims about consent, the AIWC and WIA forged an alliance with Indian nationalists to become supporters of the Child Marriage Restraint Act. As Mrinalini Sinha has demonstrated, this feminist-nationalist convergence on child marriage produced a liberal politics that placed at its core a "normative citizen-subject," unmarked by considerations of caste, class, or religion.[42]

However, the operations of the act illustrate the stark limitations of this conjugal politics in practice. Once the legislation came into effect in April 1930, a number of parents avoided prosecution by leaving British India to perform weddings of their underage daughters. In Madras Presidency, this could mean an excursion into French enclaves, such as Yanam near Cocanada. The *Madras Mail* reported that ninety weddings were performed in Yanam on one July day in 1934, and that "the brides and bridegrooms are the children of people whose homes are in British India territory." Arriving on "trains and motor buses . . . girls between the ages [of] five and ten were hurriedly married to boys of fifteen and eighteen." Moreover, as the *Madras Mail* noted, many parents did not even bother to leave British India, since there had been so few prosecutions for infringement of the Sarda Act.[43] For instance, in the first ten years of its operation, the Madras government prosecuted only one case.[44] Nationalists were largely complicit in ignoring these enforcement issues. As a result, the WIA and AIWC stood virtually alone in attempting to popularize the new law, and met with very limited success.[45]

The effect of the Child Marriage Restraint Act was certainly more symbolic than material; as scholars have noted, its importance lies in a proliferation of political discourses around marriage rather than in a transformation of conjugal practices.[46] I would add, further, that the act crystallized a realignment of politics and the family in colonial India. In the child marriage debates, families neither constituted the polity as they had in precolonial regimes, nor fully entered the novel spheres of mass politics created by Indian nationalism. Instead, nationalists limited their interventions on marriage to the legislative arenas sanctioned by the colonial state. These legislative debates were conducted in English and accessible only to a small minority of the population; their audience was only slightly expanded by the publication of nationalist articles on the Child Marriage Restraint Act in the English-language press. However, during the 1920s, Indian nationalism as a whole was not limited to these colonially sanctioned spheres of debate and action but found further mass expression in a politics comprised of boycotts, demonstrations, and civil disobedience. As a "political space of [nationalism's] own making,"[47] this agitational politics both transcended the existing structures of political representation under colonial rule and also helped to reshape them.

Indian nationalism excluded conjugality—and the family more broadly—from this potentially radicalizing political arena. In other words, although nationalists sought to position the Child Marriage Restraint Act as a vehicle of anticolonial response to Mayo's *Mother India,* they did not make conjugality a site for mass mobilization either against colonial patriarchy or against the colonial state more generally. In this, the marriage question stood apart from other arenas of nationalist cultural politics such as the propagation of *khadi* (handspun cloth) or the picketing of liquor stores. Unlike these activities, which mobilized cultural practices to challenge indigenous hierarchies as well as the colonial state, conjugality did not become a subject for resistant cultural practice. Instead, Indian nationalists referred to the conjugal relationship when speaking about the nation but removed family life from the content of their political action.

This simultaneous centrality and marginalization of families as the subject of politics in India resonated with the transnational development of bourgeois domesticity during the nineteenth and twentieth centuries.

Drawing from Malthusian and eugenic principles of racial degeneration, as well as claims about companionate marriage and female education, this politics of domesticity justified its "public" interventions through reference to a "private" sphere centered on women (especially mothers) in the family. For instance, as Anna Davin has demonstrated for early-twentieth-century Britain, debates about poverty focused on mothers but figured motherhood in class-undifferentiated terms, thus occluding the material impact of poor living conditions or work environments on maternal and infant health. In colonial contexts, similar debates were overlain with racism, whereby indigenous culture itself was held to produce incompetent mothers and, implicitly, undeveloped politics.[48] Mayo is perhaps the preeminent, but hardly the only, example of this discourse in colonial India.

Insofar as child marriage legislation was figured as a specifically nationalist response to colonial racism, it rejected the imperialist attempt to blame bad mothering on Hindu/Muslim culture. However, as part of a transnational bourgeois discourse of domesticity, the Indian nationalist reform of child marriage produced an undifferentiated vision of conjugality and maternity that ignored the material impact of class and caste. Therefore, in recasting the child wife of Brahmanical patriarchy into an "educated mother of the race," nationalist interventions sought to universalize the practice of an emergent middle class as critical to a specifically "Indian" cultural politics. Consequently, only the body of the (implicitly middle class) child wife could stand in for the national body politic, representing both the current degradation of Indian tradition and the potential future redemptive power of an Indian modernity.[49]

This relentless nationalist gaze on the suffering body of the child wife/mother allowed no room to focus on the body or subjective experience of the child prostitute or child laborer. In this sense, claims of national unity mandated an intervention in the marriage age while rendering other forms of gendered oppression outside the purview of reform. Moreover, nationalism's gestures toward the "Indian-ness" of its cultural politics remained deeply embedded in its claims about upper-caste (patriarchal) tradition. Nationalists were thus in a position of "modernizing" marriage without entirely repudiating the "traditionalized" conjugal forms of Brahmanical patriarchy. The severe limitations of Indian nationalist conjugality—as expressed in the content and enforcement of child marriage legislation—were part of this patriarchal balancing act.

Forging the Dravidian Nation: Self Respect Marriage and Tamil Politics

On 29 June 1929, during the height of debate about the Child Marriage Restraint Act, the town of Karaikudi witnessed an unusual wedding ceremony, likely the first of its kind in the vicinity. The ceremonies began with the arrival of Periyar E. V. Ramaswami, who was escorted to the *pantal* (tent) where the wedding was to take place. The bride and groom—both adults—joined him in the tent to exchange wedding rings and rose garlands. The groom vowed in Tamil: "I take Marakatavalli with my complete mind to be my life companion. Whatever rights I expect from her, I also give her. We will live together with affection [*aṉpu*]."[50] The bride took the same vows, and Ramasami proclaimed that they were married according to the principles of the Self Respect movement.

Despite this pronouncement, the wedding of Marakatavalli with Cho. Murugappan lacked virtually all the rituals that legally constituted a Hindu marriage. There were no Brahman priests, no religious ceremonies, no Sanskrit prayers, and Murugappan did not tie a *tāli* (wedding necklace) around his bride's neck. Moreover, Marakatavalli and Murugappan were hardly typical of Tamil brides and grooms. Marakatavalli was a widow; although widow remarriage had been explicitly legalized since 1856, it remained a rare practice among some higher castes even by 1929. Moreover, the bride and groom did not belong to the same endogamous descent group, or *jāti*. A wedding between members of two different *jātis,* which Self Respect activists termed a *kalappu maṇam* (literally, "mixed marriage"), was perhaps even more unusual than widow remarriage. Nevertheless, according to activists present at the ceremony, the wedding of Marakatavalli and Murugappan exhibited the ideal qualities of a *cuyamariyātait tirumaṇam* (Self Respect wedding): "It was a widow remarriage, a mixed marriage, and a love marriage; it avoided useless customs and extravagant expense."[51]

Marakatavalli and Murugappan's Self Respect wedding was part of a conjugal discourse and practice that far exceeded the limited changes suggested by the Child Marriage Restraint Act. Although Self Respect activists advocated the abolition of child marriage, their marriage reforms went much further in developing new wedding styles, new structures of endogamy, and new modes of challenging patriarchy.[52] Linked to the larger ideological formations of Dravidian nationalism in the Tamil region, Self Respect marriage reforms inaugurated models of conjugality—rooted in an anti-caste politics—that challenged the limitations of Indian nationalism.

Founded in 1925 by Ramasami, a former Congress activist, the Self Respect movement focused its politics on religious, caste, and gender hierarchies in Tamil society. In its early years, the movement spread rapidly throughout the Tamil districts of Madras Presidency, and Self Respect Leagues were established in Madras and in other towns and cities. By the late 1920s, it was well enough established to hold district- and presidency-wide conferences, many of which included women's meetings. In fact, women played an active role in the movement from its outset, with several women activists rising to positions of prominence and leadership in Self

Respect politics. In addition to marriage, the Self Respect movement championed a broad range of other causes concerning Tamil non-Brahman identity and political power; among its most dramatic campaigns, from 1938 to 1940, was the successful reversal of the Congress government's imposition of Hindi in schools.[53]

The Self Respect movement's "non-Brahman" constituency was wide-ranging. Like its Justice Party predecessor, it included members of fairly elite "forward" non-Brahman castes. At the same time, activists in the movement made efforts also to reach out to "backward" and "untouchable" castes. Particularly with the radicalization of Self Respect politics in the wake of economic depression in the 1930s, the movement developed a substantial lower-caste and working-class base that was distinct from both the Justice Party and the core targets of Indian nationalist cultural politics.[54] The eclecticism of Self Respect ideology accommodated these various social groups, and its claims ranged from a left-leaning socialism to more moderate demands for non-Brahman representation in politics.

Across these ideological and sociological differences, Self Respect activists remained consistent in targeting marriage as a critical site for building a unified Dravidian national community composed of non-Brahman Tamil speakers or, more rarely, of speakers of all Dravidian languages in southern India. Self Respect weddings represented a distinct sphere of political action that rejected the gender, caste, language, and religious hierarchies that had marked conventional Tamil marriage practice. These weddings first occurred as early as 1925 with the inauguration of Self Respect, were increasing in number by the time of Marakatavalli and Murugappan's ceremony in 1929, and continued even after Indian independence in 1947. The political implications of these marriage reforms were manifold. On the most immediate level, a Self Respect wedding provided an important vehicle for the movement to disseminate its propaganda. For example, an article in the Self Respect newspaper *Kuṭi Aracu,* titled "A Reformed Wedding," in Kovai notes that the wedding of Indiramani and Duraiswami took only "three minutes." Following the brief ceremony, Ramasami spoke for forty-five minutes on the role of marriage within the movement. That evening, at a concert held to celebrate the wedding, five hundred copies of *Kuṭi Aracu* were sold to the guests.[55] In this account, the wedding appears as the mere background for the movement's political interventions in Kovai. Similarly, at weddings of activists such as of Kuncitam and S. Gurusami in 1929, the bride and groom themselves spoke about Self Respect before the assembled wedding guests.[56] Self Respect slogans posted around the wedding hall, and a procession through the main streets of the locality, extended the message of Self Respect weddings to an audience beyond only the guests. Indeed, as *Kuṭi Aracu* notes about several weddings throughout the 1920s and 1930s, the mere rumor that a Self Respect ceremony might occur drew curious onlookers to the vicinity.[57]

These politicized weddings were rooted in a gendered discourse that, at least rhetorically, rejected the patriarchal norms of Tamil families. For example, as Ramasami argued, "many people say that marriage is divine, [but] in actuality it is about women's abject subservience. If this is divine marriage, we have no choice but to reject divine marriage, which is in fact a slave marriage."[58] Claiming that religious rituals merely justified women's slavery within the conjugal relationship, Ramasami advocated a kind of wedding ceremony—and a broader ideology of marriage—that would liberate, rather than subjugate, women. Female activists in the movement developed this critique further, as in the case of S. Kuncitam, who claimed that, "in the name of marriage, our parents sell us like goats and cows to men whom we do not like. Having sold us thus, they leave us to a cruel fate of lifelong tears." Ending such hardship, Kuncitam argued, would require not only a transformation of weddings but a change in the very structures and ideologies that shaped women's lives; she exhorted women to become educated, independent, and fight for their own rights.[59] Beyond marriage, the movement also addressed questions of sexual freedom, with a consistent emphasis on women's autonomy.[60]

Unlike Indian nationalism and the all-India women's movement, Self Respect marriage did not develop an ambivalent modification of "tradition" to support claims about modernity. Less concerned with the reform of traditional practice than its outright rhetorical rejection, the movement's wedding ceremony offered activists the opportunity to demonstrate their commitment to rationalist progress:

> In each and every action [in the wedding] we must break the bonds that subordinate us to Brahmans. We should not check horoscopes: one bond (*kaṭṭu*) is broken. We must not care for the *muhūrtam* (auspicious time); another bond is broken. The wedding took place during *rāhukālam* (an especially inauspicious time); yet another bond is broken. In this way, we must become perfect rationalists (*pakuttaṛivuvāti*). *Rāhukālam,* horoscope, and other such practices are not suitable to rational thinking.[61]

These attempts to rationalize conjugal norms opened up a vast terrain for the movement's critique of Brahmanical religion and caste. In terms of marriage, this appraisal centered on the figure of the Brahman priest, or *purohit,* within conventional weddings: "The major qualification a *purohit* has today is that he must be of a high *jāti*. We have no interest in his behavior or character. We tell him to perform rituals he does not understand in a language we do not understand. Then we give this man money and fall at his feet." Such behavior implied inferiority on the basis of caste, yet Ramasami argued: "We do not agree that we belong to a low caste."[62]

The criticism of the Brahman *purohit* extended to challenge any religious basis for marriage at all: "Why must we invite God to our weddings?

What is the relation between God and a wedding? What is the necessity of God? When we go to a restaurant or go to the latrine do we invite God then?"[63] Further, as quoted in the chapter's epigraph, Ramasami maintained that weddings required no religious or caste foundation: "Divinity, custom, and *sastra* are all opposed to the progress, rationality, and freedom of the people. That is why Self Respect marriage leaves no room for these regressive and anti-freedom concepts."[64] Once again, the rhetorical impetus here is not simply to reform Tamil-Indian conjugality to suit modern norms. Rather, the Self Respect movement consistently emphasized the fundamental, paradigm-shifting nature of the *cuyamariyātait tirumaṇam,* as opposed to the insistence of Indian nationalism to return to the true spirit of tradition.

Within the de-sacralized, de-traditionalized space of Self Respect, the wedding was figured as a secular, contractual relationship. Activists thus discouraged the use of conventional terms like *kalyāṉam* or *kanyā tānam* to describe a Self Respect wedding, coining instead the phrase *vāḻkkai oppantam* (life contract). Ramasami, for example, frequently compared marriage to a business contract: "Everyone will agree that if two friends want to start a business together, they will need to make a contract [*oppantam*] . . . So also, running a life is like running a business. Just as you need to make efforts to start a business together, so also a man and woman must jointly create a relationship together."[65] Self Respect weddings, therefore, represented the public proclamation of that contract, a moment when "a man and woman join together, become bound to each other, and make known to others that they will live their life jointly." Marital vows were essential to this contract, so that the central feature of a wedding was when "the bride and groom speak their vows to each other, exchange garlands as a sign of their agreement, and thus take their decision."[66]

In this way, although figured very differently from Indian nationalism, notions of consent were at the core of Self Respect's contractual conjugality. Far exceeding claims about the body, the movement drew rhetorical connections between consent and compatibility, equality, and companionship in marriage. In Ramasami's terms, "if the couple is of one mind and one life, then they may live together. But if they are not suited to each other—if life becomes like hell—the couple has the right to separate, marry more suitable persons, and to live a pleasurable and happy life."[67] Thus, consent once given could be revoked and marriage contracts broken. Such freely chosen contracts could aspire toward a conjugal equality that far surpassed conventional "slave" marriage: "The married couple should behave as friends. You should not say 'I am a man' and become dominant. You should think that both are friends, and live that way; no one should tolerate dominance."[68]

Self Respect publications typically represented the consenting partners of a Self Respect "*vāḻkkai oppantam*" as individual subjects who rejected social and familial constraints; the Self Respect wedding was an expression of such individuality. For instance, the marriage of Teyvanayakam Pillai and Tanapakkiyam in 1935 was among many described in these terms. The movement's newspaper, *Kuṭi Aracu*, prominently featured the wedding under the headline "Love Marriage," and explained that the families of the bride and groom did not approve of the attachment. Despite this opposition, at eight o'clock one evening, Tanapakkiyam went alone to Teyvanayakam's house and gave her consent to the marriage, which occurred at his home the next day.[69] The couple's actions—especially Tanapakkiyam's solitary trek to her lover's home at night and the public announcement of a wedding the next morning—emphasize the bride's individual defiance against parents and custom. This account presents a profound disjuncture with conventional marriage practice, and renders consent all the more valuable for its rejection of familial and social norms. This is not to imply, of course, that Tamil men and women had never defied family or community in order to marry. Rather, the significance lies in the movement's consistent valorization of such defiance; although not all Self Respect weddings exhibited these characteristics, those that did were considered to represent the movement's highest ideals.

This emphasis on the individual existing in opposition to social constraints, a quintessentially modern theme, was linked to the Self Respect movement's specific critique of caste and patriarchy in Tamil society. As such, Self Respect ideologies did not render social hierarchies beyond the purview of an individualist politics—differing from liberal nationalism and feminism in this regard—but instead demanded their rejection as the necessary basis for the formulation of a Tamil individual subjectivity. In other words, the central feature of the individual marrying subject became the explicit disavowal of caste and, if necessary, family preference as the organizing features of conjugal arrangements.

The movement gave great rhetorical prominence to instances of *kalappu maṇam* (mixed or inter-caste marriage), many of which also challenged parental and kin dictates about marriage choice. Such marriages, as in the case of Tanapakkiyam and Teyvanayakam, highlighted individual choice at the expense of social categories such as caste or lineage which conventionally had played a far greater role: "In Self Respect marriage, we don't pay attention to *jāti, vakuppu, kulam,* or *kōtram* [Skt. *gotram*], but only to the qualities of the bride and groom."[70] In the movement's construction of both individual and society, brides and grooms did not enter into marriage as members of a particular caste, clan, or household/family but instead as individuals capable of giving consent. This abstraction of the conjugal couple from kinship and caste relations represented a marked shift in Tamil conceptions of family and society. Conjugality now stood at a remove from the social networks within which it had conventionally been embedded.

Ideally for Self Respect activists, the *kalappu maṇam* forged relationships of kinship and endogamy essential to the Dravidian national community. For instance, when Dhanalakshmi Ammaiyar conducted a "mixed widow remarriage" of two couples in Devakottai in 1935, she argued that caste differences led to conflicts in Tamil society that prevented unified national or political work. Eliminating such difference was absolutely essential to the modernizing progress of the nation (*tēcam*, Skt. *deṣam*), because mixed marriage would abolish caste distinctions "from the very root."[71] Dhanalakshmi's conception of the national community was open-ended; it was unclear whether she referred to a Tamil-Dravidian nation or an Indian one. Its boundaries—the nation's insiders and outsiders—were equally porous, since the text does not explicitly exclude anyone from participating in the newly endogamous national community.

Other mixed marriages marked the boundaries of both nation and endogamy more deeply, particularly after 1938, when leaders called for a separate Dravidian nation distinct from an Indian counterpart. In this context, Dravidians were not considered simply a community with a shared history, language, or territory—although each of these aspects was important to Dravidian nationalism and the target of much ideological work.[72] "Dravidians" were also defined and demarcated as a community of inter-marriage distinct from Tamil Brahmans. In uniting this community through the bonds of kinship, marriage—quite literally—could forge the nation. Thus, in the words of one *Kuṭi Aracu* editorial, mixed marriages were absolutely necessary "if we want the Dravidian nation truly to become one nation."[73] In E. V. Ramasami's terms, this nation would ignore distinctions between such non-Brahman castes as "Nayudu, Chettiyar, Padaiyacci, or Pillai." Rather, "except for Brahmans, we are all of one *jāti*. We may call it Dravidian."[74] This neologism—this endogamous "Dravidian *jāti*"—mapped the boundaries of the Dravidian nation.

Indian and Dravidian Politics of Conjugality

Like the Indian nationalist politics of conjugality, the Self Respect movement saw the family as essential to the (Dravidian) nation. The modernizing progress of Tamil society hinged upon the reorganization of its domestic life—including kinship and sexuality as well as marriage—along contractual, secular, and rational lines. Further, despite notable differences in content, both the Self Respect movement and Indian nationalism tended to isolate these domestic reforms from wider social transformations. Telescoping the "women's question" into a debate about marriage, Self Respect ideologies sometimes de-emphasized the larger socioeconomic context within which families were figured within the putative Dravidian nation. To this extent, and like Indian nationalism, Self Respect weddings resonated with a global politics of domesticity that rendered the transformation of home and family essential to claims about a middle-class modernity.

However, unlike in Indian nationalism, the Self Respect movement did not position marriage solely as a trope for articulating other political goals. Instead, perhaps echoing Tamil precolonial histories, marriage alliances could actually construct the polity. Effective marriage choice—now represented as crossing caste boundaries and defying social convention—could produce the nation itself. The Dravidian nation, in other words, was imagined in and through family networks, and the Self Respect *kalappu maṇam* was central to forging these radical connections between non-Brahman Tamils. Rather than relying on existing arenas of political expression, moreover, Self Respect activists created a new political space around their wedding practice. Without reference to the colonial legislatures, where battles over child marriage were fought, the movement transformed weddings themselves into politicized gatherings. The *cuyamariyātait tirumaṇam* demonstrated an image of national communion that, as Benedict Anderson asserts, was so crucial to a nationalist imaginary.[75] With its flamboyant rejection of conventional practice, the wedding became a form of political theater, whereby the bride and groom dramatically overcame tradition and culture.[76] The movement's newspapers further emphasized these performative aspects, headlining weddings that most violated conventional norms, and printing photographs of the married couple and important guests.

The new political sphere of Self Respect weddings engaged new social groups, thus extending the movement's reach beyond the upper-caste, middle-class focus of Indian nationalist cultural politics. For instance, we find regular reports of Self Respect weddings among the working-class residents of Perambur, an industrial suburb of Madras city. These weddings occurred among Tamil laborers in the Kolar gold fields, as well as in the Tamil diasporas of Sri Lanka and Malaysia. Although more rarely, Self Respect newspapers also reported weddings among members of "Adi Dravida" (literally, "first Dravidian" or "untouchable") castes—many of whom were marginalized both by Indian nationalism and by the Dravidian movement's focus on "non-Brahman" or caste-Hindu political identity. In this way, the Self Respect wedding created a public domain that was largely invisible to more conventional arenas of political debate about the family.

During the movement's most radical phase in the early 1930s, the question of marriage helped to raise deeper issues about caste and gender equality. Left-leaning Self Respect activists lamented the gap between the movement's theoretical stance and its wedding practices, and also questioned whether marriage reform could produce the fundamental transformations that the Dravidian nation needed to fulfill its egalitarian aspirations. For example, S. Nilavati, a forceful champion of women's rights who was prominent in the movement during the 1930s, criticized couples who had a Self Respect wedding but did not pursue the goals of the movement: "Couples may give financial and other reasons for a Self Respect wedding. But afterwards even those who have had a mixed widow remarriage continue their lives with no thought about the movement. The couples who pay attention to Self Respect principles are few."[77] Thus, for Nilavati, even a "mixed widow remarriage," the most radical Self Respect challenge to conventional Tamil practice, did not necessarily produce the proper subjects of Dravidian nationalism; marriage alone did not inspire the requisite social change. Calling for a political praxis that extended beyond marriage, she demanded that activists take up the women's question more seriously. Even E. V. Ramasami occasionally argued that Self Respect weddings were not an end in themselves but only one means toward achieving the larger goal of eliminating caste and class oppression.[78]

These sharp-edged challenges to the transformative power of marriage in producing an egalitarian nation were, however, gradually marginalized from Self Respect debates. Indeed, in contrast to the 1920s and 1930s, the politics of Self Respect conjugality appears radically diminished in both rhetoric and practice by the 1940s, when both *cuyamariyātait tirumaṇam* in particular, and critiques of patriarchy more broadly, became much less central to the political goals of Dravidian nationalism. This shift was partly the result of the increasing distance between the Self Respect movement and the potentially radicalizing mass mobilizations against colonial rule spearheaded by Indian nationalists in the 1940s; the former, which centered its politics on caste rather than anticolonialism, remained apart from the Indian independence struggle. Facing a greatly reduced membership in the wake of the Quit India demonstrations of 1942, in which the Self Respect movement did not participate, Ramasami merged Self Respect with the more conservative Justice Party to form the Dravidar Kazhagam (Dravidian Association, DK) in 1944. Although advocating *cuyamariyātait tirumaṇam,* DK ideologies were less interested in the anti-patriarchal content of marriage reform.[79] Scholars have noted these shifts to suggest that the earlier politics of Self Respect "mobilized [women] to contest patriarchy," but that, ultimately, the movement "failed to create a new anti-patriarchal consciousness even among its own followers."[80] In other words, although its ideologies exceeded the limited reforms suggested by the mainstream of Indian nationalism—and, as such, represent a different modern legacy than the politics of the Indian nation-state—ultimately anti-patriarchal practice did not remain at the core of Dravidian nationalism.

Marriages and Nations

The Tamil process of nationalizing marriage during the 1920s and 1930s was neither singular nor unitary. Even as Indian nationalism sought to assert its authority over conjugality, there emerged an alternative and vibrant conjugal ideology, promoted by the Self Respect movement, which was not collapsed into Indian nationalism's aspirations. My point here, however, is not to celebrate the mere emergence of alternatives—a historical misreading given the actual limitations of the Self Respect movement's anti-patriarchal critique. Rather, building upon the work of historical recovery undertaken by scholars of the Dravidian movement, this chapter has sought to develop a history of nationalizing marriage that does not echo Indian nationalism's own erasure of alternative cultural politics.[81] Such a history accounts for how the modernizing conjugality of Indian nationalism was shaped not only in relation to orthodox "tradition" and the colonial state—as nationalists themselves claimed—but also in contest with alternative visions of what constituted modernizing progress for the nation and its families. To do otherwise simply echoes Indian nationalism's own hegemonic discourses about Indian modernity.

Any attempt, however, to situate Indian and Dravidian nationalist cultural politics within the same field confronts an immediate contradiction: the almost complete absence of public dialogue and debate between these two different visions of conjugal reform. Despite the historical simultaneity of their conjugal politics—both developed in the context of mass nationalism in the 1920s and 1930s—Indian and Dravidian nationalist discourses about marriage existed at a rhetorical disjuncture. Indian nationalist positions dominated a sphere of debate, defined by the colonial state, and centered on legislative assemblies, state-initiated investigations, and English-language media. Indeed, if we view these terrains as representing the entirety of public discussion about marriage in the Tamil region, Indian nationalist formulations appear to have won the day. However, although largely absent from these spheres, Self Respect marriage developed into a powerful political current within the Dravidian movement. The weddings themselves constituted a public expression of the movement's politics. They were documented and debated almost exclusively within Tamil-language publications and political activity, but they did not enter the legislative arena. In this regard, Indian nationalism did not successfully remove alternative conjugal politics from public debate in late colonial Tamil Nadu; however, it did assert authority over the legislative reformulation of marriage. Consequently, although child marriage was not the only point of contention about conjugality during this period, it was the only one to receive state scrutiny and legislative intervention.

In postcolonial scholarship, Indian nationalism has remained—with some justification—at the center of investigation into histories of patriarchy, modernity, and gender. This is partly because Indian nationalist ideologies were so successful in setting the terms of debate, especially in relation to the colonial state. Thus, as we have seen, the rhetorical force of

Indian nationalism both helped to make *Mother India* a target of public debate and worked to make the Child Marriage Restraint Act the primary vehicle of nationalist response. Indeed, on occasion, the dominance of the Indian nationalist position even functioned to deny other ideologies a public platform from which to debate.[82] Despite this dominance, however, the existence and proliferation of Self Respect marriage suggests the extent to which alternative models of gender, family—and, indeed, modernity itself—took hold during the 1920s and 1930s in Tamil Nadu. Consequently, historical inattention to these alternatives reinscribes Indian nationalist dominance yet again.

De-centering Indian nationalist conjugal politics through attention to *cuyamariyātait tirumaṇam* opens the possibility for a fuller examination of indigenous responses to colonial domination, and resituates the child marriage debates within a much broader field of discourse about conjugality and nationality. The complex representation of marital consent within Self Respect weddings introduced possibilities for Tamil subjectivity far exceeding the limited reforms produced by Indian nationalist claims about female bodily consent. The movement's attention to class, gender, and caste hierarchies in its production of an individual marrying subject called into question the refusal of Indian nationalism to engage these categories in its production of a national citizenry. Nationalist categories have also been challenged by various subaltern populations, and historians of the Subaltern Studies school have amply documented forms of resistance that have gone unnoticed in elitist historiographies. Some scholars have noted the parallels between these subaltern politics and the Dravidian movement, suggesting that the latter's anti-caste politics marks its subaltern status vis-à-vis the dominant ideologies of Indian nationalism.[83] I argue, instead, that Self Respect marriage disrupted the closures of Indian nationalism in somewhat different ways. Although indeed a challenge to the "hegemonic project of national modernity," *cuyamariyātait tirumaṇam* consciously posited alternative modern and nationalist forms.[84]

In making this claim, I differ from some theorists whose work investigates the hegemonizing aspirations of Indian nationalism while locating alternatives primarily within the interstices or fragmentary ruptures of nationalist thought. In addition to these fragmentary disruptions, I emphasize that Indian nationalist claims were contested on their own terms from the very outset by organized movements like Self Respect. The *cuyamariyātait tirumaṇam* was thus not solely a "fragmented resistance [to the] normalizing project" of Indian nationalism, to borrow Partha Chatterjee's terms, but also offered an alternative imagination of national culture itself.[85] In other words, the language of nationalism, as well as of modernity, progress and universalism, was not ceded, a priori, to Indian nationalist claims but contained alternative trajectories that we cannot afford to dismiss as inevitably marginal to Indian modernity. Despite the foreclosure of these alternative possibilities in later decades, when the Self Respect movement retreated from its anti-patriarchal rhetoric and practice, the project of nationalizing marriage illuminates the multiplicity not only of marriage reform but of nation and national identity themselves.

FOUR

Marrying for Love: Emotion and Desire in Women's Print Culture

> In our day, the groom does not see the bride; the bride does not see the groom . . . Marriage has become merely a commercial exchange. Because of this, couples share no reciprocity or unity, and become separated from each other.
>
> *Muthulakshmi Reddi, "Remarriage," 1937*

> In order to conduct our domestic duty, we cannot think that one person is higher or lower than the other; we must consider them [husband and wife] to be equals. Justice requires that they establish the same affection and the same trust.
>
> *Ma. Antalammal, "Chastity," 1913*

The critiques of contemporary marriage practices expressed in the epigraphs to the chapter, the first by a prominent activist on women's issues and the second by a lesser-known contributor to a Tamil women's magazine, were both part of an emergent print culture directed at women that developed in late colonial Tamil Nadu. This culture, exemplified in periodical texts such as *Grihalakshmi* (Lakshmi of the home) and *Peṇ Kalvi* (Women's education), constructed a novel paradigm that made the emotional content of conjugal life the centerpiece of reform. Along these lines, Muthulakshmi Reddi and Ma. Antalammal referenced a companionate conjugal ideal, rejecting those elements of Tamil marriage practice that prevented husbands and wives from becoming companions with "the same affection and the same trust."

This emotional paradigm, I suggest, marked a departure from the existing frameworks of Tamil debate on families and familial relationships.

This chapter investigates the emotional paradigm through a reading of magazines, some edited by men and some by women, published from the 1890s to the 1940s and designed for a female readership.[1] In referencing emotions, the magazines typically used the Tamil terms "*uṇarcci*" or "*uṇarvu*," which may be translated in English as "emotion," "feeling," or "sentiment"; my translations of the terms are based on context. The magazines' focus on "emotion" was linked to the rearticulation of family life examined thus far. The texts developed their critiques of conjugality in relation to a wider sphere of public debate about marriage; for example, articles advocated for legal reform and invoked nationalist discourses to demand social change. At the same time, however, by focusing fierce and critical attention on the affective experience of conjugality, these women-centered texts brought into public discourse issues and concerns beyond the purview of legal, feminist, and Indian and Dravidian nationalist sites of reform. This critique marked the components of companionship (particularly affection, pleasure, and romantic love) as the "natural" attributes of married life. It challenged existing Tamil customs and social practices, claiming that they placed "unnatural" restrictions on conjugal emotion. Muthulakshmi's and Antalammal's interventions, published in two important women's magazines of the time, contributed to developing this emotional paradigm.

Historical scholarship on women's magazines in India has focused on the opportunities they created for women writers and readers. For instance, in her study of early-twentieth-century Urdu women's magazines, Gail Minault argues that, despite some limitations of access and ideology, the magazines "at least gave women a place where their voices could be heard."[2] Himani Bannerjee's research on Bengali texts takes this argument further to suggest that magazines functioned as a "wide communicative space" for women which filled the gap created by the disappearing culture of the *zenana* or *andar mahal* (women's quarters). Although, as we have seen, colonial relations of rule disrupted the cultural practices of these female-centered spaces, Banerjee suggests that women's magazines attempted to create another "social, moral and cultural space for and by women."[3] In other words, as the *zenana* of precolonial households was pathologized under the weight of colonial and nationalist discourses, developing print cultures offered new vocabularies for women's communication. In this regard, the magazines were a nineteenth- and twentieth-century version of long-standing conceptions about women's communities in India, representing both continuity and a break with the past.

I employ Bannerjee's formulation of the women's magazine as a modern communicative space with some qualifications. First, the social space of the magazines did not include all women, as they were restricted to those who were literate in Tamil or in English. For the time period under discussion, this restriction meant that most readers came from the urban middle classes—the same social group that was central to the public reformulation of the family. Second, although designed for women, the magazines did not exclude men. Particularly in the nineteenth century, as both Bannerjee and Minault note, many magazines for women were edited, and largely written, by men. In this sense, the communicative space of the magazines was never exclusively female, and was perhaps less indicative of the concerns of women's own communication than of the subjects that male social reformers deemed appropriate for a female audience. The magazines thus drew two kinds of boundaries around women's communicative space, both demarcating the legitimate subjects of female reading, and including only a limited group of women within this reading public.

Moreover, the conditions for the existence of Tamil women's magazines were different from those that had created female communicative spaces in the past. On the one hand, the magazines grew out of a developing culture of print capitalism in the Tamil region where women were one segment of a wider, largely middle-class market of readers. Echoing developments in other parts of the colonial world, this culture of print, which included periodical literature as well as novels, used nationalist ideologies as a legitimating paradigm.[4] In this context, Tamil prose joined the cause of social and national reform, offering a fertile terrain for discourse about the family. On the other hand, the creation of magazines meant specifically for women developed from engagements with "the woman question," which, as we have seen, was thoroughly embedded in debates about family and domesticity in colonial Tamil Nadu. On this basis, I emphasize that the magazines did not represent an already existing women's community but rather shaped a female reading public according to the demands of ideology, politics, and the market for print. Consequently, its membership—the community of women readers—was markedly different from the interaction of female kin, servants and slaves, and service providers who constituted the female-oriented spaces of precolonial households.

In tracing the chronological development of this colonial reading community and its emotional paradigms, I follow Francesca Orsini's periodization of women's magazines in Hindi, which are paralleled in the history of Tamil texts. The first phase, from the beginnings of women's publishing in the 1890s until World War I, focused on reforming women into more "appropriate" forms of domesticity. In the subsequent decades of the 1920s to the 1940s, which Orsini terms a "radical-critical phase,"[5] I demonstrate that the magazines offered a more thoroughgoing challenge to women's oppression within the family by developing a more complex discourse of emotion.

The magazines' focus on the emotional lives of female subjects marks a significant moment in the history of Tamil families for several reasons. First, references to emotional companionship supported an ongoing privatization of marriage and kinship; in this regard, the magazines echoed nationalist claims that the family was a "private" sphere distinct from "public" political activity. Second, the magazines linked family privacy to conceptions of individual subjectivity that defined the private sphere in new ways. Third, the magazines did not simply invoke "emotion" but actively shaped its meanings by associating emotional life with domesticity, interiority, and femininity. As a result, they produced new notions of identity in which one's "inner feelings" emerged as primary markers of the self. The women's magazines were at the forefront of privileging this supposed interiority over kinship, familial relations, or caste as identity markers. Therefore, in producing novel paradigms of emotion, the magazines also produced distinct conceptions of "the family" that were less concerned with the politics of marriage alliance than with the affective bonds sustaining the conjugal couple.

Educating Wives, 1890–ca. 1920

The earliest examples of Tamil periodical literature date from the 1840s, but only about fifty years later, during the late 1880s and 1890s, were they published in any significant numbers, and specifically for women. This growth in Tamil publishing was made possible, in part, by a rise in female literacy.[6] Literate women, by the late nineteenth century, although only a small percentage of the overall Tamil population, represented a potential community of readers for these new magazines. This growing female readership—prompted by an increase in formal education for girls and women—sparked debates about whether boys and girls could share the same curriculum, or whether girls required different subjects of instruction. Some magazines sought to fill this perceived curricular gap by creating a body of writing that included both general topics and those relating directly to women. For example, articles about household hints accompanied writing on general science, medicine and hygiene, geography and history.

This section examines three magazines directed at women.[7] Two of these were published exclusively in Tamil: the first is *Peṇmati Pōtini* (Women's enlightenment), edited by two women, N. S. Pittarammal and Minampikai Ammal, and published monthly from Madras beginning in 1891;[8] the second, *Mātar Maṉōrañjiṉi* (Brightener of women's minds), was edited by a man, C. S. Ramaswamy Iyer, and published monthly from Madras beginning in about 1899.[9] The third, the *Indian Ladies Magazine,* began in 1901 as an English-language monthly edited by Kamala Sattianadhan, a well-known writer and scholar who belonged to a prominent Christian family in Madras.[10] Although not published in Tamil, the magazine's content and perspectives were deeply rooted in the cultural politics of the Tamil region, and its articles resonated with the issues brought up in the Tamil texts.

In identifying the purpose of female education, all three magazines focused on motherhood and wifehood. Rather than challenging women's oppression within the family, the texts sought to educate women to become more "efficient" and "capable" wives and mothers. In so doing, they established a model of what I term "appropriate domesticity." Among many examples of this model is a series of articles appearing in *Peṇmati Pōtini* in 1892. Titled "Domestic Life of the English," the series described English habits and customs for its Tamil readers to emulate.[11] Articles focused on practices of child care, hygiene, and household management. Underlying this advice to Tamil women, as the author makes clear in the first installment of the series, was the notion that in England husbands went to work outside the home and wives took responsibility for all household activity. This was the model the author assumed and advocated for Tamil families.

The emphasis that the series "Domestic Life of the English" placed on separating home from work reflected transformations in English culture and economy dating from the late eighteenth and early nineteenth centuries. As Leonore Davidoff and Catherine Hall have demonstrated, the shift of the locus of production away from the home—and the concomitant reconstruction of the home as a female domain and haven from outside turbulence—was central to the culture of a developing English middle class under capitalism. Indeed, this cultural shift (which both reflected and contributed to a changing economic situation) marked the boundaries of the middle class; by "making domesticity the practice of a class," men and women reformulated their class identity while developing a domestic ideal.[12] According to Davidoff and Hall, this model of bourgeois domesticity became well established in England by the mid-nineteenth century. The articles in *Peṇmati Pōtini,* published several decades later, imply that this domestic model was an essential and immutable feature of English culture that Tamils would do well to adopt.

Despite *Peṇmati Pōtini*'s claims, however, English domesticity was clearly not a pre-formulated metropolitan norm that could simply be replicated in the colonies. Not only were English ideals produced, in part, through a rejection of the domestic practices of colonized others, but Tamils (like other colonized populations) also engaged in a process of translation that substantially transformed European models. Missionaries were critical in this negotiation. For example, in the Tamil context, they maintained that European domestic arrangements, with their gendered divisions of labor, were central to Western civilizational and moral superiority. As elite households struggled with the crises provoked by the colonial administration, missionaries led an ideological attack on the domestic arrangements of Tamil families, focusing on the *zenana* "as an absence, a lack, which the West could fill."[13] Rejecting the physical separation of men from women that the *zenana* represented, they advocated a re-gendering of Tamil domesticity along the lines of Victorian separate spheres. However, Tamils did not simply adopt these domestic models but developed them in relation to locally specific ideologies and aspirations.[14] For example, many articles in *Peṇmati Pōtini* and the other magazines selectively appropriated precolonial discourses in the service of their modern domestic aims. Some writers referenced long-standing Tamil and Indian traditions that feminized interior spaces in order to buttress their own claims about women's domestic roles.[15] Similarly, one article, "The Duties of Hindu Wives," in advising women to obey their husbands, referenced Vatsyayana's *Kamasutra*.[16]

Thus, far from being a mere imposition of European norms, the magazines' model of appropriate domesticity represented a "convergence of late nineteenth century Tamil and Victorian morality" that helped to restructure Tamil ideas about the family.[17] These "Tamil" moral discourses, moreover, were specifically upper-caste and often explicitly Brahman in origin. Writers especially linked Brahmanical representations of female chastity and spiritual cooperation between husband and wife to Western and Christian conceptions of companionate marriage.[18] In this way, the combined rhetorical force of Tamil Brahman and English Victorian ideals denounced the diverse, sometimes non-monogamous, conjugality of lower classes and non-Brahman castes. Along these lines, both European missionaries and upper-caste Tamils deployed discourses of "appropriate domesticity" to challenge the elite households of non-Brahman *zamindars*, on the one hand, and, on the other, the domestic arrangements of economically marginal peasant and tribal families.

The resonance of this developing domestic ideal for some Tamil readers was linked to socioeconomic and ideological changes in the family that occurred from the late nineteenth century on. Specifically, the texts assumed a privatization of the family characterized by a fixed residence, rooted in the conjugal relationship, and isolated from non-blood related kin or other household dependents. This framework of family life would have been incomprehensible to many Tamils, but by the 1890s, as we have seen, it was gaining currency among upwardly mobile urbanizing social classes. Women of these classes both witnessed, and contributed to, a transformation of the domestic realm. Professional and especially administrative occupations removed men's productive work from the home; moreover, since men from these groups often left rural areas and moved to Madras and other cities, their wives were in the position of creating households apart from mothers-in-law and other senior kin. In these new households, the conjugal couple was increasingly central, and women assumed greater responsibility for the care and early education of their children.

Within this context, as Judith Walsh argues, it became necessary for "the Western-educated to adjust their home lives and family relations to the teachings of the educational system . . . [and] the requirements of occupations that demanded implicitly or explicitly that such men appear hardworking, well organized, efficient, and clean."[19] In developing their domestic models, the magazines sought to transform wives into suitable partners in this enterprise. The *Indian Ladies Magazine* was at the forefront of this endeavor. Its editor, Kamala Sattianadhan, came from a family that was committed to models of companionate marriage and a Christian-inspired domesticity. For example, Sattianadhan's mother-in-law, Anna Sattianadhan, authored a domestic manual that was among the first in Tamil to propagate these ideals; other members of the Sattianadhan family wrote about and advocated companionate conjugality as essential to Christian morality.[20] A prolific writer and scholar in her own right, Kamala Sattianadhan wrote a number of articles for the *Indian Ladies Magazine* urging Tamil women—both Hindu and Christian—to become companions to their husbands and educated mothers of their children.

Other contributors to the magazine made similar arguments. For instance, in "Our Wives," A. K. Sabha argued that, particularly for "English educated Indians,"

> [marriage] becomes almost a chaotic gloom. Their wives cannot give a particle of literary pleasure or amusement nor are they able to enjoy any of their much-dreamt of marriage blessings. There is little in our marriages to bind up the magic tie of matrimony, little to contribute to any happiness . . . A true reciprocated love is the essential tie of marriage. In cases of servile obedience we rarely meet with unmixed happiness.[21]

Implicit in Sabha's complaint was the notion that wives ought to be their husbands' preeminent companions and that they, rather than other members of an extended family, should share in his emotional life. In fact, echoing other discourses about conjugality, Sabha's text separated the marital relationship from other kinship relations, and located husband and wife at the center of family life. His article also hinted that gender hierarchies were responsible for the lack of companionship in marriages.

However, as became apparent in one response to "Our Wives" penned by "an Indian Girl" and appearing in the next issue, Sabha's desire for change in marriage did not take "women's point of view into consideration at all." The anonymous author argued that Sabha wrongly blamed women for the problems of marriage. Women, she claimed, would become educated companions to men if they could, but women depended upon men—and particularly husbands—to educate them in true companionship. After all, the "Indian Girl" added in an ironic reference to child marriage, husbands were in contact with their wives from a very young age; rather than blaming women, men needed to take the initiative for reform.[22]

The dialogue between Sabha and the "Indian Girl" prefigures subsequent discourses that situated a companionate domesticity at the heart of their marriage ideals. Despite such references, however, neither the *Indian Ladies Magazine* nor the Tamil magazines *Peṇmati Pōtini* and *Mātar Maṉōrañjiṉi* consistently made marriage itself an object of reform during this period.[23] Although the magazines sought to educate women into an "appropriate" wifehood, they paid little attention to the broader structures that shaped families in the Tamil region, implying that emotional companionship only required the individual efforts of women within the newly constituted domestic sphere.

Visions of Companionship, ca. 1920–1940s

The 1920s marked a significant shift in the content, ideology, and production of women's magazines. Magazines became more numerous during this period, as did women writers and editors. This publishing boom in women's magazines was consonant with an increase in the output of Tamil publishers overall, which began in the 1920s and continued through the interwar years. Alongside women's magazines there appeared a number of periodicals designed for the general public, as well as an increase in the publication of novels—many of them appearing first in serial form in the magazines. The community of women readers was also on the rise, and, by the end of this period, women constituted an important segment of Tamil readers overall.[24] This developing women's print culture was heavily influenced by an upsurge in women's political activity, including, as discussed in chapter 3, diverse forms of agitation around marriage and family. Women's magazines published from the First World War to the 1940s reflect this contentious ideological context, in which nationalist and feminist movements redefined both conjugality and politics.

This section examines four women's magazines, in Tamil and English, each of them committed to social reform and women's issues. Three of the magazines were edited by women. The earliest of these three, *Peṇ Kalvi* (Women's education), edited by S. Thayarammal, pursued "the object of enlightening and elevating ladies."[25] The *Indian Ladies Magazine,* re-launched during the interwar years after a hiatus, was still edited by Kamala Sattianadhan.[26] A third important magazine edited by women was the organ of the WIA, *Stri Dharma* (Women's duty), in which articles in Tamil and Hindi regularly supplemented the English sections of the magazine.[27] The one male-edited magazine, S. Krishnan's *Grihalakshmi* (Lakshmi of the home), inaugurated in 1937, was published monthly in Madras.[28] Although *Grihalakshmi* was not officially associated with the WIA, its editors and writers were committed to many of the association's campaigns. The thematic content of all these magazines reflected a middle-class and upper-caste perspective. Echoing the larger women's movement's neglect of working-class women's issues, they only rarely carried news or opinions on these subjects.

Like their earlier counterparts, a few articles and editorials from this period continued to develop models of "appropriate" domesticity for their female readers. Others broke with earlier magazines by representing women's oppression within the family as an explicitly political question. Like nationalist interventions in family life, these texts politicized conjugality, casting it as a public problem that required reform. However, the political content of the magazines differed from both their nineteenth-century predecessors and contemporary nationalists. When writing about marriage, authors demanded not that wives change to become suitable emotional companions to their husbands but rather that the social norms and economic practices supporting patriarchal marriage be transformed to suit the conjugal couple's emotional needs. Specifically, many magazines criticized marriage through the metaphor of the market, and condemned the exchange of brides and grooms on the basis of monetary, caste, or kinship considerations. This kind of exchange, they claimed, both instituted and perpetuated women's oppression. By contrast, the magazines represented marriage as a relationship in which an emotional bond between husband and wife assumed primacy over other matters.

The new focus on transforming society, rather than wives, emerged around the question of dowry. Relatively marginal to other public debates about marriage, dowry was represented in the magazines as the quintessence of an inappropriate commercialization of family relationships.[29] For example, a cartoon in *Peṇ Kalvi* demonstrated the disastrous impact that dowry had on brides and their families.[30] In the cartoon, potential grooms and their fathers are pictured at the far left; written on the turbans of the grooms are their dowry demands, ranging from Rs. 2000 to Rs. 6000, and some clasp diplomas in their hands. The grooms' fathers make their monetary demands even more explicit in the accompanying caption: "Look here! Our sons have earned F.A. and B.A. degrees. They are going on to study for their B.S. degree. If you give us the money written on their turbans, we will have our sons marry your daughters." At the center of the cartoon—literally caught in the middle of the grooms' demands and their daughters' plight—are the parents of the potential brides. Their caption indicates that they cannot pay such huge amounts in dowry, "even if [they] sell house and home." At the right of the cartoon, the daughters—the potential brides—are all committing suicide: two by hanging, a third by jumping into a well, a fourth by setting herself on fire, and the last by decapitating herself with a knife. Their caption reads, "Oh, parents! Do not lament! . . . This is our fate. For our sake, do not suffer in poverty, losing

“Problems Caused by Dowry,” *Peṇ Kalvi*, March 1914

house and home." The brides' only alternative to the ruinous prospects of high dowry payments is death.[31] Thus, the cartoon suggests that, because of these dowry payments, marriage, quite literally, has become a market populated by demanding grooms and exploited brides.

A number of short stories in the magazines suggested further that marriage had not only become a marketplace but a starkly unequal one, where grooms and their families set the terms of exchange. C. Kanakavalli's story, "Susila's Wedding," which appeared in *Grihalakshmi,* recounts the financial and emotional impoverishment that accompanies commercialized marriage. The plot centers on Susila, a Brahman girl whose parents, themselves formally educated, allow her to attend school. Her father Gopal Ayyar, however, is determined that Susila marry before puberty, and he travels to Madras in search of a son-in-law. Bewildered by the big city, he is forced to pay for the services of a marriage mediator, who introduces him to Gunasagaran, a student at Madras Presidency College. Ultimately the combined cost of the mediator, the dowry, and the wedding arrangements drain Gopal Ayyar of his entire life savings. Here the narrator notes that none of these payments, of course, will contribute to Susila's marital happiness. When she finally enters her conjugal home, she is ill-treated and abandoned by her husband and his family: "Susila's condition was truly pitiable. Gopal Ayyar became desperately poor. And what was lost? The life of a woman!"[32] "Susila's Wedding" clearly advocates the separation of commercialized market relations from the conjugal domain.

A number of articles and short stories sought to replace conjugal commerce with an emotional bond between husband and wife. For instance, in an essay in *Grihalakshmi,* S. Komalam condemns child marriage as merely the "buying and selling of eggplants and plantains." According to Komalam, Tamil parents viewed daughters as a "burden that they are eager to shove off onto the groom's family." As a result, girls were married at the earliest opportunity and forced into relationships that held no possibility of a "unified life" between husband and wife. Komalam asserts, however, that marriage should not to be modeled on the ethics of trading vegetables; parents should instead help their educated, adult daughters in choosing husbands to their own liking.[33]

N. Yagneswara Sastry developed a related argument in an essay in *Stri Dharma,* where he examined the emotional toll of child marriage. Since religious sanctions requiring the marriage of prepubescent girls pressured fathers to find suitable grooms for their daughters, "bridegrooms become the dictators of marriage terms and make money at the cost of their fathers-in-law—one reason for a parent's disrelish [*sic*] of girls." Once such a commercialized marriage had taken place, Sastry added, the "average educated Hindu" spent little time with his wife. In this sort of relationship, there was no "spontaneity of feeling, mutuality of sentiment and discriminative taste." Referring explicitly to European practices, Sastry suggests that the inauguration of "courtship" between potential brides and grooms would lay the foundation for companionate marriages.[34]

Several authors emphasized that the commercialization of Tamil society overall had contributed to destroying the conjugal relationship. An essay by K. V. Swaminathan in the *Indian Ladies Magazine* argued that an obsessive focus on monetary benefits had edged out questions of "personal worth and inborn similarity" in choosing marriage partners: "The material standards that we find in Indian Society today must be eliminated at the earliest possible moment, because, with such standards, it is impossible to make ideal marriages the general rule."[35] Muthulakshmi Reddi, in the article cited in the epigraph to the chapter, similarly criticized marriage as a "commercial exchange." Condemning the customary practices associated with enforced and celibate widowhood, the article suggested that commerce had replaced affection and emotional attachment in marriage.[36] Both these authors claimed that emotions and sentiments were stifled in contemporary marriage practices, claims that marked the beginning of an emotional standard for conjugality.

In these texts, writers called for the conjugal relationship to function as an anti-market. Having been corrupted by the growing commercialization of the Tamil economy, marriage needed to be resituated within an affective realm that prioritized emotional exchange. Therefore, in contrast to colonial law and anticolonial politics—whose turn to conjugality had been prompted, in part, by certain kinds of market relations—the women's magazines strenuously excluded the market from their representations of conjugal companionship. In these texts, appropriate forms of conjugality depended upon their effective separation from the depredations of capital.

Some writers invoked an emotional paradigm of marriage in order to challenge women's subordination in the family and society. For instance, Ma. Antalammal, quoted in the second epigraph above, argued that true *aṉpu* (affection) between husband and wife was possible only when they were equals.[37] A short story, "Susila," published in the *Indian Ladies Magazine*, also explored the relationship between equality and emotional companionship. The title character, sixteen-year-old Susila, escapes from her uncle's home to avoid being forced into marriage with a much older man. Braving the censure of her caste members (Brahman Aiyars), she trains as a nurse and supports herself financially. The story concludes on a triumphal note: "Later, she [Susila] was able to marry a doctor with whom she fell in love."[38] By creating a character who not only left her natal family but also became financially independent outside marriage, the author envisions a "new woman" who would be capable of creating a companionate and loving marital relationship.

Writing in *Stri Dharma*, G. Sumati Bai developed an even more forceful challenge to family patriarchies. In "The Facts of Marriage—No Fancy of Man," she argues that women's subservient role would end with the "dawn of a new cultural revolution in India" brought about by Indian and Dravidian nationalism, as well as by the Indian women's movement. Sumati Bai envisions a new kind of marital relationship in which:

> the master-and-slave unions of bossing husbands and servile wives will have no honourable recognition in the new age of reason. Justice would then be the criterion of law and life. Man and woman would be free to meet as comrades and *love alone shall then unite them.*[39]

By connecting love with justice and reason, this passage opens the door to a social critique based on a discourse of emotion. Asserting the primacy of love becomes the grounds for criticizing various marital practices. The full expression of such love depended upon transformations both in the "private" domestic sphere and in the "public" world of nationalism and an Indian "cultural revolution."

Within this logic, nationalism offered a non-market public context for the reformulation of marriage. In other words, while rejecting commercial exchange as an appropriate conjugal model, the magazines emphasized nationalist bonds of solidarity and resistance. An article by "Mrs. Munshi," titled "Dominion Status in Matrimony," that appeared in *Stri Dharma* begins with a critique of "traditional" Indian concepts of marriage, which Munshi locates in the *Mahabharata:* "You know very well what Dharmaraja did in the *Mahabharata.* He staked his wife in gambling. She was no more to him than a mere chattel or coin. This ideal of marriage is deeply ingrained in Indian men and women."[40] Such a position was completely inappropriate to contemporary Indian society, where young women were using their newly acquired education and freedom to serve the country. Therefore, she demanded:

> Just as the Dominions become more loyal to the British Commonwealth on possessing the "right to secede," so also would the husband and wife be more loyal to each other if the relation is based on freedom. In short, women also want dominion status in matrimony with the right to secede . . . The women who brought the British Government to its knees will find it easy enough to bring their fathers, husbands and sons to their knees.[41]

Munshi's text linked nationalist mobilizations to the intimate relations of husbands and wives, thus weaving anticolonialist sentiment into the very fabric of discussions about conjugality.

Despite the differences between the magazines considered here, the contents of each disavowed a market-based exchange in marriage that supported oppressive gender relations. In replacing this marriage market with emotional companionship, however, the magazines were also redefining the terms by which affective expression could be understood and represented. They emphasized certain sentiments, so that love (*kātal*) and affection (*aṉpu*) became central to denote ideal forms of a desexualized conjugality.[42] More broadly, the magazines' insistence on separating companionate marriage from the transactions of the market, or on distinguishing emotional ties from commercial exchange, was significant in itself. In diametric opposition to the "public" and anonymous nature of the market—exemplified in the *Peṇ Kalvi* cartoon—the magazines tended to represent marital emotion as both private and individualized. Conjugal love and affection were not to be bargained over publicly as in the case of a trade in property, but were to be situated firmly in the "privacy" of the domestic sphere. The family, and especially marriage, thus emerged as a site of resistance to the encroachments of capital. This domesticated privacy of conjugal life, however, was not rendered impervious to social change. Thus, although primarily concerned with the domestic expression of marital emotion, some texts also sought to replace the oppressive transactions of marriage-as-market with a more liberating public context of nationalist mobilization.

Desire and Pleasure in Marriage: *Mātar Maṟumaṇam*, 1936–1939

Among the women's magazines published between the 1920s and the 1940s, one stands out in terms of ideology and content: *Mātar Maṟumaṇam* (Widow remarriage), edited by Marakatavalli. Marriage occupied a dominant place in the content of the magazine; essays, short stories, and poetry focused on widow remarriage in particular, but also launched a wide-ranging challenge to oppressive marriage practices more generally. As in the other magazines, the social critique in *Mātar Maṟumaṇam* was based on an appeal to emotional companionship. However, the magazine also extended the realm of emotion beyond marriage to take up questions of romantic love (*kātal*) and pleasure (*iṉpam*) among widows who were denied the possibilities of "family life" (*kuṭumpa vāḻkkai*).

The plight of widows had been a long-standing concern for social reformers. Among upper castes, widowhood was permanent and enforced; a widow and her family faced social ostracism if she remarried. This restriction held true both for adult women and for "child widows" who were married before puberty and whose husbands had died prior to consummation of the marriage. Widows' sexuality was strictly controlled, typically through the imposition of restrictions on clothing, ornaments, food, and social activity. Brahman communities imposed especially severe constraints on widows, but lower castes also emulated these practices as a marker of social prestige. Since the mid-nineteenth century, reformers had campaigned against permanent and enforced widowhood, and their efforts resulted in the passage of the Widow Remarriage Act of 1856, which legally recognized the right of widows to remarry.[43] The change in law, however, was largely ineffective in altering social practice, and the editor of *Mātar Maṛumaṇam* saw the need for reform in Tamil society even eighty years later.

The question of marriage reform held a personal resonance for the magazine's editor, Marakatavalli, as she herself was a widow who had remarried in a Self Respect ceremony in 1929.[44] Although the magazine reflects Marakatavalli's commitment to Self Respect principles, there is little evidence about her direct involvement in the movement's activities by 1936, when *Mātar Maṛumaṇam* first appeared. Marakatavalli began publishing the magazine as part of her efforts with the *Mātar Maṛumaṇam Cakāya Caṅkam* (Widow Remarriage Assistance Society). Under her editorship, the magazine was published monthly in the town of Karaikudi beginning in August/September 1936 and continued until at least 1939.[45] Articles focused on women's issues, and, though addressed to women, the magazine enjoyed a male readership as well.

Although the magazine's ideology was eclectic, drawing on the Indian women's movement, Gandhian ideals, and Dravidian nationalism, it consistently criticized the role of custom in shaping gender norms. A cartoon titled "Open the Door!" which appeared in an early issue encapsulates this criticism by picturing a woman imprisoned, literally, in the cage of "religious and caste custom."[46] A young male "social reformer" is attacking the cage with an ax, and his caption reads, "You won't open the door [of the cage]? Just one chop and the bars will fall to pieces. Just watch!" The social reformer's efforts cause the two other men in the cartoon—a Brahman Hindu priest and an older Brahman man—to lament that "scripture, religion, and caste are all gone, lost beyond rescue." "Open the Door!" thus offered an unambiguous rejection of caste and religion while making an explicit argument for social change. Furthermore, the drawing took a clear position about obstacles to change, suggesting that the male Brahman orthodoxy benefited from existing custom. This outright rejection of custom, which resonated with Self Respect ideologies but was largely absent from the other magazines examined here, placed *Mātar Maṛumaṇam* among the more radical social critiques of its time.

The drawing also implies that only male social reformers have the ability to open the doors of custom's cage; the imprisoned woman—a widow—waits passively to be rescued, silent in the face of conflict between men representing the forces of tradition and change. The volume's cover illustration, in which a kneeling widow seeks the blessing of a man clearly identifiable as Gandhi, makes a similar point.[47] Here, too, it is the male nationalist-social reformer, and not the widow, who has the agency to initiate change. Even when the drawings did not look explicitly toward men to champion reform, the magazine did not provide visual representations of

கதவைத் திறங்கள்!

சீர்திருத்தக் காரன்:— கதவைத் திறக்கமாட்டீர்களா? ஒரே வெட்டு. அடைப்பு தூளாகிறது. பாருங்கள்!

பெரியவர்:— விதவையை அடைத்துப்போட வேண்டுமென்று சாஸ்திரத்தில் சொல்லியிருக்கிறது.

சாஸ்திரி:— போச்சு சாஸ்திரம் மதம் ஜாதி யெல்லாம் முழுகிப் போச்சு.

"Open the Door!" *Mātar Maṛumaṇam* 1, no. 3 (October/November 1936). Reproduced from the original held in the collection of Roja Muthiah Research Library.

"Widow Remarriage," *Mātar Maṛumaṇam*, cover of each issue of vol. 1 (1936). Reproduced from the original held in the collection of Roja Muthiah Research Library.

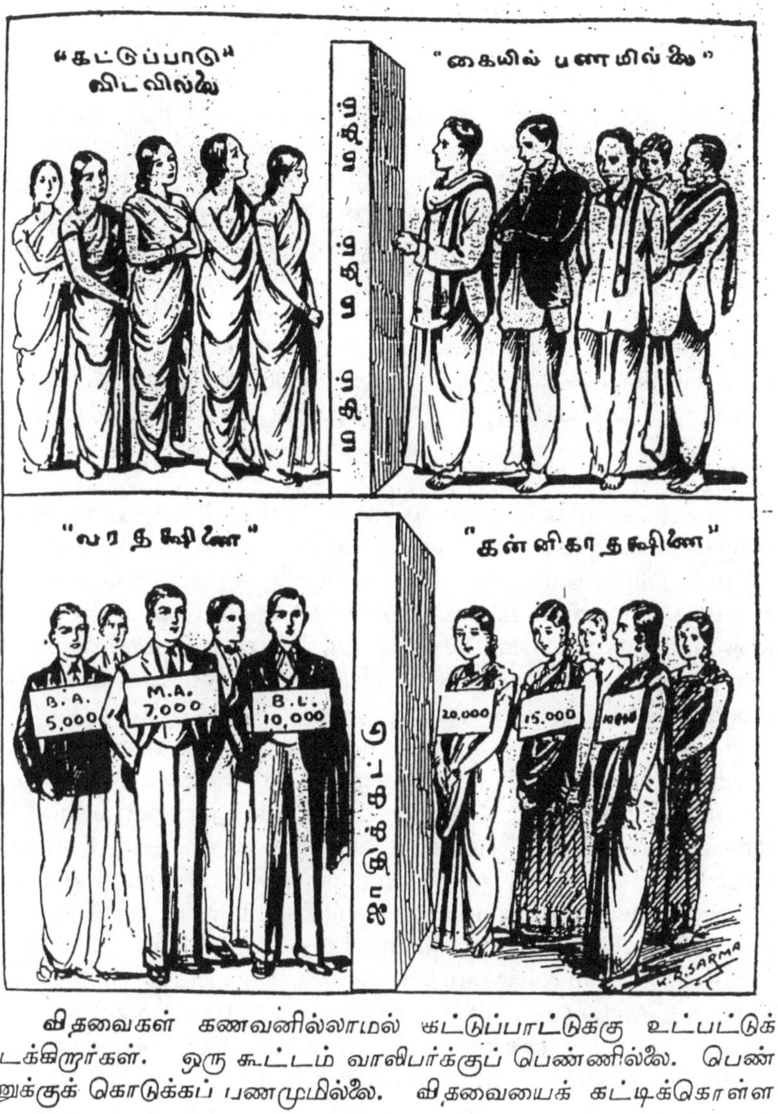
"கட்டுப்பாடு" விடவில்லை
"கையில் பணமில்லை"
"வரதக்ஷிணை"
"கன்னிகா தக்ஷிணை"
B.A. 5,000
M.A. 7,000
B.L. 10,000
20,000
15,000
K. R. SARMA
விதவைகள் கணவனில்லாமல் கட்டுப்பாட்டுக்கு உட்பட்டுக் கிடக்கிறார்கள். ஒரு கூட்டம் வாலிபர்க்குப் பெண்ணில்லை. பெண்ணுக்குக் கொடுக்கப் பணமுமில்லை. விதவையைக் கட்டிக்கொள்ள

"Religion and Caste Custom," *Mātar Maṛumaṇam* 1, no. 1 (August/September 1936). Reproduced from the original held in the collection of Roja Muthiah Research Library.

women's ability to intervene; a cartoon lamenting how religious and caste customs resulted in barriers to marriage is one example.[48] Based on these images, one might argue that the magazine participated in a long-standing nationalist discourse on the "women's question" in India that sought to recast women in order to modernize patriarchal gender relations.[49]

I suggest, however, that *Mātar Maṛumaṇam* actually provided the tools to challenge such representations of women. In an article on remarriage, for example, S. Nilavati addressed women directly:

> Push out the betrayals of womanhood that have spread in this world! However many tasks you have accomplished, however many tasks you will accomplish in the future—in the matter of widow remarriage you must not be slow and cautious, sisters! You yourselves have the power to break your chains.[50]

Nilavati was an activist closely associated with the Self Respect movement during its radical phases in the 1930s; the most anti-patriarchal aspects of Dravidian politics are echoed in her assertion that women themselves fight for change. Throughout the text, moreover, Nilavati turns specifically to widows as agents of reform. Thus, although this article appeared under the cover illustration of Gandhi and the widow, Nilavati does not assume that widows are either passive or silent.

The discourse of love, pleasure, and desire was a consistent presence throughout these contradictory representations of widows in *Mātar Maṛumaṇam*. Invocation of a widow's desire—and the very portrayal of the widow as a desiring subject—complicated notions of agency and social change in these texts. For instance, a number of essays and short stories looked to the widow's romantic love (*kātal*) as a force to challenge social norms. In the short story "Shankaran's Love," published in 1938, the protagonist is an urban college student who receives a letter from his childhood friend, Ambujam, while visiting his native village. Ambujam, a child widow, writes of her love for Shankaran and hopes that her widowhood will not prevent their marriage. Shankaran, however, fearful of the social opprobrium attached to widow remarriage, refuses Ambujam. In response, she writes an impassioned letter:

> Love is not related to caste (*jāti*) or social customs. It does not recognize such things. It does not permit these stupid and meaningless beliefs. You have seen me, and I have also met you. We love each other. Where did the meaningless custom of caste come in?[51]

In this passage, all social divisions are irrelevant in the face of Ambujam's love for Shankaran. Neither the lovers' caste backgrounds nor the caste-based sanctions against widows remarrying can interfere with this love. Indeed, in making this claim, the text removes marriage entirely from its conventional context of kin and caste alliance. The narrative thus portrays Ambujam not only as an upper-caste widow prohibited from marriage but also as an individual woman whose love makes marriage possible.

Ambujam's vision, however, remains an unattainable goal. After rejecting her, Shankaran learns that he himself is the illegitimate child of a widow. He is now overcome with remorse over his rejection of Ambujam, but, in the glare of the sentimentalist genre of the text, it is too late. He tears open Ambujam's last letter only to find a suicide note: "When you have forsaken me, I have no purpose in this world." She will wait for him in another world "where there is superior knowledge, where caste (*jāti*) and customs do not hold back the progress of humanity . . . where differences between high and low, rich and poor, do not exist. Where true love is victorious."[52] The author consistently portrays Ambujam as having the courage to challenge the customs associated with widowhood; only she, not Shankaran can take the initiative to remarry. Despite her scathing critique of Tamil society, however, Ambujam is ultimately dependent on Shankaran's love. With no possibility of a life outside marriage—nowhere does the author speak of any option other than marriage for child widows—Ambujam needs a man with sufficient love or compassion to marry her. Thus, the text's emphasis on love provides the impetus for radical transformation of marriage ideologies, even while foreclosing other alternatives for women. The widow's love can only be a transformative force with the support of a potential husband.

The suffering of widows deprived of the possibility of remarriage is also a common theme in the fictional pieces of *Mātar Maṟumaṇam;* in many of them, the widow herself, as first-person narrator, conveys a sense of urgency to the project of widow remarriage. In one short story, a widow describes the moment she learned of her husband's death: "They took away all my ornaments; I was without silk clothes, plaited hair, or *tilak*. Calling me cursed and inauspicious, they threw me into a corner. Since that night . . . memories of that time flash before my eyes like a movie." Finally, in despair at her wasted life, the widow decides, "I will follow the path of death while calling it pleasure (*iṉpam*). I choose this path. I have chosen it! I will be free from this compassionless society. From today, I am auspicious again."[53]

Many other stories also focus on the moment when a woman learns of her widowhood. In the following passage, the narrator describes her reactions to her husband's death years earlier:

> I thought of my life. I thought of the condition I had been in until the previous day. I thought of the past. I thought of my stage in life. I thought of the many desires (*ācai*) I had. I realized that all my ideas and plans had been snatched away from me. Oh, I had so many desires. I wanted to

> live with my husband, to have children. But these desires were scattered like cotton in the wind . . . From that day until now, tears have been my only companions . . . Can't you [readers] do something to wipe away our tears? Society has pushed us aside like unwanted trash. But we are not trash. We are human beings. We were born, raised, and lived as your younger sisters, mothers, and daughters. You have thrown us into the trash heap. Will you now help us, and treat us as humans?[54]

Again this narrative depicts widows as victims, dependent entirely on the compassion of others, yet I suggest that the passage also introduces further possibilities. Widowhood, for the narrator, represents the "snatching away" of her desires. Unlike the texts about companionate marriage discussed in the previous section, here the widow openly reveals her desires, among them a life with husband and children. Elsewhere in the text, the narrator refers to the loss of jewels and colored clothing, of social interaction and family life, of music, education, and other sources of happiness. Thus, desire (*ācai*) becomes integral to the arguments about widow remarriage.

Invoking a widow's desire was not unusual in itself, since containment of that desire lay at the root of the social restrictions traditionally placed on upper-caste widows. Their physical appearance—plain clothing and shaved head—was meant to eliminate the possibility of widows becoming the *objects* of sexual desire. This text, however, was radical in portraying widows as desiring *subjects*. Whereas the discourse of widows as objects was rooted in descriptions of external conditions—clothing, food, and so on—their portrayal as desiring subjects called attention to the interior emotional experience of widowhood.[55] In a distinctly modern move, these texts depict the widow's "inner" self as her true identity. Documenting this interiority also meant asserting its existence by bringing the widow's "interior" emotional life into the "exterior" public discourse of the magazine, where it served as a call to action. Such documentation necessarily challenged the social conventions of widowhood, which mandated against its expression.

The transgressive nature of a widow's desire, and the way it was used to challenge social norms, is further elucidated in a short story by Bharati Dasan.[56] Ironically titled "The Well-Being of Widows!" the story describes the relationship between Devaki, a widow, and her cousin, Sundaram. After many years of separation, Devaki learns that Sundaram has married, and, typical of widows in this literature, she dies of sorrow. Sundaram is puzzled by her death, as he cannot fathom that Devaki had feelings for him: "She used to write letters to me. But they were not love letters, because, after all, she was a widow! How could she have felt love toward anyone?" When Sundaram discovers many letters that Devaki never mailed, he is finally convinced both of her love for him and of a widow's ability to love at all, and this prompts him to acknowledge that "many widows in this country seem well from the perspective of outsiders" but this well-being is merely a sham.[57] Bharati Dasan thus exposes the false assumption that widows, simply because of their widowhood, are outside the realm of desire. In a poem published in the inaugural issue of *Mātar Maṟumaṇam*, Bharati Dasan expands this pronouncement by suggesting that the sanctions of celibate widowhood mandate against natural sentiments. Titled "Restrictions That Harm Love (*kātal*)," the poem makes the following appeal:

> O Goddess of Nature *(iyaṟkkai),* who has given us youth,
> and sentiment *(uṇarvu),* and pleasure *(iṉpam)* in life,
> The mean-spirited people of our country
> Have outlawed love in the name of widowhood![58]

Widow remarriage thus emerges as the fulfillment of "natural" love; celibate widowhood, by contrast, is an unnatural constraint upon sentiment.

This appeal to "natural" sentiments is even more explicit in an essay by Ma. Pichai which claims that "feelings of pleasure (*iṉpa uṇarcci*) are common to everyone." The author focuses on *iṉpam,* a term that connotes both joy and pleasure, including sensual pleasure. Given that all human beings seek *iṉpam,* Pichai argues, "there is no reason why they [child widows] should live without feelings of pleasure." Adding that *iṉpam* is a "natural feeling," the author warns that, when deprived of outlets for their pleasure, young widows will follow "harmful paths,"[59] clearly implying sexual relations outside marriage. Thus, a widow's potential sexuality is as central for Pichai as for Brahmanical patriarchy. Indeed, Pichai's text mirrors the logic underlying traditional Brahmanical restrictions on upper-caste widows. But whereas Brahmanical patriarchy demands that sexuality be contained through celibacy, Pichai sees a widow's desire as the basis for ending this unnatural enforcement of celibacy.

As in other narratives about widows' desire, Pichai also explores the emotional interiority of the widow as subject. By positing *iṉpam* as a "feeling" (*uṇarcci*) everyone experiences, widows and non-widows alike, he highlights the discrepancy between the widow's inner life and its outer expression. Yet, in calling for these two aspects to be united—for the widow to express her desires and pleasures—Pichai focuses on the ways in which feelings are contained; in other words, celibacy should be replaced by marriage.

In another short story, presented as a dialogue, a daughter convinces her mother to support widow remarriage:

> When the husband dies, what will happen to her [the widow's] beauty and youthful status? What will result from social customs that fetter human feelings (*maṉita uṇarcci*) and human rights (*urimai*)? Prostitution and unnecessary slander will be the only result.[60]

Disregarding a widow's "human feelings" thus produces disordered sexuality—"prostitution"—that can only be controlled by allowing widows to remarry. Echoing Self Respect discourses, the text also links the concept of "human feelings" to a notion of logic and reason in the organization of socio-sexual relations. Throughout the story, the daughter rationally refutes each of her mother's objections to widow remarriage, culminating in the daughter's assertion of the widow's emotions and rights. The demands of reason and emotion unite to sanction the remarriage of widows in defiance of custom and social practice.[61]

By validating a widow's desire, the narratives in *Mātar Maṟumaṇam* complicate the portrayal of widows as passive objects of reform. This is not to say, however, that *Mātar Maṟumaṇam* accords an unproblematic agency to widows; the emphasis on their pitiable conditions, and their frequent deaths when unable to remarry, precludes any such interpretation. Nevertheless, the magazine raises the possibility that widows' desire should be an impetus for, and set the terms of, social change. This text also offers more explicit references to female sexuality than any of the other magazines considered here. Indeed, more than through representations of the companionate marital relationship, it is in the interior subjective suffering of widows that desire and pleasure are most elaborated. These are not the domesticated, privatized sentiments that developed in the context of other magazines' portrayals of marriage. Rather, in *Mātar Maṟumaṇam*'s figure of the widow, the modern subject develops an interiority that is rooted in sexuality and the expression of "natural" feelings. That said, the magazine's emphatic answer to the question of desire is remarriage. As we have seen, this both undercuts widows' agency (they die if they cannot remarry), and perhaps functions as another politics of containment of female sexuality.

Emotion, Interiority, and Women's Print Culture

Tamil women's magazines changed significantly over time, moving from a reformist emphasis on "appropriate domesticity" at the turn of the twentieth century toward a more radical critique of gender relations within the family by the 1920s and 1930s. However, upon examining these texts in terms of language and vocabulary, similarities and continuities across periods are also apparent. In particular, the magazines' focus on several Tamil terms—*kātal* (romantic love), *iṉpam* (pleasure), and *aṉpu* (affection)—transcend the texts' ideological differences and set their discourse apart from other sites of public debate about the family examined thus far.

The term *kātal,* romantic love, is at the heart of stories about couples whose relationships challenge established social divisions. In a magazine like *Mātar Maṟumaṇam,* and in the most progressive writing in *Grihalakshmi* or *Stri Dharma,* romantic love operates in two ways. On the one hand, the texts define oppressive social practices as those that restrain the expression of love between a heterosexual couple. On the other hand, love also emerges as the crucial force whereby young couples challenge these oppressive practices. In this way, *kātal* offers the power to reform the family as well as society; it also places the conjugal couple at the center of social change. What is significant here is not just the reference to *kātal;* classical Tamil literature was also concerned with heterosexual romantic love and lovers.[62] The difference is that, in these magazines, *kātal* was inextricably linked both to marriage and to a drive for women's freedom.

The second term, *iṉpam,* denotes joy or pleasure, including sensual pleasure. *Iṉpam* appears regularly only in *Mātar Maṟumaṇam,* which is, not coincidentally, the only magazine to address questions of desire and sexuality. Like its portrayal of romantic love, the text represents the concept of pleasure as a force for social change. By proclaiming that a widow's desire for *iṉpam* is natural, writers challenged the social customs that denied these women pleasure. At the same time, however, they situated "feelings of pleasure" (*iṉpa uṇarcci*) exclusively within marriage.

Aṉpu was probably the most frequently used of these three terms. Although usually translated as "affection" in English, the word carries a wide range of connotations; unlike *kātal,* it is not restricted to a romantic or sexual relationship but can apply to relationships between friends, between parents and children, and so on.[63] The women's magazines represent *aṉpu* as the basis of the bond between husband and wife. The presence or absence of this quality, however, also has important social implications. The expansive use of the term *aṉpu* is apparent in the following passage from *Peṇ Kalvi:* "Without *aṉpu* there is no womanhood; without womanhood there is no world. Without the world, everywhere there is nothingness."[64] *Aṉpu* almost acquires characteristics of the sublime; it is elevated beyond the realm of mundane life into something that sustains the world. When we consider that, for many writers, the term *aṉpu* also encapsulated the best qualities of a conjugal relationship, we may begin to understand how the magazines' emphasis on emotion represented a significant shift in the very terms by which marriage was understood.

Through the elaboration of emotion, the magazines contributed to the privileging of conjugality—over and above kinship, caste, and patrilineage—that was also occurring in various other contexts. Traces of this decentering may be seen in *Stri Dharma*'s criticism that child marriage prevented any "mutuality of sentiment"[65] between husband and wife, or in the *Indian Ladies Magazine*'s attack on the joint Hindu family because it impeded the emotional relationship of the conjugal couple.[66] In these cases, the demands of extended kin relations and the maintenance of caste-based marriage conventions gave way to other considerations. *Mātar Maṟumaṇam* took this position further in its condemnation of any practice—whether the celibacy of widows or the enforced submission of wives—that gave primacy to caste or kinship norms. At its most radical, *Mātar Maṛumaṇam* suggested that caste-based endogamy and caste sanctions against widow remarriage should be disregarded and replaced by love and pleasure. Therefore, although the emotional paradigm offered a distinct logic for foregrounding conjugality, it nevertheless supported the claims of mercantile and professional classes, Indian and Dravidian nationalists, and feminists who argued that marriage reform was central to transforming social, political, and economic relations in the Tamil region.

Moving beyond most other sites of debate about conjugality, however, the magazines used emotion to demarcate new boundaries of "private" and "public" in Tamil society. They explicitly contrasted their emotional paradigm of marriage to the "public" transactions of the market; the texts situated conjugality in a domestic realm that stood in opposition to forms of commercial exchange. Furthermore, the emphasis on privacy was accompanied by a feminization of emotional expression. Addressing a female reading public, and concerned with the emotional development of female subjects, the magazines created a feminized discourse of love, affection, and pleasure. Although drawing from Tamil precolonial traditions, this gendering of emotion held new implications for defining privacy and domesticity in the colonial era.[67]

Scholarship in women's history has identified the permeability and contingency that attend the boundaries between private and public; the feminized privacy of emotion was no exception. This is most apparent on the level of reading, since the magazines constructed their private paradigms through the public market for print. The logic and technologies of print capitalism—including the market of text and advertisement—thus shaped the putative "privacy" of the female reading "public." In addition, the magazines' discussion of marital emotion was never isolated from the public politics of women's movements and nationalist mobilizations. Instead, it existed in relationship with, and yet remained distinct from, the politicization of the familial imaginary that occurred in these contexts. Thus, rather than assuming the privacy and femininity of the emotional paradigm, I suggest that these texts must be read as actively creating a new private sphere around the expression of *kātal, iṉpam,* and *aṉpu.*

This focus on the private or domestic expression of marital emotion raised a further question for the magazines: if the marrying subject was no longer marked primarily (or exclusively) by ascriptive identities, what ought to determine marriage choice? Who were the proper subjects for a new ideology of marriage that was not about reproducing the patrilineal, caste-endogamous order? To answer these questions, the magazines elaborated new notions of identity, in effect theorizing a female subject of conjugality. For all the texts considered here, the themes of love, affection, and pleasure mapped the contours of the marrying subject; these emotions were the new guides for choosing marriage partners. But consistently in *Mātar Maṟumaṇam,* and in fragmented fashion in other texts, there also developed a model of emotional interiority.

In other words, the texts represented *kātal, iṉpam,* and *aṉpu* not merely as the components of emotional companionship but also as the "inner feelings" central to widowed women's subjectivity. Thus, the widow's inner self marked the boundaries of her identity and her unique individuality; communitarian affiliations were rejected in favor of an individuated subject developed within a female print culture. In this regard, magazines like *Mātar Maṟumaṇam* fractured generic notions of "Woman" as the ground for debate about nation, caste, or community, instead substituting individuated widowed women whose interior subjective suffering mandated conjugal reform.

I situate the Tamil magazines' development of this (female) emotional subject of conjugality within a broader history of bourgeois subjectivity that extends beyond the Tamil region. The expression of emotions and sentiments—typically linked to the exercise of reason—played a critical role in this history globally. As in the case of the widows in *Mātar Maṟumaṇam,* emotional experience distinguished each individual subject from others and marked the boundaries of identity. The "private" subject individuated by emotional life thus developed hand in hand with a "public" subject of civil society and the state.[68] Print culture played an important role in developing this notion of subjectivity in both colonial and metropolitan contexts.[69] The act of reading printed text, as we have seen, both exemplified privatized emotional experience and linked the reader to a public market of print capitalism. Simply put, it was an individualized act that also brought the reading subject into a wider reading public.

In this regard, I suggest that the female communicative space of the women's magazines not only reconstituted women's communities in the wake of colonial rule but also participated in a global repositioning of self and identity in the context of modernity. Thus, the texts' emotional paradigm, although explicitly focused on reforming marriage, at once gestured toward the reformulation of the Tamil citizens-subjects who would create these conjugal relationships. On the one hand, this reformulation called for social and political change; writers demanded shifts ranging from the abolition of child marriage to the overthrow of the colonial regime. On the other hand, it required the production of (female) subjects marked and individuated by their emotional experiences. And, in elaborating this experience, the women's magazines spoke publicly about much that remained "unsayable" within other sites of debate about Tamil families.

CONCLUSION

Families and History

> Sex disqualifications can no longer be countenanced. The Hindu Woman through her all-around progress has earned the right to all the privileges and responsibilities of an enlightened nation . . . We are capable, and if not, we must be made capable to shoulder the responsibility of managing an absolute estate.
>
> ***Women's Indian Association (Madras Branch) to the Government of Madras, 1944***

> The fundamental basis of [the] Hindu economic structure, namely, the joint family, is now sought to be completely abolished . . . *The system of division [of joint property] is practically pakistanic in its aspect.*
>
> ***C. Rajagopolachari to the Hindu Law Committee, 1947***

Tamil activists combined a critique of the family with a redefinition of community, identity, and politics in the late colonial era. For writers, reformers, feminists, and nationalists, the family provided a rich vocabulary for speaking about the concerns confronting Tamil citizens/subjects in the context of colonial domination. This dense network of meanings and debates may be termed a "familial imaginary" whereby Tamils—both implicitly and explicitly—referenced family life to address other social, political, and economic relationships. We have seen the familial imaginary at work in several different contexts: *zamindari* attempts to reimagine households and royal authority, professional and mercantile initiatives to reconfigure property relations, Indian and Dravidian campaigns to nationalize marriage, and, finally, Tamil women's magazines' discourses of emotion and interiority around the conjugal couple. In each of these cases, the Tamil familial imaginary did not limit its horizons to reforming the family but made the family central to re-envisioning Tamil social relations more broadly.

The demise of colonial rule did not signal the end of this familial imagination. Rather, as the above epigraphs suggest, feminists and nationalists continued to debate the importance of the family for the community and the (postcolonial) state. Thus, Congress leader C. Rajagopalachari argued that the preservation of the Hindu joint family and its economic relationships was essential to the survival of a Hindu-Indian nation. Speaking against the reform of Hindu family law, he suggested that not only a nation, but also its families, could become "pakistanic." Writing in favor of legal reform, the Madras Branch of the Women's Indian Association claimed that women's contribution to the nation, through anticolonial struggle, mandated their legal equality within families. In both cases, a powerful familial imaginary linked the fate of the Indian nation to the condition of its families. This connection both opened the doors for pressing progressive demands for women's equality within families and the nation, and offered the justification for deferring reform in the name of defending India against its Pakistani "other." This inter-penetration of family and nation—with its origins in the colonial politics of nationalizing marriage—cast a long shadow over the postcolonial familial imaginary.

My use of the term "imaginary" here does not imply the essential falsity or inaccuracy of either colonial or postcolonial Tamil representations of family life.[1] I do not suggest that an "imagined" family existed entirely apart from the material conditions that were changing family structures and family life during the nineteenth and twentieth centuries. Rather, invoking a Gramscian analysis of ideology that emphasizes its material effects, I have examined the co-development of Tamil debates about the family alongside shifts in gender, political authority, property ownership, and individual subjectivity.[2] The Tamil familial imaginary thus formed a set of malleable discourses and ideologies through which Tamils made sense of their changing society; at the same time, their "imaginary" construction of family ties shaped their interventions in social and political relationships that extended beyond the household.

Attention to the familial imaginary, I suggest, allows us to foreground the dynamics of family history in the production of "the family" as a ground for political debate during colonial rule. Recognizing that the family was not an empty discursive category awaiting (anticolonial or postcolonial) appropriation, a focus on the Tamil familial imaginary can make visible the interaction between the family as an institution, as a mode of organizing social relations, and as a site of proliferating discourse. On one level, this process of re-historicizing the family has important implications for understanding gender, nation, and community in colonial India. On another level, the colonial history also illuminates how the family became such an important ground of debate in the immediate aftermath of Indian independence in 1947.

Colonialism and the Tamil Familial Imaginary

The conditions of colonial rule—and specifically the development of the colonial state—helped to set the broader context for historical changes in the Tamil familial imaginary. As we have seen, the demise of precolonial polities represented a profound disjuncture in the connections between households and ruling authority. Removed from state power, and regulated by the colonial law, the politicized households of Tamil elites gradually gave way to a depoliticized "family" characterized by blood kinship. Novel relations of economy and affect crystallized around this newly domesticated family during the late nineteenth and early twentieth centuries. These changes provided the context for nationalist appropriations of the family, and, beginning in the 1920s, Indian and Dravidian nationalists injected new political content into the ostensibly apolitical family of colonial rule. However, in contrast to households under precolonial regimes, families within a nationalist framework did not produce their own political authority. Instead, nationalists invoked the family to make various claims about the relationship between Indian or Dravidian citizens.

Conjugality became especially important to this process of re-imagining familial relationships. Placing the conjugal couple at the normative center of family relations, activists displaced—but did not eliminate—other household configurations. The husband-wife relationship became an entry point through which nationalists, feminists, and others could advocate social and political reform in the Tamil region. In the case of the activist E. V. Ramasami, for instance, the "slavish" state of Tamil marriage symbolized the slavery of non-Brahman Tamils to ideologies of caste; *cuyamariyātait tirumaṇam* was meant to forge the nation on new grounds. For contributors to the WIA's magazine, *Stri Dharma,* the enslavement of wives echoed and perpetuated the subordination of an Indian/Dravidian nation to colonial rulers. Wives who fought the tyranny of the latter, they suggested, would have no difficulty challenging the familial authority of their husbands. In this way, the state of Tamil conjugality served as an indicator of social problems; marriage reform offered one means for their solution.

Yet even as discourses of conjugal reform referenced the public politics of nation and state, they also figured marriage as quintessentially private and domestic. In the case of the women's magazines, writers even produced a private sphere of interiority and emotion by investigating the conjugal relationship. This development of a "private" domestic realm around the family in Tamil Nadu was part of a "global and intersecting" history of bourgeois domesticity in the modern era.[3] In common with both British and other colonial domesticities in the nineteenth and twentieth centuries, Tamil domestic ideals marginalized certain issues of gender, class, and caste hierarchy from the terrains of public debate. When conjugality and the family were called into question, in other words, not all aspects of domestic life were equally available for contestation and change. Rather, practices specific to middle classes and upper castes stood in for claims about Tamil domesticity overall; women's rights were often subordinated to calls for familial, and national, unity.

Although this process of selective reform resonates across the history of domesticity in both colonial and metropolitan contexts, the content of domestic ideals was, of course, locally specific. In colonial India, as we have seen, the separation of a private domestic sphere from public politics coincided with the political marginalization of colonial subjects overall. Indian and Dravidian nationalists championed conjugality as the crux of home and nation within this context of political disenfranchisement. Other changes in Tamil society supported this emphasis on the husband-wife relationship. The development of new forms of economic activity—at least among professional and mercantile interests—prompted the creation of new discourses about property that centered on the conjugal couple. Models of companionate marriage, invoked both by Christian missionaries and by Tamil women writers, revalued conjugality in producing family and community. Feminists who attacked women's oppression within the family highlighted marriage as a key site for reform. As a result, a Tamil conjugal family ideal developed through points of intersection between colonial domestic discourses, shifts in state authority and political economy, and the emergence of nationalist and feminist ideologies that privileged the family as a site of (anticolonial) resistance. In other words, Tamil debates about the family were at once locally specific and enmeshed in a wider circulation of capital and ideas within the British Empire.

Historians have noted, moreover, that modern discourses of domesticity often held contradictory implications for gender ideologies and for women's lives. In the Tamil case, these contradictions hinged upon representations of the conjugal family. On the one hand, attention to conjugality perforce drew attention to women, and revalued women's roles in producing the domestic sphere of both home and nation. On the other hand, women also bore the burden of tensions within the Tamil politics of conjugality. For example, when men's competing interests strained at the boundaries of the "Hindu joint family," women mediated between divergent models of property ownership. Within an emergent nexus of conjugality and capital, the limited reform of women's rights to property thus opened new avenues for male individual rights without challenging the patriarchal underpinnings of joint ownership. Similarly, when debates about child marriage raised questions of women's autonomy in familial relationships, Indian nationalism retreated to a politics grounded in women's bodies—rather than in their autonomous consent to marriage. Even the more thoroughgoing reforms of Self Respect marriage did not fully address the implications of women's equality within family and nation but, instead, eventually reneged on the anti-patriarchal promise of *cuyamariyātait tirumaṇam*. In each of these examples, when reforms in marriage raised the possibility of a systematic change in gender relations, the family debates appeared to redirect, or perhaps foreclose, these changes. The Tamil familial imaginary, despite important changes over time, continued to naturalize gender hierarchies within marriage.

Confronting these limitations, some women took advantage of tensions in the family debates to articulate their own claims to authority, resistance, and emotional/political subjectivity. Thus, Menakshi Sundra Nachiar defended her status as *zamindarni* of Uttumalai by developing a model of "dharmic conjugality" that inserted political authority into her definition of wifehood. Similarly, numerous widows who exercised their rights under the Hindu Women's Rights to Property Act sought to expand their access to coparcenary property by demanding the privileges of male ownership. From the 1920s on, these efforts were supplemented by emergent political organizations that claimed to represent women—*qua* women—to the state and to the Indian/Dravidian nation. Women's published writing about family life gave further impetus to these activist representations of female subjectivity. For example, the complex interiority that characterized women's writing in Tamil magazines refused to make a generic vision of "Woman" the ground for family debates by demonstrating women's individualized and privatized experiences of marriage and widowhood.

Further examination of women's agency—both within their families and in the family debates—would benefit from more investigation of families as sites of lived experience. This kind of research would require, as Antoinette Burton has suggested, a redefinition of the historical archive itself to include memory, oral history, and women's historical imagination.[4] Attention to these sources, which implies a radical re-historicization of women's family lives, might begin by examining individual family histories. For example, how did members of families respond to, and further, debates about a Tamil familial imaginary? To what extent did normative ideals of conjugality transform the experiences of conjugal couples? How did women's writing about emotion shape emotional experiences within families? Considering these questions may allow for a more nuanced analysis of women's agency that would resist essentialized representations of "the family" as an ahistorical component of national identity. It is my hope that this book, with its attention to historical currents that transformed ideas about family life in the Tamil region, can provide a framework for further investigation—a re-archiving of sorts—of family histories.

Family, Community, and Nation in the Aftermath of Colonial Rule

Examination of the colonial history of families may also illuminate the ongoing renegotiation of family and politics in postcolonial India. I close this volume with a brief excursion into the postcolonial familial imaginary, suggesting how debates about the family mediated significant historical changes in the first decade after Indian independence. As in the colonial case, postcolonial appropriations of the family adopted the rich vocabulary of family relations to confront wider questions about national community and identity. In particular, postcolonial references to the family helped to cement a deeply problematic relationship between "women" and religious "community" that had its roots in the colonial regime but had been transformed significantly under the politics of the nation-state. As a result, in the wake of independence and partition, women bore the burden of contradictions and tensions in the postcolonial state's rearticulation of the family. My account of this process is not meant to be comprehensive but rather to suggest how restoring a historicity to families challenges the efforts of the postcolonial state to identify "the family" with a singular set of gendered and political meanings.

In the first decade following Indian independence, debates about the family centered on the creation of a new code of Hindu law. Intended to replace the Hindu personal laws developed under colonial rule, these legal reforms marked a watershed in the history of gender and politics in independent India. The government's decision, under Prime Minister Jawaharlal Nehru, to reform Hindu law can be traced to two immediate factors; the first relates to specific developments within the colonial law, and the second to the broader legal context of the postcolonial state, as represented in the Indian Constitution. Regarding the former, the creation of a Hindu Code developed from a reevaluation of Hindu personal law that began in the last years of colonial rule. Prompted by irregularities and inconsistencies resulting from the application of the Hindu Women's Rights to Property Act (1937), in which widows gained some rights of coparceners, legal reformers determined that only a comprehensive set of legal changes could resolve these contradictions. The result was the Hindu Code Bill, which was first introduced before the legislature in February 1947. Following independence in August of that year, the broader constitutional context allowed—and perhaps facilitated—the passage of legal reforms directed exclusively at Hindus rather than at all Indian citizens. In other words, despite its claims about secular democracy, the Indian Constitution did not mandate the creation of a uniform set of civil laws applicable to all Indians but, instead, made this task a non-enforceable "directive principle." In the wake of the violence and instability engendered by partition, legal reformers limited their attention to the codification of Hindu personal law; they neither developed a uniform civil code nor engaged in the comprehensive reform of Muslim or other religious personal laws.

Legislative debate on the Hindu Code Bill began in 1948, when it was introduced before the Indian Constituent Assembly. However, faced with massive opposition, the bill lapsed. The provisions of the Hindu Code were finally passed by the first elected Indian Parliament, or Lok Sabha, as a series of five separate acts between 1954 and 1956.[5] These acts, among the most contentious to be debated by the Lok Sabha in its early years, made several important changes in the existing Hindu laws governing families, especially regarding marriage and property ownership. Notably, the Hindu Marriage Act introduced monogamy as a requirement for all Hindus, including men and women. For the first time, it also made legal provisions for divorce; under colonial law, the courts sometimes acknowledged "customary" divorce procedures, but the right to divorce was not uniformly applied. The Hindu Succession Act also made significant changes; most important among them, daughters were provided with some access to joint family property. However, the act retained the Mitakshara coparcenary as constituted by colonial law, continued to exclude women from becoming coparceners, and gave sons greater property rights than daughters.[6]

Thus, although the revised Hindu law provided women with greater rights, it did not offer them legal equality; in Archana Parashar's terms, legal reforms "were mainly meant to unify and modernize the law, rather than 'liberate' Hindu women."[7] The gender inequality built into the Hindu Code was apparent to feminist activists at the time, as suggested by the Madras WIA's position, cited in the epigraph above. As numerous feminist scholars have since demonstrated, the Hindu Code not only helped to entrench a system of personal law based on religion into the framework of the postcolonial regime but reestablished a stark gender hierarchy that flew in the face of constitutional claims of equality for all citizens.[8] Moreover, given that much of the Hindu Code centered on laws governing family relations, reference to the family was central to naturalizing women's ongoing legal inequality.

To some extent, postcolonial debates about the Hindu Code adopted colonial discourses about nationalizing marriage. As under the colonial regime, "the family" figured as a critical site at which reformers sought to redefine the nation and national identity. However, following the partition of the subcontinent in 1947, questions about the "Hindu-ness" of the Indian nation—and its families—took center stage. In other words, although assumptions of religious identity underlay debates about the family even in previous decades, after 1947 the postcolonial familial imaginary gave increasing importance to the family in articulating and preserving a Hindu-Indian national identity. In Tamil Nadu, moreover, the Dravidian movement continued to raise questions about the legitimacy of Indian nationalist ideologies even after 1947, and it crosscut claims about "Hindu" families with assertions of a non-Brahman, or Tamil, family produced via reformed marriage practices.

Within this fraught context, the Hindu Code Bill provoked serious opposition from those who were reluctant to see any change in existing property and family relations. Opponents of the proposed Hindu Code made various arguments against reform, but in each case they equated reform of the family with a threat to the Hindu community. Specifically, they argued that in the wake of the creation of a Muslim-majority Pakistan, any legal change in family relationships threatened the survival of Hindu identity in India. Numerous witnesses appearing before the Hindu Law Commission thus cast their defense of the familial status quo as a Hindu-Indian national necessity. Among them was N. Natesha Iyer, who testified that legal reform would "Muslimize Hindusthan" since "the draft [code] is 90 per cent [*sic*] Muhammadan law."[9] Similarly, the Congress leader C. Rajagopalachari, in contrast to his support for conjugality and capitalist development in the 1920s, adamantly opposed the Code's introduction of female heirs to joint family property. As cited in the epigraph, he maintained that "the fundamental basis of [the] Hindu economic structure, namely, the joint family is now sought to be completely abolished . . . *The system of division [of joint property] is practically pakistanic* [*sic*] *in its aspect.*"[10] Rajagopalachari thus aimed to preserve joint families to defend the "Hindu community" from the perceived threats of a Muslim/Pakistani other.

Significantly, this identification of the Hindu community with the Indian nation occurred through the mediation of the family. Within the postcolonial familial imaginary, the family essentially stood in for the religious community, and, in turn, this community was central to national identity. Family reform—or the lack thereof—was raised to the level of national self-defense. In this nexus of family-community-nation, the question of women's rights receded still further. For example, as we have seen during the early twentieth century, opponents of women's rights to joint property claimed that including widows as coparceners would threaten landholding classes. Within a postcolonial framework, opponents of reform maintained that women's ownership threatened the Indian nation itself. And in the aftermath of partition, framing the question of women's rights in this way provided a powerful incentive against reforming family law along gender egalitarian lines.

The arguments against the Hindu Code took an especially stark form in debates about the principle of monogamy. The introduction of this principle for Hindus contrasted with the Muslim law, which, in the absence of postcolonial reform, continued to allow polygamous marriage for men. Hindu nationalist organizations challenged this discrepancy, which they represented as an attack on Hindu patriarchal privilege. According to the Madras Branch of the Hindu Mahasabha: "The New Hindu Code based on monogamy may get the credit of having converted the whole of India into a vast Pakistan."[11] Claiming that allowing polygamy among one "community" while prohibiting it in another would result in a Hindu demographic crisis, the Mahasabha demanded a return to the colonial Hindu laws of marriage. These arguments erased any distinction between family, community, and nation. Conjugal reform—in this case, the rejection of polygamy—posed a threat to the supposedly Hindu character of the postcolonial nation. Although the Mahasabha represented an extreme view even among those opposed to legal reform, its rhetoric contributed to a wider dissolution of the family into the (Hindu) community and nation. As anti-reform discourses merged the family into these other politicized spaces, little room remained for discussion of women's equality.

As an analysis of family history might suggest, however, this construction of the "Hindu family" as a metaphor for a Hindu community/nation vacated other familial imaginings. It disregarded the historicity of families in favor of an ahistorical, emptying out of multiple axes of economy and affect within familial networks. In other words, participants in the Hindu Code debates linked the family so intimately to national preservation that they effectively removed from the discussion other modes of representing and understanding families and family life. Families as mediators of lived experience, as sites for the expression of power and ruling authority, as the nexus of emotional relationships producing individual subjectivity—none of these potential meanings disrupted the rhetorical juggernaut that merged family into Hindu community and nation in the first postcolonial decade. As a result, the historical process of nationalizing marriage, whereby conjugal reforms helped to elaborate nationalism, was turned on its head. Rather than advocating family reforms in the name of strengthening the nation, debate about the Hindu Code Bill introduced claims about national self-defense to limit the horizons of reform in family law.

Attention to the history of families allows us to challenge these postcolonial closures of meaning. Without collapsing the "family" into community and nation, we must instead investigate the historical factors that combined to make familial relationships so salient to constructing new modes of politics and identity in colonial and postcolonial India. Focusing on this historical process will also begin to unravel a family politics that, throughout the colonial era and beyond, has depended upon the inequality of women. If this volume, with its attention to the historical production of a conjugal family ideal, contributes to this conversation, then it will have served its purpose.

Notes

Introduction

1. *Deivanai Achi v. R.M.Al.Ct. Chidambaram Chettiar* [Appeal no. 446 of 1949 and Civil Miscellaneous Petition no. 3507 of 1951]. The Madras High Court of Judicature's judgment in this case is included in Government of Madras Order no. 3448 [Home (General)], 24 November 1954. The initials preceding Chidambaram Chettiar's name refer to the initial letters of three or four generations of his ancestors, which together formed a family name (*vītu vilacam*) among the Nagarattar caste. Prior to the 1930s, according to David Rudner, this name was also used as a business name (*to<u>l</u>il vilacam*) (*Caste and Capitalism in Colonial India: The Nattukottai Chettiars* [Berkeley: University of California Press, 1994], 109). The names of both litigants in this case would have made their caste affiliations apparent to contemporary Tamils.

2. *Deivanai Achi v. R.M.Al.Ct. Chidambaram Chettiar,* Government of Madras Order no. 3448 [Home (General)], 24 November 1954.

3. Ibid.

4. In addition to Tamil, the other major Dravidian languages are Kannada, Malayalam, and Telugu. The Dravidian movement sometimes addressed members of these other linguistic groups, but it was strongest in the Tamil districts. Tamil speakers were at the heart of Dravidian conceptions of the nation, and the leaders of the movement spoke Tamil.

5. Of course, by its very definition, a court case represents an unusual, rather than typical, social event. Therefore, I do not assume that the particular circumstances of Chidambaram and Rangammal will explain Tamil marriage forms in general, but instead examine how social and legal conflicts over their wedding became linked to broader historical debates about families in colonial society.

6. *Deivanai Achi v. R.M.Al.Ct. Chidambaram Chettiar,* Government of Madras Order no. 3448 [Home (General)], 24 November 1954.

7. The Hindu Non-Conforming Marriages (Registration) Bill, 1954, reprinted in Government of Madras Order no. 3448 [Home (General)], 24 November 1954.

8. Response of the Government of Madras to the Hindu Non-Conforming Marriages (Registration) Bill, 1954. Government of Madras Order no. 3448 [Home (General)], 24 November 1954.

9. See, for example, "Weddings without Hindu Priests," in the Dravidian movement's newspaper, *Viṭutalai,* 5 May 1954. Reprinted in Government of Madras Order no. 3448 [Home (General)], 24 November 1954. Although the movement was unsuccessful in passing such legislation following Chidambaram's case, these weddings were finally legalized in the immediate wake of the Dravida Munnetra Kazhagam's (DMK, a Dravidian political party) defeat of the Congress and ascent to power in 1967—again testifying to the symbolic and rhetorical importance of such weddings for Dravidian nationalist ideologies.

10. This is not to imply, however, that a conjugal or nuclear family form was fully achieved—or even universally aspired to—among merchant and professional groups. Sociological evidence suggests that various types of joint property ownership or co-residence or both continued into the postcolonial era (A. M. Shah, *The Family in India: Critical Essays* [New Delhi: Orient Longman, 1998], 1–13). See also Yuko Nishimura, *Gender, Kinship and Property Rights: Nagarattar Womanhood in South India* (Delhi: Oxford University Press, 1998).

11. For example, Susan Glosser's study of twentieth-century China suggests that the inter-penetration of familial and national reform characterizes the politics of domesticity in colonial contexts and distinguishes it from family reform in Western Europe and the United States. Glosser adds that in China this emphasis on the nation overshadowed other motivations for reform, including claims about individual rights and privacy (*Chinese Visions of Family and State, 1915–1953* [Berkeley: University of California Press, 2003], 20).

12. For a classic statement on the reconstitution of patriarchies in colonial India, see Kumkum Sangari and Sudesh Vaid, "Recasting Women: An Introduction," in *Recasting Women: Essays in Indian Colonial History*, ed. Kumkum Sangari and Sudesh Vaid (New Brunswick, N.J.: Rutgers University Press, 1990). In a recent study, Judith Walsh demonstrates that families, in particular, were an important site for recasting "new" patriarchies in colonial Bengal; see *Domesticity in Colonial India: What Women Learned When Men Gave Them Advice* (Lanham, Md.: Rowman and Littlefield, 2004). Walsh argues that an intergenerational shift in power away from older men, and especially older women, toward younger men was critical to transforming patriarchal practices within families. Nor was this shift limited to colonial India; for a discussion of such trends in China during about the same time, see Gail Hershatter, "State of the Field: Women in China's Long Twentieth Century," *Journal of Asian Studies* 63, no. 4 (November 2004): 994–1016.

13. Stephanie Coontz, *The Social Origins of Private Life: A History of American Families, 1600–1900* (London: Verso 1988), 12–14.

14. Perhaps the most well-known example of this disjuncture in colonial India was the Brahmo Samaj leader Keshub Chandra Sen's decision to marry his minor daughter to the ruler of the princely state of Cooch Behar. This contradicted the minimum age of marriage that the Samaj itself had advocated in its campaign for a reformed marriage law. Sen's decision helped to motivate a split in the Brahmo Samaj. See, for example, Sailen Debnath, "Cultural Imperialism in British India: A Case Study of Cooch Behar Marriage in 1878," in *The Kingdom of Kamata Koch Behar in Historical Perspective*, ed. P. K. Bhattacharya (Calcutta: Ratna Prakashan, 2000), 23–31.

15. Indrani Chatterjee, ed., *Unfamiliar Relations: Family and History in South Asia* (Delhi: Permanent Black, 2004).

16. For further discussion of this point, see Indrani Chatterjee, "Introduction," in idem, *Unfamiliar Relations*, 21.

17. An important exception to this trend of neglecting the family in political studies is Pamela Price, *Kingship and Political Practice in Colonial India* (Cambridge: Cambridge University Press, 1996).

18. For useful reviews of this kind of research on Western families, see Michael Anderson, *Approaches to the History of the Western Family, 1500–1914* (Cambridge: Cambridge University Press, 1980; rev. ed., 1995); Tamara K. Hareven, "The History of the Family and the Complexity of Social Change," *American Historical Review* 96, no. 1 (February 1991): 95–124. This neglect of the family may be partly because of a lack of sources; the fertility, mortality, and marriage records so central to Western reconstructions are not readily available in the Indian context. However, more recent scholarship utilizing sources that until now were relegated exclusively to "literary" rather than "historical" realms suggests possibilities for further study. See Ramya Sreenivasan, "Honoring the Family: Narratives and Politics of Kinship in Pre-colonial Rajasthan," in Chatterjee, *Unfamiliar Relations*, 46–72.

19. An important exception here is Veena Oldenburg's *Dowry Murder: The Imperial Origins of a Cultural Crime* (New York: Oxford University Press, 2002).

20. For example, T. N. Madan, "The Hindu Family and Development," in *Family, Kinship and Marriage in India*, ed. Patricia Uberoi, 416–434 (Delhi: Oxford University Press, 1993); and Shah, *The Family in India*. Another important area of sociological and anthropo-

logical research on the family is the study of kinship; see Louis Dumont, *Affinity as a Value: Marriage Alliance in South India, with Comparative Essays on Australia* (Chicago: University of Chicago Press, 1993); Leela Dube, *Women and Kinship: Comparative Perspectives in South and South-East Asia* (Tokyo, New York, and Paris: United Nations University Press, 1997).

21. Uberoi, "Introduction," in idem, *Family, Kinship and Marriage in India,* 33.

22. For the Tamil region, for instance, David Rudner's study of the Nagarattar merchant caste has pointed to the numerous intersections between the construction of families, the production of caste organization and identity, and the development of the colonial political economy (Rudner, *Caste and Capitalism*).

23. Partha Chatterjee, *The Nation and Its Fragments: Colonial and Postcolonial Histories* (Princeton, N.J.: Princeton University Press, 1993), 6. See also idem, *Nationalist Thought and the Colonial World: A Derivative Discourse* (Minneapolis: University of Minnesota Press, 1986); and idem, "The Nationalist Resolution of the Women's Question," in Sangari and Vaid, *Recasting Women,* 233–253.

24. Tanika Sarkar, *Hindu Wife, Hindu Nation: Community, Religion, and Cultural Nationalism* (Bloomington: Indiana University Press, 2001), 38, 39.

25. Indrani Chatterjee makes a similar argument in "Introduction," 4.

26. Sumit Guha, "The Family Feud as a Political Resource in Eighteenth-century India," in Chaterjee, *Unfamiliar Relations,* 90–91.

27. For example, G. Arunima, *There Comes Papa: Colonialism and the Transformation of Matriliny in Kerala, Malabar c. 1850–1940* (Delhi: Orient Longman, 2003); Malavika Kasturi, *Embattled Identities: Rajput Lineages and the Colonial State in Nineteenth-Century North India* (New Delhi: Oxford University Press, 2002).

28. Coontz, *The Social Origins of Private Life,* 15.

29. Jan Lewis, "The Republican Wife: Virtue and Seduction in the Early Republic," *William and Mary Quarterly* (3rd series) 44, no. 4 (October 1987): 707–709; Janaki Nair, *Women and the Law in Colonial India: A Social History* (New Delhi: Kali for Women, 1996), 38–43.

30. For example, Leonore Davidoff and Catherine Hall, *Family Fortunes: Men and Women of the English Middle Class, 1780–1850* (Chicago: University of Chicago Press, 1991); Mary Ryan, *Cradle of the Middle Class: The Family in Oneida County New York, 1790–1865* (Cambridge: Cambridge University Press, 1983; reprint).

31. Laura Engelstein, *The Keys to Happiness: Sex and the Search for Modernity in Fin-de-Siècle Russia* (Ithaca, N.Y.: Cornell University Press, 1992), 7.

32. Davidoff and Hall, *Family Fortunes,* esp. 180–192, 357–396.

33. Sarkar, *Hindu Wife, Hindu Nation,* 23–52.

34. John Comaroff and Jean Comaroff, "Home-Made Hegemony: Modernity, Domesticity, and Colonialism in South Africa," in *African Encounters with Domesticity,* ed. Karen Tranberg Hansen (New Brunswick, N.J.: Rutgers University Press, 1992), 67.

35. Ann Laura Stoler and Frederick Cooper, "Between Metropole and Colony: Rethinking a Research Agenda," in *Tensions of Empire: Colonial Cultures in a Bourgeois World,* ed. Ann Stoler and Frederick Cooper (Berkeley: University of California Press, 1997), 37 n. 1.

36. Davidoff and Hall, *Family Fortunes;* Ryan, *Cradle of the Middle Class.*

37. Dipesh Chakrabarty, "The Difference-Deferral of a Colonial Modernity: Public Debates on Domesticity in British Bengal," in Stoler and Cooper, *Tensions of Empire,* 373–405; Dipesh Chakrabarty, *Provincializing Europe: Postcolonial Thought and Difference* (Princeton, N.J.: Princeton University Press, 2004); Ann Laura Stoler, *Carnal Knowledge and Imperial Power: Race and the Intimate in Colonial Rule* (Berkeley: University of California Press, 2002); Karen Tranberg Hansen, ed., *African Encounters with Domesticity* (New Brunswick, N.J.: Rutgers University Press, 1992).

38. Indeed, this notion has been thoroughly discredited by various empirical studies. For a discussion of the Indian scholarship, see T. N. Madan, "The Hindu Family and Development," in Uberoi, *Family, Kinship, and Marriage in India*, 416–434.

39. Stephanie Coontz offers an example of the complexity of these connections in her arguments about American families in the revolutionary period, suggesting that "we can examine how the social relations of an emerging market economy interacted with the ideology of the American Revolution, and the demography of the middle class to produce the private family with the woman at its domestic center, without concluding that the private family with the woman at its domestic center is an inevitable component of any industrialization process" (*The Social Origins of Private Life*, 17). Similarly, the point here is not to assert that particular normative relations within families necessarily had to be so within the context of colonial capitalism; rather, I consider the conjunction—and mutual reinforcement—of particular claims about the family with arguments about political economy.

40. Katherine A. Lynch, "The Family and the History of Public Life," *Journal of Interdisciplinary History* 24, no. 4 (Spring 1994): 671. Lynn Hunt's work on the French Revolution powerfully documents these intersections of "private" life and the language of "public" politics, as in *The Family Romance of the French Revolution* (Berkeley: University of California Press, 1992).

41. Lynne Haney and Lisa Pollard, "In a Family Way: Theorizing State and Familial Relations," in *Families of a New World: Gender, Politics, and State Development in a Global Context*, ed. Lynne Haney and Lisa Pollard (New York: Routledge, 2003), 5.

42. For example, Nancy F. Cott, *Public Vows: A History of Marriage and the Nation* (Cambridge, Mass.: Harvard University Press, 2000); Joan Landes, *Women and the Public Sphere in the Age of the French Revolution* (Ithaca, N.Y.: Cornell University Press, 1988); Lewis, "The Republican Wife"; Glosser, *Chinese Visions of Family and State;* Sarkar, *Hindu Wife, Hindu Nation;* and Lynn Hunt, *The Family Romance of the French Revolution.*

43. Gayatri Spivak, "The Rani of Sirmur: An Essay in Reading the Archives," *History and Theory: Studies in the Philosophy of History* 24, no. 3 (1985): 247–272.

44. Antoinette Burton, *Dwelling in the Archive: Women Writing House, Home and History in Late Colonial India* (Oxford: Oxford University Press, 2003), 5, 27.

45. Gauri Viswanathan, *Outside the Fold: Conversion, Modernity, and Belief* (Princeton, N.J.: Princeton University Press, 1998), esp. 98–111.

1. Colonizing the Family

1. Nicholas Dirks, "From Little King to Landlord: Colonial Discourse and Colonial Rule," in *Colonialism and Culture*, ed. Nicholas Dirks (Ann Arbor: University of Michigan Press, 1992).

2. Bernard Cohn, "Recruitment of Elites in India under British Rule," in *Essays in Comparative Social Stratification*, ed. Leonard Plotnicov and Arthur Tuden (Pittsburgh: University of Pittsburgh Press, 1970), 132. Madras Presidency was known for the ryotwari system of land tenure which originated there; however, in practice, its patterns of land control and distribution were not very different from those in other parts of colonial India, including primarily zamindari areas such as Bengal. For instance, during the latter half of the nineteenth century, approximately 30–40 percent of land in districts across British India (excepting Awadh and Punjab) was held by a small number of large landholders; the rest was held by a larger number of small landholders. The Madras evidence is consistent with that pattern (Cohn, "Recruitment of Elites," 131). Moreover, as Burton Stein notes, the development of the Madras ryotwari system under Thomas Munro was directed against various forms of communal landholding, and was not necessarily more egalitarian in its land distribution than the zamindari system (Burton Stein, *Thomas Munro: The Origins of*

the Colonial State and His Vision of Empire [Delhi: Oxford University Press, 1989], 58–133). In other words, the differences between zamindari and ryotwari systems were not as stark as contemporary commentators suggested.

3. Pamela Price, *Kingship and Political Practice in Colonial India* (Cambridge: Cambridge University Press, 1996), 6.

4. Ibid., 58–70.

5. Nicholas Dirks, *The Hollow Crown: Ethnohistory of an Indian Kingdom* (Cambridge: Cambridge University Press, 1987).

6. Indrani Chatterjee, "Introduction," in *Unfamiliar Relations: Family and History in South Asia*, ed. Indrani Chatterjee (New Brunswick, N.J.: Rutgers University Press, 2004), 9–17.

7. David Gaunt, "Kinship: Thin Red Lines or Thick Blue Blood," in *Family Life in Early Modern Times, 1500–1789*, The History of the European Family series, vol. 1, ed. David I. Kertzer and Marzio Barbagli (New Haven, Conn.: Yale University Press, 2001). On the development of "medieval era" practices under the Mughals, consider Ruby Lal's analysis of the fluidity and inter-penetration of household and polity: *Domesticity and Power in the Early Mughal World* (Cambridge: Cambridge University Press, 2005).

8. Indrani Chatterjee, *Gender, Slavery and Law in Colonial India* (New Delhi: Oxford University Press, 1999), 34–124.

9. Ibid., 36–44.

10. Pamela Price, "Honor, Disgrace and the Formal Depoliticization of Women in South India: Changing Structures of the State under British Colonial Rule," *Gender & History* 6, no. 2 (August 1994): 246–264; idem, "Kin, Clan, and Power in Colonial South India," in Chatterjee, *Unfamiliar Relations*, 192–221; Ramya Sreenivasan, "Honoring the Family: Narratives and Politics of Kinship in Pre-Colonial Rajasthan," in Chatterjee, *Unfamiliar Relations*, 46–72.

11. David Ludden, "Patriarchy and History in South Asia: Interpretive Experiments," *Calcutta Historical Journal* 17, no. 2 (1995): 5–7.

12. André Wink, *Land and Sovereignty in India: Agrarian Society and Politics under the 18th Century Maratha Svarajya* (Cambridge: Cambridge University Press, 1986), 27–28.

13. Sumit Guha, "The Family Feud as Political Resource in Eighteenth-Century India," in Chatterjee, *Unfamiliar Relations*, 78, 83.

14. Chatterjee, "Introduction," 21.

15. Price, "Kin, Clan and Power," 211–214.

16. Burton Stein, *Peasant State and Society in Medieval South India* (Delhi: Oxford University Press, 1994), 22, 23, 24, 434. Stein adopted his model from Aidan Southall's study, *Alur Society* (Cambridge: W. Heffer, 1956).

17. Price, *Kingship and Political Practice*, 29; idem, "Honor, Disgrace," 248.

18. See, for example, David Ludden; *Peasant History in South India* (Princeton, N.J.: Princeton University Press, 1985); Sanjay Subrahmanyam, *Penumbral Visions: Making Polities in Early Modern South India* (Ann Arbor: University of Michigan Press, 2001); Stein, *Peasant State;* Sanjay Subrahmanyam and David Shulman, "The Men Who Would Be King? The Politics of Expansion in Early 17th Century Northern Tamilnadu," *Modern Asian Studies* 24, no. 2 (1990): 225–248.

19. Subrahmanyam and Shulman, "The Men Who Would Be King?" 228, 246–247.

20. For example, see Michael H. Fisher, "Becoming and Making 'Family' in Hindustan," in Chaterjee, *Unfamiliar Relations;* William Dalrymple, "White Mughals: The Case of James Achilles Kirkpatrick and Khair un-Nissa," in Chatterjee, *Unfamiliar Relations;* and Durba Ghosh, *Sex and the Family in Colonial India: The Making of Empire* (Cambridge: Cambridge University Press, 2006).

21. Ludden, "Patriarchy and History," 10.

22. Burton Stein, "Introduction," in *The Making of Agrarian Policy in British India, 1770–1900,* ed. Burton Stein (Delhi: Oxford University Press, 1992), 10–12.

23. Price, "Honor, Disgrace," 260.

24. Price, *Kingship and Political Practice,* 189. However, the colonial state was not entirely successful in dissolving indigenous "segments" of ruling authority to secure a monopoly for itself. Alternative sources of political authority remained outside the boundaries of colonial control; so-called criminal castes and tribes are one such example. See David Ludden, "Anglo-Indian Empire," in Stein, *The Making of Agrarian Policy in British India,* 183–184.

25. Ludden, "Anglo-Indian Empire," 158.

26. Ludden, "Patriarchy and History," 10.

27. For a discussion of caste, see Nicholas Dirks, "Castes of Mind," *Representations,* no. 37 (Special Issue: *Imperial Fantasies and Postcolonial Histories*) (Winter 1992): 56–78.

28. Price, "Kin, Clan, and Power," 213.

29. Bernard Cohn, "The Census, Social Structure and Objectification in South Asia," *An Anthropologist among the Historians and Other Essays* (Delhi: Oxford University Press, 1987), 237.

30. G. Arunima, *There Comes Papa: Colonialism and the Transformation of Matriliny in Kerala, Malabar c. 1850–1940* (New Delhi: Orient Longman, 2003), 42–43, 70.

31. D. A. Washbrook, "Law, State, and Agrarian Society in Colonial India," *Modern Asian Studies* 15, no. 3 (1981): 649–721.

32. Stein, "Introduction," 17.

33. Ibid., 20.

34. C. A. Bayly, *Indian Society and the Making of the British Empire* (Cambridge: Cambridge University Press, 1988), 152.

35. Arunima, *There Comes Papa,* 106–127.

36. Veena Talwar Oldenburg, *Dowry Murder: The Imperial Origins of a Cultural Crime* (Oxford: Oxford University Press, 2002), 99–174.

37. Similarly, the power of landowning classes also did not commence with colonial rule. In particular, landlords of various kinds were also empowered within the commercializing economy of the eighteenth century, but their status and power was taken to new levels by the colonial state (Stein, "Introduction," 23).

38. Eliza F. Kent, *Converting Women: Gender and Protestant Christianity in Colonial South India* (New York: Oxford University Press, 2004), 140–150.

39. Ibid., 128–140; quote at 140.

40. For a discussion of colonial intervention in the families of laborers and prisoners, see Samita Sen, "Offences against Marriage: Negotiating Custom in Colonial Bengal," in *A Question of Silence? The Sexual Economies of Modern India,* ed. Mary E. John and Janaki Nair, 261–291 (New Delhi: Kali for Women, 1998); and Satadru Sen, "Domesticated Convicts: Producing Families in the Andaman Islands," in Chatterjee, *Unfamiliar Relations,* 261–291.

41. Price, *Kingship,* 40–44. To fund litigation, many zamindars turned to Nattukottai Chettiar, or Nagarattar, creditors (ibid., 96–105). Despite this financial involvement, the colonial state—in the name of preserving the "native aristocracy"—attempted to prevent merchant families from gaining control over the land but was not always successful (Dirks, "From Little King to Landlord," 199). An emergent class of lawyers, largely Tamil Brahmans, were the chief financial beneficiaries of zamindari litigation (Pamela Price, "Ideology and Ethnicity under British Imperial Rule: 'Brahmans,' Lawyers and Kin-Caste Rules in Madras Presidency," *Modern Asian Studies* 23, no 1 [1989]: 162–167).

42. For further discussion of the testimony-gathering process, see Price, "Kin, Clan and Power," 198–199.

43. Pamela Price's research on zamindari legal disputes in Madras Presidency pro-

vides several examples of these gendered conflicts: see her "Honor, Disgrace" and "Kin, Clan, and Power."

44. The case is *Sundaralingasawmi Kamaya Naik v. Ramasawmi Kamaya Naik* (P.C. No. 40 of 1897). All subsequent references to "Saptur litigation" refer to this case. The estate was composed of seventeen villages and, according to the 1891 census, had a population exceeding sixteen thousand (Saptur litigation, Supplemental Record of Proceedings, document no. 1, exhibit S, pp. 3–8) in a total area of 123 square miles (W. Francis, *Madura,* vol. 1, *Madras District Gazetteers* [Madras: Government Press, 1914], 329).

45. Saptur litigation, Supplemental Record of Proceedings, document no. 1, exhibit S., pp. 1, 2–3.

46. In her testimony, Nagammal noted that she borrowed Rs. 70,000 from one "Arunachalam Chetti," to whom she would pay Rs. 300,000 if awarded the estate (Saptur litigation, Supplemental Record of Proceedings, document no. 120, pp. 154–155). Nagammal did not specify her exact relationship with the zamindar of Paraiyur, which, like Saptur, was located in the Tirumangalam taluk (subdivision) of Madurai district. It included thirty villages and an area of 21 square miles. Like the Saptur family, the zamindari household in Paraiyur was classified as belonging to the "Tottiyan" caste (Francis, *Madura,* 328). These caste connections likely rendered Nagammal's claims to status in Saptur more believable in the eyes of the law.

47. Saptur litigation, Supplemental Record of Proceedings, document no. 120, p. 240.

48. Ibid., document no. 26, p. 51.

49. Ibid., document no. 98, p. 153.

50. Saptur litigation, Record of Proceedings, document no. 175, judgment of the Madura District Court in original suit no. 21 of 1889 (delivered on 19 December 1890).

51. Saptur litigation, Judgment of the Lords of the Judicial Committee of the Privy Council in P.C. no. 40 of 1897.

52. Edgar Thurston and K. Rangachari, *The Castes and Tribes of Southern India,* vol. 7 (New Delhi: Asian Educational Services, 1987 [1909]), 190–191. The entry under "Tottiyan" references the Saptur case to note that the presence of a dagger indicates "inequality in the caste or social position of the bride" but would not invalidate the marriage (191).

53. The estate was left unsettled by the colonial administration after the initial zamindari assessments of 1803–1805 (Francis, *Madura,* 313–314).

54. The case is *Kamulammal v. T. B. K. Visvanathaswami Naicker* (P.C. No. 45 of 1919). Subsequent references to "Bodinayakanur litigation" refer to this case.

55. Bodinayakanur litigation, Supplemental Record of Proceedings, document no. 163, quotes at 435, 435, 436.

56. Ibid., quotes at 436, 440, 443.

57. Ibid., document no. 188, quotes at 504, 504, 505, 506.

58. Ibid., quotes at 518, 522, 512, 514.

59. Bodinayakanur litigation, Record of Proceedings, document no. 193 (District Court of Madura [West], O.S. no. 31 of 1902), pp. 554, 592.

60. Ibid., document no. 217 (High Court of Judicature at Madras, Appeal no. 118 of 1906), p. 759.

61. Ibid, p. 759.

62. Price, *Kingship,* 15. On the redistributive responsibilities of a *dharmic* ruler in relation to the constraints of colonial rule, see 190–191.

63. Located in the Tenkasi taluk and headquartered in Verakeralampudur, Uttumalai was the third largest zamindari in Tirunelveli district. The estate comprised 63 villages, including both irrigated and dry lands over an area of 126 square miles. Its population was estimated at 51,246 (H. R. Pate, *Tinnevelly,* vol. 1, *Madras District Gazetteers* [Madras: Government Press, 1917], 467–471). See also Dirks, "From Little King to Landlord," 187–188.

64. The village of Kurukalpatti was in the Tenkasi *taluk* (subdivision) of Tirunelveli district, and was not the headquarters of a zamindari estate. The village of Chokkampatti, also in Tenkasi *taluk,* had once been the headquarters of a zamindari estate of the same name, but by the time of the lawsuit, it had been broken up into twelve subdivisions, or *mittahs,* which had passed out of the ownership of the original zamindari title-holders (Pate, *Tinnevelly,* 92, 274–275, 454). The village of Chokkampatti was one such *mittah.* Presumably, the Uttumalai zamindar's uncle in Chokkampatti was the holder of a title to this *mittah,* but his exact status is not apparent from witness testimonials, which sometimes refer to him as the "Zamindar of Chokkampatti."

65. *Annapurni Nachiar v. Menakshi Sundra Nachiar and G. S. Forbes* (P.C. No. 54 of 1899). Forbes was the collector of Tinnevelly and agent of the Court of Wards. Subsequent references to "Uttumalai litigation" are to this case.

66. Uttumalai litigation, Record of Proceedings, document no. 523, p. 434. According to the Head Assistant Magistrate of Tirunelveli's records, Annapurni's forceful entry into the palace was secured by a party of about five hundred people who accompanied her. See Uttumalai litigation, Record of Proceedings, document no. 426, p. 294 (Proceedings of the Head Assistant Magistrate of Tirunelveli, 24-6-1889 in Criminal Miscellaneous case no. 5 of 1889).

67. Uttumalai litigation, Record of Proceedings, document no. 3, p. 9.

68. Ibid., document no. 523, pp. 431–445, quotes at pp. 433, 436.

69. Ibid., document no. 523, pp. 433–441, quotes at pp. 443, 440.

70. Ibid., document no. 604 (District Court of Tinnevelly, O.S. no. 15 of 1892), p. 605.

71. Price, "Honor, Disgrace," 251–252.

72. As Indrani Chatterjee notes, similar principles underlay the colonial legal system across the subcontinent. The laws governing both Hindus and Muslims privileged the marriage rituals of parents to determine the rights of children and sought to insert all women into caste-ranked systems of marriage (*Gender, Slavery and Law,* 93–98, 225–226).

73. Price, *Kingship,* 73–76.

74. Ibid., 35–36.

75. Antoinette Burton examines the *zenana* as a "pathologized" space in *Dwelling in the Archive: Women Writing House, Home and History in Late Colonial India* (Oxford: Oxford University Press, 2003), 8.

76. Kent, *Converting Women,* 138–140.

77. This rejection was not entirely complete. As Pamela Price argues in her study of "honor" in twentieth-century Dravidian movements, some elements of a precolonial "monarchical cosmology" were rearticulated in modern Tamil politics (*Kingship,* 189, 198–199).

78. Burton, *Dwelling in the Archive,* 11.

2. Conjugality and Capital

1. Tyagaraja Iyer did concede that daughters should be allowed some limited property rights, and suggested that they receive one-third of a son's share. Whether this would be bestowed in the form of jewelry and moveable property or in land would be at the discretion of their fathers and brothers. After a woman married, Tyagaraja Iyer added, she would acquire "legal rights upon her husband and his family for her maintenance" and thus did not require equal ownership rights with her brothers (Government of Madras Order No. 174 [Law (General)], 19 January 1935).

2. D. A. Washbrook, "Law, State, and Agrarian Society in Colonial India," *Modern Asian Studies* 15, no. 3 (1981): 653–656, 711–712.

3. Janaki Nair, *Women and the Law in Colonial India: A Social History* (New Delhi: Kali for Women, 1996), 147.

4. See, for example, Ratna Kapur, *Feminist Terrains in Legal Domains: Interdisciplinary Essays on Women and Law in India* (New Delhi: Kali for Women, 1996); and Nair, *Women and Law in Colonial India.*

5. For example, see Kumkum Chatterjee, *Merchants, Politics, and Society in Early Modern India: Bihar 1733–1820* (Leiden: E. J. Brill, 1996); Burton Stein, "Eighteenth Century India: Another View," *Studies in History* 5, no. 1 (1989): 1–26; Lakshmi Subramaniam, *Indigenous Capital and Imperial Expansion: Bombay, Surat, and the West Coast* (Delhi: Oxford University Press, 1996); D. A. Washbrook, "Progress and Problems: South Asian Economic and Social History, c. 1720–1860," *Modern Asian Studies* 22, no. 1 (1988): 57–96. Of course, mercantile activity and property rights have a history that precedes the eighteenth century. See, for example, Sanjay Subrahmanyam, *The Political Economy of Commerce: Southern India, 1500–2002* (Cambridge: Cambridge University Press, 2002).

6. Washbrook, "Progress and Problems," 70, 80–81.

7. For example, Yuko Nishimura, *Gender, Kinship, and Property Rights: Nagarattar Womanhood in South India* (Delhi: Oxford University Press, 1998); David Rudner, *Caste and Capitalism in Colonial India: The Nattukottai Chettiars* (Berkeley: University of California Press, 1994).

8. R. Suntharalingam, *Politics and Nationalist Awakening in South India, 1852–1891* (Tucson: University of Arizona Press, 1974), 24–57, 104–150.

9. Pamela Price, "Ideology and Ethnicity under British Imperial Rule: 'Brahmans,' Lawyers, and Kin-Caste Rules in Madras Presidency," *Modern Asian Studies* 23, no. 1 (1989): 151–177. In the case of lawyers, much of this income derived from zamindari litigation, leading some contemporaries to argue that the work of lawyers was leading to the demise of the zamindari classes.

10. See, for example, C. J. Baker, *The Politics of South India, 1920–1937* (Cambridge: Cambridge University Press, 1976), 85–168; Rudner, *Caste and Capitalism,* 5, 64–67.

11. Washbrook, "Law, State, and Agrarian Society," 649–721; Bina Agarwal, *A Field of One's Own: Gender and Land Rights in South Asia* (Cambridge: Cambridge University Press, 1994), 158–180.

12. Bernard S. Cohn, *Colonialism and Its Forms of Knowledge: The British in India* (Princeton, N.J.: Princeton University Press, 1996), 57–75; Duncan M. Derrett, *Religion, Law, and the State in India* (New York: Free Press, 1968), 274–320.

13. Agarwal, *A Field of One's Own,* 200–201.

14. Nair, *Women and Colonial Law,* 37.

15. Lucy Carroll, "Daughter's Right of Inheritance in India: A Perspective on the Problem of Dowry," *Modern Asian Studies* 25, no. 4 (1991): 793.

16. Property falling under the zamindari settlement was a notable exception to this system. Concerned with the fragmentation of estates among the "native aristocracy," the colonial laws maintained that zamindari landholdings were impartible (i.e., they could not be partitioned) and would descend to a single owner.

17. Under colonial law in Madras, this was the case whether the property in question was moveable or immoveable. Vijnaneshwara himself appears to distinguish between the two, suggesting that the father's power to dispose of immoveable property is restricted by the rights of the sons, whereas the disposal of moveable property is fully under the father's control. In this view, fathers would have greater rights to give moveable property to daughters. Later south Indian commentators on the Mitakshara, however, elided this distinction (John D. Mayne, *Mayne's Treatise on Hindu Law and Usage,* 13th rev. ed. [New Delhi: Bharat Law House, 1993], 543–544). Within the colonial legislation and case law discussed here, no distinctions of ownership were made based on whether property was moveable or immoveable. In actual practice, however, women likely had greater access to moveable property, whether as part of a dowry or as gifts after marriage (for example, see S. J. Tambiah and

Jack Goody, *Bridewealth and Dowry*, Cambridge Papers in Social Anthropology 7 [Cambridge: Cambridge University Press]). Inheriting or controlling immoveable property—notably land—has proven to be considerably more difficult for women.

18. Mayne, *Mayne's Treatise*, 898. The precedent-setting case for the limitations of a woman's estate was *Kasinath Bysack v. Hurrosundery Dossee* (4 *Indian Law Reports* 979 [1826]).

19. Mayne, *Mayne's Treatise*, 878–887.

20. The ongoing operation of caste and village councils, or *panchayats*, alongside the colonial law produced a system of legal pluralism that Erin Moore defines as "multiple legal orders operating within the same social field" (*Gender, Law and Resistance in India* [Tucson: University of Arizona Press, 1998], 86).

21. Agarwal, *A Field of One's Own*, 249–291; Srimati Basu, "The Personal and the Political: Indian Women and Inheritance Law, in *Religion and Personal Law in Secular India: A Call to Judgment*, ed. Gerald James Larson (Bloomington: Indiana University Press, 2001).

22. Agarwal, *A Field of One's Own*, 82–193; G. Arunima, *There Comes Papa: Colonialism and the Transformation of Matriliny in Kerala, Malabar c. 1850–1940* (New Delhi: Orient Longman, 2003). I borrow the term "masculinization" of the economy from Veena Oldenburg, *Dowry Murder: The Imperial Origins of a Cultural Crime* (New York: Oxford University Press, 2002), 133–134.

23. Given this context, perhaps it is not surprising that during at least some periods of medieval and early modern history some women in southern India had greater rights to control property than would be subsequently granted to them under colonial law (Kanakalatha Mukund, "Turmeric Land: Women's Property Rights in South India: A Review," *Economic and Political Weekly* 27, no. 17 (1992): WS2–WS6; idem, "Women's Property Rights in South India: A Review," *Economic and Political Weekly* 34, no. 22: 1352–1358; Leslie Orr, *Donors, Devotees, and Daughters of God: Temple Women in Medieval Tamilnadu* (New York: Oxford University Press, 2000).

24. Their turn to the colonial legal system in this period roughly coincides with a trend toward increasing litigation overall beginning in the latter half of the nineteenth century and continuing into the twentieth (Washbrook, "Law, State, and Agrarian Society," 670); Government of Madras, *Annual Reports on the Administration of Madras Presidency, 1922–1947* (Madras: Government Press). This increase may suggest that the law had a growing impact on property relations, at least among the relatively elite classes whose disputes entered the civil courts.

25. Bhashyam Iyengar, "The Law of Hindu Gains of Learning," *Madras Law Journal* 10 (1900): 6.

26. Price, "Ideology and Ethnicity," 163–164; Suntharalingam, *Politics and Nationalist Awakening*, 197–198.

27. *Swadesamitran*, 6 March 1891, translated from the Tamil and reprinted in *Madras Native Newspaper Reports* (1891).

28. Government of Madras Order No. 2708 (Home [Judicial]) 17 November 1916.

29. Ibid. Subbarayulu Reddi held numerous posts in local government in the South Arcot district of Madras Presidency (D. A. Washbrook, *The Emergence of Provincial Politics: The Madras Presidency, 1870–1920* [Cambridge: Cambridge University Press, 1976], 57).

30. Government of Madras Order No. 2708 (Home [Judicial]), 17 November 1916.

31. The Southern India Chamber of Commerce was founded in 1919 by a prominent member of the Nagarattar caste and held a reserved seat in the Madras Legislative Council to represent business interests (Rudner, *Caste and Capitalism*, 155). Among the members of the Madras Landowners' Association who opposed the bill was the Maharaja of Bobbili, one of the leading zamindars in the Tamil region. See Government of Madras Order No. 2708 (Home [Judicial]), 17 November 1916. Of course, since the bulk of zamindari estates

were deemed impartible, the Hindu Coparceners' Partition Bill would have had limited effect on zamindars; only lands that were owned by zamindars but were not part of the zamindari estate itself would be subjected to partition. Nevertheless, perhaps as a testament to the strong sentiment against any partition of land among these groups, zamindars joined other landholders to criticize the proposed bill.

32. Government of Madras Order No. 2708 (Home [Judicial]), 17 November 1916.

33. Ibid., statements of V. Appanna Sastry, M. Venkataraghavalu Reddi, and T. E. Ramanuja Achariyar.

34. Ibid., statements of M. Verghese, C. S. Nataraja Iyer, C. Rajagopala Achariyar, and C. P. Ramaswamy Ayyar. The latter was a prominent lawyer in Madras and became the Home Minister in 1921.

35. Ibid., statement of C. P. Ramaswamy Ayyar.

36. Ibid., statement of C. Rajagopalachari.

37. The Madras Mahajana Sabha was established in 1884 with a membership composed of merchants and professionals (largely lawyers, doctors, and journalists). It explicitly excluded "official" members, that is, those employed by the state (Suntharalingam, *Politics and Nationalist Awakening*, 208–230).

38. Government of Madras Order Nos. 1359–60 (Home [Judicial]), 28 June 1917.

39. Government of Madras Letter No. 750 (Home [Judicial]), 4 April 1917.

40. Baker, *The Politics of South India*, 255–264.

41. For a discussion of changes in state support for individual property rights, see Washbrook, "Law, State and Agrarian Society," 711–712.

42. For example, see Geraldine Forbes, *Women in Modern India*, pt. 4, vol. 2 of *The Cambridge History of India* (Cambridge: Cambridge University Press, 1998), 112–119.

43. Other attempts included the Hindu Widows' Rights of Inheritance Bill (1930), which gave a widow an absolute right of inheritance over her husband's share of joint property; the Hindu Widows' Rights of Maintenance Bill (1933), which fixed a widow's rate of maintenance; and the Hindu Women's Inheritance Bill (1935), which allowed women to inherit property from their natal families.

44. *Indian Legislative Assembly Debates* 6, no. 1, 5 (September 1933), reprinted in Government of Madras Order No. 3847 (Law [General]), 28 November 1933.

45. Government of Madras Order No. 174 (Law [General]), 19 January 1935. The association making this claim was the Stri Bharat Dharma Mandal, whose membership was composed of women. But unlike organizations like the WIA and AIWC, which remained in existence for many years, had widespread memberships, and published journals and pamphlets about their position, conservative women's groups like the Stri Bharat Dharma Mandal were narrowly focused on one legal reform or another.

46. Ibid., statement of P. C. Tyagaraja Iyer.

47. Government of Madras Order No. 2180 (Law [General]), 19 May 1930, statement of the Collector of Tirunelveli (Tinnevelly).

48. Harbilas Sarda, *Speeches and Writings* (Ajmer: Vedic Yantralaya, 1935), 90, 76.

49. Government of Madras Order No. 2180 (Law [General]), 19 May 1930, statement of P. Kunku Panikkar.

50. Editorial, "Women's Status in the New Constitution," *Stri Dharma* 14, no. 6 (1931): 230.

51. Umeshwari Nehru, "The Hindu Law of Inheritance," *Stri Dharma* 15, no. 2 (1931): 71.

52. Nehru, "The Hindu Law of Inheritance," 74.

53. Although scholars have emphasized the importance of the case law in analyzing legal discourses and institutions (see Marc Galanter, *Law and Society in Modern India* [Delhi: Oxford University Press, 1989], 5; and Nair, *Women and Law in Colonial India*, 17),

much historical scholarship on the laws regarding women remains focused on legislative and political debates. For example, see Archana Parashar, *Women and Family Law Reform in India* (New Delhi: Sage, 1989); Tanika Sarkar, *Hindu Wife, Hindu Nation: Community, Religion, and Cultural Nationalism* (Bloomington: Indiana University Press, 2001), 226–249. Although this research has been immensely valuable for analyzing the workings of gender in relation to colonial and postcolonial discourse, I maintain that attention to the case law is essential for understanding the intersections of the law with social practice.

54. My arguments about judicial interpretation are based on a review of all recorded cases appearing before the Madras High Court from 1937 to 1965 concerning the Hindu Women's Rights to Property Act. After 1965, the numbers of such cases declined, as, by then, most widows were subject to the revised Hindu Code laws that were passed in the 1950s.

55. The depositions and testimonies I used in analyzing the zamindari cases were unavailable to me in the cases concerning the Hindu Women's Rights to Property Act. Instead, I focus on judicial decisions coming from the Madras High Court.

56. *Rathinasabapathy Pillai and another v. Saraswati Ammal,* 41 *All India Reporter* (*AIR*) Madras 307 (1954).

57. Ibid., 309.

58. The exception was *Manorama Bai v. Rama Bai,* 44 *AIR* Madras 269 (1957). For additional cases following the dominant trend of legal interpretation, see *Umayal Achi v. Lakshmi Achi and others,* 86 *Madras Law Journal* (*MLJ*) 70 (1944); *Dhanam alias Dhanalakshmi Ammal and another v. Varadarajan,* 103 *MLJ* 176 (1952); *Subramanian v. Kalyanarama Iyer* and others 103 *MLJ* 575 (1952); *Ramalingam Pillay and another v. Ramalakshmi Ammal and ten others, Indian Law Reports* (*ILR*), Madras Series 7 (1958) *Alamelu Ammal v. Chellammal,* 116 *MLJ* 269 (1959); *Lakshmi Ammal and others v. Ramachandra Reddiar,* 47 *AIR* Madras 568 (1960).

59. *Movva Subba Rao v. Movva Krishna Prasadam, ILR,* Madras Series 257 (1954).

60. Ibid., 264, 262, 265.

61. *Manicka Gounder v. Arunachala Gounder, AIR,* Madras Series 1016 (1961).

62. Ibid., 1020, 1021.

63. *Ramaiya Konar v. Mottaya Mudaliar,* 101 *ILR,* Madras Series 314 (1951).

64. Ibid., 325.

65. Mayne, *Mayne's Treatise,* 722.

66. *Ramaiya Konar v. Mottaya Mudaliar,* 101 *ILR,* Madras Series 314 (1951), 322–323.

67. Ibid., 322. Because chastity was not mentioned explicitly in the 1937 act, there was some judicial dispute about the proper interpretation of the law. The Bombay High Court had decided in 1941 that the Hindu Women's Rights to Property Act eliminated previous requirements of chastity (*Akoba Laxman v. Sai Genu, ILR* Bombay Series 438 [1941]). The question of chastity did not come before the Madras High Court until 1951, in the case discussed here. Although it first appeared before only two judges, "given that there is no decided case throwing light upon the question and as the question is an important one," these judges referred the case to a full bench of the Madras High Court. The Madras court's decision in *Ramaiya Konar v. Mottayya Mudaliar* disagreed with the Bombay court's decision in 1941, establishing chastity as a necessary requirement under the 1937 act. However, the terms of inheritance would soon change with the passage of the Hindu Succession Act in 1952.

68. Women were excluded because the subject of agricultural land was reserved for legislation by provincial governments; the Hindu Women's Rights to Property Act, however, was passed by the central legislature and so did not apply to agricultural land. A number of provincial governments sought to correct this inconsistency, and the Madras government amended the law in 1948 to include all property (see Government of Madras Order No. 174 [Home (General)], 16 January 1948). Perhaps reflecting the strong resistance

to women's ownership, however, the amendment was not retroactive. A widow's rights were based on the date of her husband's death, as in the case of Nallammal, who did not succeed to agricultural land because the amendment only applied to the property of a Hindu dying intestate after 26 November 1946, and her husband Krishnaswami Naicker had died in 1942 (see *Subba Naicker v. Nallammal and others, MLJ* 536 [1949]). The exclusion of agricultural land also sparked litigation concerning the rights to agricultural profits and the very definition of "agricultural land." Given that much inherited property in India was agricultural land, this exclusion had a massive impact on women's rights. For further discussion of agricultural land, see *Parappagari Parappa and another v. Parappagari Nagamma and two others, ILR* Madras Series 183 (1954).

69. This was not entirely unknown, however, as evidenced in *Ramalingam Pillay v. Ramalakshmi Ammal, ILR* Madras Series 7 (1958).

70. Washbrook, "Law, State, and Agrarian Society," 711–712.

3. Nationalizing Marriage

1. Mrinalini Sinha, "The Lineage of the 'Indian' Modern: Rhetoric, Agency, and the Sarda Act in Late Colonial India," in *Gender, Sexuality, and Colonial Modernities,* ed. Antoinette Burton (London: Routledge, 1999), 207.

2. Frederick Cooper, *Colonialism in Question: Theory, Knowledges, History* (Berkeley: University of California Press, 2005), 147.

3. Partha Chatterjee, "The Nationalist Resolution of the Women's Question," in *Recasting Women; Essays in Indian Colonial History,* ed. Kumkum Sangari and Sudesh Vaid (New Brunswick, N.J.: Rutgers University Press, 1990), 237–240.

4. Judith Walsh demonstrates the transnational character of this domestic discourse by comparing Indian developments with domesticity in England and the United States (*Domesticity in Colonial India: What Women Learned When Men Gave Them Advice* [Lanham, Md.: Rowan and Littlefield, 2004]). For a discussion of the importance of domestic ideals to middle-class identity, see Leonore Davidoff and Catherine Hall, *Family Fortunes: Men and Women of the English Middle Class, 1780–1850* (Chicago: University of Chicago Press, 1987); Kristin Mann, *Marrying Well: Marriage, Status, and Social Change among the Educated Elite in Colonial Lagos* (Cambridge: Cambridge University Press, 1985); and Eliza Kent, *Converting Women: Gender and Protestant Christianity in Colonial South India* (New York: Oxford University Press, 2004), 127–163. Tanika Sarkar suggests that domesticity acquired a magnified importance in colonial contexts because of the constraints placed on indigenous capital; as she argues for nineteenth-century Bengal, "since the new economic man did not appear . . . it would be the new domestic woman who had to carry the image of a class" (*Hindu Wife, Hindu Nation: Community, Religion and Cultural Nationalism* [Bloomington: Indiana University Press, 2001], 43–44).

5. Citing Karl Marx, Guha elaborates this point as follows: "Thanks to the historical conditions of its formation, the Indian bourgeoisie could strive towards its hegemonic aim only by constituting 'all the members of society' into a nation and their 'common interest' into the 'ideal form' of nationalism" (*Dominance without Hegemony: History and Power in Colonial India* [Cambridge, Mass.: Harvard University Press, 1997], 101).

6. Meera Kosambi, "Girl Brides and Socio-Legal Change: Age of Consent Bill (1891) Controversy," *Economic and Political Weekly* 36, nos. 31–32 (3–10 August 1991): 1858.

7. For example, Rakhmabai published a series of letters in newspapers in her own defense. One of these is reprinted in Sudhir Chandra, *Enslaved Daughters: Colonialism, Law, and Women's Rights* (Delhi: Oxford University Press, 1998), 213–218.

8. Geraldine Forbes, "Women and Modernity: The Issue of Child Marriage in India," *Women's Studies International Quarterly* 2, no. 4 (1979): 410.

9. Sarkar, *Hindu Wife*, 191.

10. *Mahratta*, 22 March 1891, in *Bombay Native Newspaper Reports*, 1891.

11. Sarkar, *Hindu Wife*, 51.

12. The Indian Legislative Assembly passed a bill raising the Age of Consent from twelve to thirteen in 1925. In 1927, Harbilas Sarda introduced a bill establishing a minimum marriage age which, following much discussion and modification, became the Child Marriage Restraint Act.

13. Katherine Mayo, *Mother India* (London: Jonathan Cape, 1927), 29. According to Mrinalini Sinha, Mayo's "connections with the official British propaganda machine quickly discredited Mayo's credentials as a champion of women's issues in India." See Sinha, "Gender in the Critiques of Colonialism and Nationalism: Locating the 'Indian Woman,'" in *Feminism and History*, ed. Joan Wallach Scott (Oxford: Oxford University Press, 1996), 478.

14. Mayo, *Mother India*, 38.

15. *Muthulakshmi Reddi Papers* (*MRP*), n.d., Subject files 9 and 10.

16. For further discussion of the controversy surrounding Mayo's text, see Mrinalini Sinha, ed., *Mother India: Selections from the Controversial 1927 Text* (Ann Arbor: University of Michigan Press, 2000); and Mrinalini Sinha, *Specters of Mother India: The Global Restructuring of an Empire* (Durham, N.C.: Duke University Press, 2006).

17. Honorary Secretary of the Women's Indian Association and Chairwoman of the AIWC to Rai Sahib Harbilas Sarda, December 1927, AIWC Papers, file no. 5, Nehru Memorial Library.

18. *Madras Legislative Council Debates* (*MLCD*) 42, no. 1 (27 March 1929): 37.

19. *Indian Legislative Assembly Debates* (*ILAD*) 5 (Delhi: Government of India Press, 23 September 1929): 1252.

20. Sinha, *Specters of Mother India*, 161.

21. The Age of Consent Committee was popularly known as the Joshi Committee after its chairman, Sir Moropant Joshi, who had formerly been Home Member for the Central Provinces. Eight other members were Indian. In addition to Nehru, the committee included another woman, a British doctor (Judy Whitehead, "Modernising the Motherhood Archetype: Public Health Models and the Child Marriage Restraint Act of 1929," in *Social Reform, Sexuality and the State*, ed. Patricia Uberoi [New Delhi: Sage, 1996], 201).

22. *ILAD*, 4 (4 September 1929): 263.

23. Age of Consent Committee, *Evidence, 1928–1929*, Vol. 4: *Oral Evidence and Written Statements of Witnesses from the Madras Presidency* (Calcutta: Government of India Central Publication Branch, 1929), statement of T. R. Ramachandra Iyer.

24. Age of Consent Committee, *Evidence*, statement of M. K. Acharya.

25. According to the 1921 Census for example, 39.8 percent of all Indian girls had been married by the age of fifteen. The comparable figure for Madras Presidency was considerably lower, at 22.8 percent; in all of British India (not including the princely states), only the Northwest Frontier Province had a lower rate, at 12.6 percent. The census figures are cited in Age of Consent Committee, *Report*, 306–309. According to S. N. Agarwala, whose census-based study includes the princely states but does not examine the districts that became East and West Pakistan in 1947, the mean age of marriage among Brahman girls in most provinces ranged from eleven to thirteen years; with a mean age of twelve, the Madras Brahman average fell within this range. See S. N. Agarwala, *Age at Marriage in India* (Allahabad: Kitab Mahal, 1962), 175, 180.

26. There was also a significant Muslim opposition to legislation on the grounds that non-Muslims did not have the authority to regulate the marriage practices of Muslims. As in the case of Tamil Brahmans, Muslim opponents of legislation emphasized that the community rather than the nation or state governed its own marriage practices.

27. *Kuṭi Aracu* (People's Rule, K.A.) (hereafter, *KA*), 22 December 1929, reprinted in E. V. Ramasami, *Periyar on Women's Rights,* ed. K. Veeramani, trans. R. Sundara Raju (Madras: Emerald, 1992).

28. Age of Consent Committee, *Evidence,* statement of T. R. Ramachandra Iyer.

29. *ILAD,* 5 (15 September 1927): 4450–4451; and *ILAD,* 5 (19 September 1929): 1116–1117.

30. The quotation is from *ILAD,* 6 (3 September 1925): 745; statement of Rama Aiyangar. Sesha Iyengar introduced an amendment to the Child Marriage Restraint Act that a minimum age of marriage would "not apply to Brahmans and other such communities in which post-puberty marriages are forbidden by their religion or custom or both." The amendment was overwhelmingly rejected. See *ILAD,* 5 (19 September 1929): 1130.

31. *ILAD,* 6 (15 September 1927): 4437.

32. Sanjam Ahluwalia, "Demographic Rhetoric and Sexual Surveillance: Indian Middle-Class Advocates of Birth Control, 1920s–1940s," in *Confronting the Body: The Politics of Physicality in Colonial and Post-Colonial India,* ed. James H. Milles and Satadru Sen (London: Anthem, 2004). Whitehead, "Modernising the Motherhood Archetype," 187–191.

33. Age of Consent Committee, *Report,* 178.

34. Sarkar, *Hindu Wife,* 218–219.

35. Muthulakshmi Reddi's message to the Third International Conference on Planned Parenthood, n.d., in *MRP,* Subject files 9 and 10.

36. Harbilas Sarda quoted this passage from a letter Bhagirathi Ammal sent to him advocating age of marriage legislation (*ILAD* 1 [29 January 1929]: 194).

37. Government of Madras Letter No. 2542 (Law [General]), 1 August 1928.

38. *Swarajya,* n.d. "Girl Mothers' Woes: Some Shocking Fallacies Exposed," in Muthulakshmi Reddi Papers (Subject files 9 and 10). The context suggests that this article was published in early 1928.

39. "An Appeal to My Educated Sisters," n.d., n.p., *MRP,* Subject files 9 and 10.

40. Colonel J. D. Crawford, who represented a European constituency in Bengal, read this statement, which appeared in a WIA telegram to legislators, during his speech to the Indian Legislative Assembly (*ILAD* 5, pt. 3 [23 March 1925]: 2842).

41. Uma Chakravarti, "Whatever Happened to the Vedic Dasi? Orientalism, Nationalism and a Script for the Past," in *Recasting Women,* ed. Kumkum Sangari and Sudesh Vaid, 27–87 (New Brunswick, N.J.: Rutgers University Press, 2000).

42. Sinha, "The Lineage of the 'Indian' Modern," 209.

43. *Madras Mail,* 3 July 1934. Reprinted in Government of Madras Order No. 2454 (Law [General]), 28 August 1934. The report added that, "owing to the large number of marriages that took place, the accommodation in Yanam was found insufficient during the last marriage season." Indeed, the initial impact of the Child Marriage Restraint Act was to encourage the early marriage of girls by parents eager for their daughters to marry before the law took effect in April 1930. Consequently, according to census statistics, the mean age of marriage in Madras Presidency in 1931 (14.92 years) was actually lower than the comparable figure in 1921 (15.31). This reversed a decades-long trend of a gradual increase in the mean age of marriage (Government of India, *Report of the Census of Madras Presidency of 1931* [Madras: Superintendent of Government Press, 1932]: 159; Agarwala, *Age at Marriage,* 228).

44. Government of Madras Order No. 2027 (Law [General]), 5 November 1931. The Child Marriage Restraint Act rendered any offense (i.e., a wedding before age fourteen) non-cognizable, which meant that the state could not prosecute cases of its own accord but had to wait for a complaint from non-officials.

45. G. Visalakshi, "The First Experiences of the Sarda Act Committee of the WIA and AIWC (Madras)," *Stri Dharma* 15, no. 8 (June 1932): 438.

46. For example, Forbes, "Women and Modernity," 416–418.

47. Guha, *Dominance without Hegemony,* 101.

48. Anna Davin, "Imperialism and Motherhood," in *Tensions of Empire: Colonial Cultures in a Bourgeois World,* ed. Frederick Cooper and Ann Laura Stoler, 135–136 (Berkeley: University of California Press, 1997). For an example of similar discourses in a colonial context, see Nancy Rose Hunt, "'Le bébé en brousse': European Women, African Birth Spacing, and Colonial Intervention in Breast Feeding in the Belgian Congo," in idem, *Tensions of Empire,* 287–321.

49. Judy Whitehead discusses these class implications further in "Modernising the Motherhood Archetype," 205–207.

50. *Kuṭi Aracu,* 7 July 1929.

51. Ibid.

52. The movement was consistent in condemning child marriage, but this was never a focus of Self Respect conjugal politics. Thus, during the height of Indian nationalist debate on legislative reform, Self Respect writing on child marriage was limited to a handful of articles that reported on Mayo's *Mother India,* welcomed the creation of an Age of Consent Committee, and editorialized on the need for child marriage legislation. See, for example, Ko. Ramasami, "Child Marriage," *KA,* 28 June 1925; Ayyamuthu, "Mother India," *KA* 5, no. 2 (12 May 1919); and "Editorial," *KA* 5, no. 11 (21 July 1919). Soon after its passage, the Self Respect movement demanded the law's enforcement and included this among its resolutions at the Second Provincial Self Respect Conference, held at Erode in 1930 (S. Anandhi, "Women's Question in the Dravidian Movement," *Social Scientist* 19, nos. 5–6 [May–June 1991]: 30–31). An article published in 1934 criticizing the government's lack of enforcement of the Sarda Act was one of the last references to the legislation that we might find in Self Respect newspapers (S. Nilavati, "The Sarda Act and the Government's Conduct," *Pakuttarivu* 1, no. 6 [30 September 1934]).

53. For more details on the activities of the Self Respect movement, see K. Nambi Arooran, *Tamil Renaissance and Dravidian Nationalism, 1905–1944* (Madurai: Koodal, 1980), 152–185; N. K. Mangalamurugesan, *Self-Respect Movement in Tamil Nadu* (Madurai: Koodal, 1979).

54. The term "forward non-Brahman" was current in Tamil politics during this period and included elite landowning and business castes such as Reddiar, Vellalar, Naidu, Mudaliar, Chettiar, and Pillai. As Marguerite Barnett notes, in the immediate precolonial period, these groups were distinct from "backward non-Brahman" castes because of their relatively high ritual status and their relationships with Brahmans. However, Brahman dominance was consolidated during the colonial period, producing a "conflict between a landowning non-Brahmin [*sic*] elite with a history of rural dominance, and a nascent urban Brahmin elite that had used the opportunities presented by British rule" (*The Politics of Cultural Nationalism in South India* [Princeton, N.J.: Princeton University Press, 1976], 17). One example of a "backward" caste that took enthusiastically to Self Respect marriage was the Nadar community. Finding in these weddings an expression of their upward social mobility that did not follow Sanskritization models, many Nadars adopted Self Respect ceremonies as their own. The extent to which Self Respect weddings spread among Nadars is apparent from the publication of a marriage manual, *Nadar Marriage Customs,* which describes a Self Respect wedding ceremony (S. A. Togo, *Nāṭār Tirumaṇac Cataṅkukaḷ* [n.p., n.d.]). On the working-class constituency of the Self Respect movement, see C. J. Baker, *The Politics of South India 1920–1937* (Cambridge: Cambridge University Press, 1976), 192.

55. "Reformed Wedding in Kovai," *KA,* 27 January 1945.

56. "Self-Respect Mixed Marriage," *KA,* 15 December 1929; "Our Achievements," *Revolt,* 19 January 1930.

57. See, for example, "Self-Respect Wedding in Pujaimedu," *KA,* 23 December 1928. According to this article, months before the Self Respect weddings of two brothers, Govindasami and Carangapani Nayudu, rumors in the village of Pujaimedu (near the town of

Cuddalore [Kadalur]) indicated that an unusual wedding was to occur. These rumors were wide-ranging, supposing the ceremony to be atheist or Brahmo Samaj or Christian. Uninvited visitors, including devadasis and musicians, were reported to have attended the ceremony to see E. V. Ramasami, who officiated. Perhaps in a telling example of how this wedding was figured in Self Respect discourse, the brides, who came from another village, were not mentioned by name in *Kuṭi Aracu*.

58. E. V. Ramasami, "Self-Respect Wedding in Chennai," *KA*, 7 April 1929.

59. S. Kuncitam, *KA*, 26 June 1932.

60. S. Anandhi, "Reproductive Bodies and Regulated Sexuality: Birth Control Debates in Early Twentieth Century Tamilnadu," in *A Question of Silence? The Sexual Economies of Modern India*, ed. Mary E. John and Janaki Nair, 139–166 (New Delhi: Kali for Women, 1998). See also *KA*, 6 April 1930, reprinted in K. Veeramani, ed., *Periyar on Women's Rights*, trans. R. Sundara Raju (Madras: Emerald, 1992), 45–46; P. Panditai Janaki, "Women's Contraception and Remarriage," *KA*, 10 May 1931.

61. E. V. Ramasami, "What Is Desirable in a Life Companion," 1958; reprinted in *Ī. Vē. Rā. Cintaṉaikaḷ*, 222–223. For Ramasami, such rational thinking required the refutation not only of upper-caste "Indian tradition" but also of its non-Brahman, putatively "Tamil" variety. Indeed, throughout his political life, Ramasami had an ambivalent relationship to Dravidian attempts to reconstruct Tamil "tradition" or to glorify the Tamil language (Sumathi Ramaswamy, *Passions of the Tongue: Language Devotion in Tamil India, 1891–1970* [Berkeley: University of California Press, 1997], 233–242).

62. Ramasami, "What Is Desirable in a Life Companion," 220. Ramasami's refusal to show honor to Brahmans by falling at their feet must also be viewed in relation to the broader politics of honor, respect, and status in Tamil society. As Pamela Price argues, Ramasami's emphasis on "Self Respect" (*cuya mariyātai*) was revolutionary in its implications because it rejected the notion that honor and respect were linked to how one was treated by others (more normative in Tamil society), and focused instead on the "inner qualities of a person" as marking honor (*Kingship and Political Practice in Colonial India* [Cambridge: Cambridge University Press, 1996], 199).

63. Ramasami, "What Is Desirable in a Life Companion," 222.

64. E. V. Ramasami, "Respect for Self—Respect for Puranas," *Pakuttarivu*, 7 October 1934. Reprinted in *Ī. Vē. Rā. Cintaṉaikaḷ*, 188–189.

65. Ramasami, "What Is Desirable in a Life Companion," 213.

66. E. V. Ramasami, "Marriage and Contract," in *Ī. Vē. Rā. Cintaṉaikaḷ*, 184, 186. This emphasis on contractual forms of marriage also resonated with Muslim and Christian practice.

67. Ibid., 186–187.

68. Ramasami continues, "A woman is like a friend to a man; she is not his slave. She is not his cook who cooks rice for him; she is his equal; she is like a friend—she is a companion to his life. They both have the same rights. She has the same rights as a man to her father's property" ("What Is Desirable in a Life Companion," 230).

69. "Love Marriage," *KA*, 17 February 1935. Fictional accounts of weddings emphasized similar themes, as in the case of the play *Kantimati, allatu Kalappu maṇam* (Kantimati, or mixed marriage). Although the author, R. Iramanatan, does not make explicit his connection to the Self Respect movement, the language and themes of the play reflect Self Respect ideologies. Published in Kuala Lumpur, in 1934, the text seems indicative of the spread of Dravidian principles to Tamils in Malaysia. However, the text itself makes no diasporic references and appears to be set in Tamil Nadu.

70. Ramasami, "Respect for Self—Respect for Puranas." Reprinted in *Ī. Vē. Rā. Cintaṉaikaḷ*, 190.

71. "Self-Respect Wedding in Devakottai: Widow Mixed Marriage," *KA*, 12 September 1935.

72. See, for example, Arooran, *Tamil Renaissance and Dravidian Nationalism: 1905–1944;* Eugene Irschick, *Politics and Social Conflict in South India* (Berkeley: University of California Press, 1969); and Ramaswamy, *Passions of the Tongue.*

73. "Editorial," *KA*, 3 November 1940.

74. Ramasami, "What Is Desirable in a Life Companion," 218.

75. Benedict Anderson, *Imagined Communities: Reflections on the Origin and Spread of Nationalism* (London: Verso, 1983; rev. ed., 1991), 6.

76. In fact, Self Respect marriage inspired theatrical productions, in which fictionalized weddings were performed as a method of spreading Self Respect ideologies. For example, *Kalappu Maṇam, allatu Pirāmaṉaṉum Cūttiraṉum* (Mixed marriage, or the Brahman and the Sudra) was performed by the Samadharma Actors' Association for Tamil workers at the Kolar Gold Fields in 1934. See *KA*, 9 September 1934.

77. S. Nilavati, "Women's Condition," *KA*, 28 April 1935. Elsewhere, Nilavati linked conventional Tamil marriage to the system of private property, arguing that, "until we receive freedom from property," neither marriage nor women's lives could undergo fundamental change (S. Nilavati, "Salem District Self-Respect Women's Conference," *KA*, 15 May 1932). For another important appraisal of the limitations of Self Respect marriage, see M. Singaravelu, "Mixed Marriage Is One Way to Destroy Caste," *KA*, 17 January 1932.

78. See, for example, his speech at a wedding in Perambur, Madras, addressed to railway workers (*KA*, 10 March 1945).

79. The conjugal politics of Dravidian nationalism were further modified after 1949, when E. V. Ramasami's marriage to a much younger woman catalyzed a split in the movement and led to the establishment of the Dravidar Munnetra Kazhagam (DMK) by C. N. Annadurai.

80. Anandhi, "Women's Question," 38.

81. Several careful analyses have shown the connections between Indian nationalist and Dravidian ideologies without collapsing the latter into a mere variant of the former. See, for example, V. Geetha, "Periyar, Women, and an Ethic of Citizenship," *Economic and Political Weekly* 33, no. 17 (25 April 1998): WS9–WS15; Sumathi Ramaswamy, "Virgin Mother, Beloved Other: The Erotics of Tamil Nationalism in Colonial and Post-Colonial India," *Thamyris* 4, no. 1 (Spring 1997): 9–39.

82. Occasionally this denial was quite explicit. For instance, when a speaker from the Non-Brahman Youth League (an organization with ties to the Self Respect movement) referred favorably to Mayo during an address about marriage reform before the National Social Reform Conference in Madras in 1927, chaos ensued. The conference proceedings were disrupted; even Muthulakshmi Reddi, who had some ties to Dravidian organizations, felt compelled to disavow the speaker's remarks (Sinha, "Lineage of the 'Indian' Modern," 217–218).

83. M. S. S. Pandian, "Beyond Colonial Crumbs: Cambridge School, Identity Politics, and Dravidian Movement(s)," *Economic and Political Weekly* (18–25 February 1995): 385–391.

84. Chatterjee, *Nation and Its Fragments*, 13.

85. Ibid. See also Dipesh Chakrabarty, *Provincializing Europe: Postcolonial Thought and Historical Difference* (Princeton, N.J.: Princeton University Press, 2000), 149–179.

4. Marrying for Love

1. Though I focus here on how emotion is written about, my intention is not to suggest that emotion is not also embodied and experienced. Mapping the relationship between changes in discourse and shifts in emotional experience would be a fruitful area for further inquiry, as, for example, in Peter N. Stearns and Jan Lewis, eds., *An Emotional History of the United States* (New York: New York University Press, 1998).

2. Gail Minault, "Urdu Women's Magazines in the Early Twentieth Century," *Manushi,* no. 48 (September–October 1988): 9.

3. Himani Bannerjee, "Fashioning a Self: Educational Proposals for and by Women in Popular Magazines in Colonial Bengal," *Economic and Political Weekly* 26, no. 43 (26 October 1991): WS50.

4. Benedict Anderson, *Imagined Communities: Reflections on the Origin and Spread of Nationalism,* rev. ed. (London: Verso, 1991), 37–46; A. R. Venkatachalapathy, "Domesticating the Novel: Society and Culture in Inter-war Tamil Nadu," *Indian Economic and Social History Review* 34, no. 1 (1997): 53–67.

5. Francesca Orsini, "Domesticity and Beyond: Hindi Women's Journals in the Early Twentieth Century," *South Asia Research* 19, no. 2 (1999): 137.

6. Sita Anantha Raman, *Getting Girls to School: Social Reform in the Tamil Districts, 1870–1939* (Calcutta: Stree, 1996), 130, 58–96. For further discussion of publishing for women, see C. S. Lakshmi, *The Face Behind the Mask: Women in Tamil Literature* (Delhi: Vilas, 1984), 102–156.

7. Although the articles in all three of these magazines were directed toward women, some subscribers were male.

8. Ma. Cu. Campantan, *Tamiḻ Itaḻiyaḷ Kalañciyam* (Storehouse of Tamil periodicals) (Chennai: Tamil Publishing, 1990), 20. Campantan does not indicate how long the magazine continued publication.

9. The exact publication dates of this magazine are disputed. According to Campantan, it was first published in 1901 (*Tamiḻ Itaḻiyaḷ Varalāṟu* [History of Tamil periodicals] [Chennai: Tamil Publishing, 1987]), 161. However, Sita Anantha Raman suggests that it was published sometime between 1899 and 1901; editorial notes in the text appear to confirm the year 1899 (*Getting Girls to School,* 130).

10. Kamala Sattianadhan (1879–1950) was from a family of Telugu Brahman converts to Christianity and was the first woman to graduate with B.A. and M.A. degrees from Madras University. For more details on her life, see Anantha Raman, *Getting Girls to School,* 140–141.

11. The first article in the series was "The Domestic Life of the English" (February 1892): 200–207.

12. Leonore Davidoff and Catherine Hall, *Family Fortunes: Men and Women of the English Middle Class, 1780–1850* (Chicago: University of Chicago Press, 1987), 184.

13. Eliza Kent, *Converting Women: Gender and Protestant Christianity in Colonial South India* (New York: Oxford University Press, 2004), 130.

14. Ibid., 165–197.

15. For instance, the second-century Tamil epic *Cilappatikkāram* includes looking after the household and cooking as among the wife's domestic duties. However, based on the eroticized descriptions of the relationship between the hero and the heroine, I suggest that the domestic realm is not desexualized in this text, as it is in the nineteenth-century women's magazines. See Illango Adigal, *Shilappadikaram* (The ankle bracelet), trans. Alain Danielou (New York: New Directions, 1965).

16. Ta. Ca., "The Duties of Hindu Wives," *Peṇmati Pōtini* (March 1892): 271–274. Although the norms emphasized in the article echo the magazine's emphasis on a desexualized female domesticity, the *Kamasutra* itself was not limited to these norms. See Kumkum Roy, "Unraveling the *Kamasutra,*" in *A Question of Silence? The Sexual Economies of Modern India,* ed. Mary John and Janaki Nair (London: Zed Books, 1998), 52–76.

17. Raman, "Old Norms in New Bottles: Constructions of Gender and Ethnicity in the Early Tamil Novel," *Journal of Women's History* 12, no. 3 (Fall 2000): 98.

18. Kent, *Converting Women,* 139.

19. Judith Walsh, *Domesticity in Colonial India: What Women Learned When Men Gave Them Advice* (Lanham: Rowman and Littlefield, 2004), 39.

20. Anna Sathianathan, writing as Annal Sathianadhan, published a widely read domestic manual, *Nalla Tāy* (The good mother) in 1862. Another important writer in the family was Krupabai Sattianadhan, wife of Anna's son Samuel, who wrote several fictionalized biographies extolling domestic virtue. After Krupabai's death, Samuel Sathianadhan married Kamala (Kent, *Converting Women*, 145–149, 181).

21. A. K. Sabha, "Our Wives," *Indian Ladies Magazine* 4, no. 8 (February 1905): 238.

22. An Indian Girl, "Our Wives: A Reply," *Indian Ladies Magazine* 4, no. 9 (March 1905): 276.

23. Occasionally, though in a fragmentary fashion, *Mātar Maṉōrañjiṉi* did challenge the social norms associated with widowhood; this led to some criticism of Tamil marriage practices. See for instance: "A Woman," *Mātar Maṉōrañjiṉi* 1, no. 8 (October 1899): 125. Quoted and translated in Anantha Raman, *Getting Girls to School*, 102.

24. Venkatachalapathy, "Domesticating the Novel," 53–67.

25. *Peṇ Kalvi* was first published from Madras city in 1900 under the editorship of S. Thayarammal (Campantan, *History of Tamil Periodicals*, 54). I examine issues from 1914 to 1916.

26. I focus on available issues of this magazine from the 1920s and 1930s.

27. I focus on issues from the 1920s and 1930s, a period that represents the height of the WIA's political activity.

28. The name Lakshmi refers to the Hindu goddess of prosperity. My reading begins with the magazine's inauguration in 1937 and continues through 1940.

29. Unlike child marriage, for instance, dowry was not the subject of legislation or significant state investigation in Tamil Nadu during the colonial period. Also, unlike many other property issues, dowry cases did not typically appear before the colonial courts.

30. *Peṇ Kalvi* 3, no. 6 (March 1914).

31. Although the cartoon did not refer to any explicitly specific incident, an article in the same issue reported on the case of Snehalata Devi, a young Bengali woman who committed suicide when her father was faced with large dowry demands. Noting that some male students in Bengal made a pact not to demand dowry, the article urged readers to support such anti-dowry movements ("The Dowry System," *Peṇ Kalvi* 3, no. 6 [March 1914]). I gloss the Tamil word *varatatcinai* (Skt. *varadakṣiṇā*) as "dowry."

32. Smt. C. Kanakavalli, "Susila's Wedding," *Grihalakshmi* 3, no. 5 (May 1939): 316.

33. Smt. S. Komalam, "Marriage without Dignity," *Grihalakshmi* 1, no. 12 (December 1937): 843–844.

34. N. Yagneswara Sastry, "The Bondswomen," *Stri Dharma* (September 1929): 389, 391.

35. K. V. Swaminathan, "A Friendly Talk: Finding Your Mate," *Indian Ladies Magazine* 10, no. 10 (July–August 1932): 463.

36. Muthulakshmi Reddi, "Widow Remarriage," *Grihalakshmi* 1, no. 8 (August 1937): 708.

37. Ma. Antalammal, "Chastity," *Peṇ Kalvi* 2, nos. 7–8 (April–May 1913): 16–19.

38. P. S. A. Krishnappa, "Susila," *Indian Ladies Magazine* 5, no. 10 (July–August 1932): 469.

39. G. Sumati Bai, B.A., L.T. "The Facts of Marriage—No Fancy of Man," *Stri Dharma* 14, no. 11 (September 1931): 450; emphasis added.

40. This episode from the *Mahabharata* refers to a game of dice between cousins in which the king Dharmaraja, having staked and lost his kingdom, his brothers, and himself, gambles away his wife, Draupadi.

41. Mrs. Munshi, "Dominion Status in Matrimony," *Stri Dharma* (July 1931): 398–399. This article is a reprint of Mrs. Munshi's speech to an unspecified meeting in Poona. In this passage, Mrs. Munshi clearly demands more freedom for women, but at the same time—

analogous to the relationship of dominion to "mother" country—it is not an absolute equality.

42. This discourse of emotion was, I believe, linked to a dominant trend of desexualizing femininity within nationalist writing. However, while noting this desexualization, Sumathi Ramaswamy argues that other idioms of sexuality also existed at the interstices of Tamil nationalist discourse. See Sumathi Ramaswamy, "Virgin Mother, Beloved Other: The Erotics of Tamil Nationalism in Colonial and Post-Colonial India," *Thamyris* 4, no. 1 (Spring 1997): 9–39.

43. Lucy Carroll, "Law, Custom, and Statutory Social Reform: The Hindu Widows' Remarriage Act of 1856," *Indian Economic and Social History Review* 20, no. 4 (1983): 363–388.

44. Marakatavalli's wedding to Murugappan is described in chapter 3. See also "Marakatavalli's Wedding: Remarriage, Mixed Marriage, Love Marriage," *Kuti Aracu* (7 July 1929).

45. A search of libraries in Chennai did not produce any subsequent issues; nor do scholarly studies of Tamil periodicals provide an ending date of publication. The journal may have ceased publication during the Second World War.

46. "Open the Door!" Cartoon in *Mātar Maṟumaṇam* 1, no. 3 (October/November 1936).

47. This illustration appeared on the cover of every issue in the first volume. In contrast to the practices of Brahmanical patriarchy among Tamils, the widow is depicted with long hair. *Mātar Maṟumaṇam* was critical of the tonsure of widows, and emphasizing the widow's hair in this image may have been part of this critique. Gandhi himself was in favor of virgin widows remarrying. In the case of non-virgin, adult widows, however, his position was more equivocal, preferring to see them as ideal servants of the nation.

48. "Religion and Caste Custom." Cartoon in *Mātar Maṟumaṇam* 1, no. 1 (August/September 1936): 33.

49. Kumkum Sangari and Sudesh Vaid, "Introduction: Recasting Women," in *Recasting Women: Essays in Indian Colonial History*, ed. Kumkum Sangari and Sudesh Vaid (New Brunswick, N.J.: Rutgers University Press, 1990), 1–26.

50. S. Nilavati, "Remarriage," *Mātar Maṟumaṇam* 1, no. 1 (August/September 1936): 12.

51. N. S. Ganapati, "Shankaran's Love," *Mātar Maṟumaṇam* 2, no. 6 (January/February 1938): 21–22.

52. Ibid., 27.

53. L. Kuruppancettiyar, "Kamalam," *Mātar Maṟumaṇam* 1, no. 4 (November/December 1936): 18.

54. Anonymous, "My Story," *Mātar Maṟumaṇam* 1, no. 8 (April/May 1937): 15.

55. Dipesh Chakrabarty identified a similar dynamic in the history of Bengali modernity, whereby "archiving and observing the Bengali widow as the subject of modernity . . . meant documenting not just the external conditions of the widow's life but her internal suffering as well." Chakrabarty suggests that these explorations of the widow's interiority were pivotal to the development of Bengali modern notions of subjectivity: "One reason why the figure of the widow may have held a special fascination for the early Bengali novelists is the fact that the unrecognized desires of the widow represented a case of complete subordination of the individual to society." The figure of the widow emerged in Bengali literature as the paradigmatic modern subject, in whom the "private experiences and desires (feelings, emotions, sentiments)" struggled with a "universal or public reason" (*Provincializing Europe: Postcolonial Thought and Historical Difference* [Princeton, N.J.: Princeton University Press, 2000], 131, 133, 129–130).

56. Bharati Dasan was a pseudonym of the poet and writer Subbarathinam (1891–1964). In the late 1920s, he became involved with the Dravidian movement and eventually became its preeminent poet.

57. Bharati Dasan, "The Well-Being of Widows!" *Mātar Maṛumaṇam* 1, no. 7 (March/April 1937): 12. Cross-cousin marriage was an accepted practice among Tamils.

58. Bharati Dasan, "Restrictions That Harm Love," *Mātar Maṛumaṇam* 1, no. 1 (August/September 1936): 1.

59. Ma. A. Pichai, "Feelings of Pleasure Are Common to Everyone," *Mātar Maṛumaṇam* 2, no. 12 (July/August 1938): 10.

60. Smt. S. P. Tirunellaiyacci, "Mother and Daughter," *Mātar Maṛumaṇam* 1, no. 6 (January/February 1937): 29.

61. See also Dipesh Chakrabarty, *Provincializing Europe*, 129–132.

62. For example, romantic love was an important theme in poetry from the classical *Caṅkam* corpus (ca. 100 BCE to 250 CE) (A. K. Ramanujan, trans., *The Interior Landscape: Love Poems from a Classical Tamil Anthology* [Bloomington: Indiana University Press, 1967]).

63. For a discussion of *aṉpu*, see Margaret Trawick, *Notes on Love in a Tamil Family* (Berkeley: University of California Press, 1992), 89–116.

64. Sri Mangalam, "The Status of Women in the Future," *Peṇ Kalvi* 5, no. 11 (August 1916): 262.

65. N. Yagneswara Sastry, "The Bondswomen," *Stri Dharma* (September 1929): 391.

66. "Editorial Notes: The Joint Family System in India," *Indian Ladies Magazine* 10, no. 10 (July/August 1932): 462–463.

67. Femininity, interiority, and emotion have a long-standing relationship in Tamil culture, beginning with the earliest available Tamil literature, the *Caṅkam* corpus of poems (ca. 100 BCE to 250 CE), in which interior landscapes were associated with women and romantic love. These poems were rediscovered, published, and disseminated beginning in the late nineteenth century (Ramanujam, *The Interior Landscape*).

68. Chakrabarty, *Provincializing Europe*, 129–132.

69. For example, see Nancy Armstrong, *Desire and Domestic Fiction: A Political History of the Novel* (New York: Oxford University Press, 1987).

Conclusion

1. The distinction here is analogous to Benedict Anderson's discussion of nations as imagined communities; in investigating nationalism, Anderson is less interested in the "falsity/genuineness" of national communities than in the "style in which they are imagined" (*Imagined Communities: Reflections on the Origin and Spread of Nationalism*, rev. ed. [London: Verso, 1991], 6).

2. Antonio Gramsci, *The Antonio Gramsci Reader: Selected Writings, 1916–1935*, ed. David Forgacs and Eric Hobsbawm (New York: New York University Press, 2000), 199–200.

3. I borrow the phrase from Mrinalini Sinha, *Specters of Mother India: The Global Restructuring of Empire* (Durham, N.C.: Duke University Press, 2006), 16.

4. Antoinette Burton, *Dwelling in the Archive: Women Writing House, Home, and History in Late Colonial India* (Oxford: Oxford University Press, 2003), 20–28.

5. These were the Special Marriage Act (1954), the Hindu Marriage Act (1955), the Hindu Succession Act (1956), the Hindu Minority and Guardianship Act (1956), and the Hindu Maintenance and Adoption Act (1956).

6. For details on the content of the laws, see Archana Parashar, *Women and Family Law Reform in India* (New Delhi: Sage, 1992), 286–292.

7. Ibid., 77–78.

8. For example, see Brenda Cossman and Ratna Kapur, "Women, Familial Ideology and the Constitution: Challenging Equality Rights," *Feminist Terrains in Legal Domains,*

ed. Ratna Kapur (New Delhi: Kali for Women, 1996); Indira Jaising, ed., *Justice for Women: Personal Laws, Women's Rights, and Law Reform* (Mapusa, Goa: The Other India Press), 1996; Christine Keating, "Framing the Postcolonial Sexual Contract: Democracy, Fraternalism, and State Authority in India," *Hypatia* 22, no. 4 (Fall 2007): forthcoming.

9. Hindu Law Committee, *Written Statements,* vol. 2, statement of N. Natesha Iyer.
10. Ibid., statement of C. Rajagopalachari.
11. Ibid., statement of the Madras Branch of the All-India Hindu Mahasabha.

Bibliography

Unpublished Documents and Collections

MANUSCRIPT COLLECTIONS

All-India Women's Conference papers. Nehru Memorial Library, New Delhi
Muthulakshmi Reddi papers. Nehru Memorial Library, New Delhi

TAMIL NADU ARCHIVES, CHENNAI

Proceedings of the following departments:
Home (General) Department
Home (Judicial) Department
Judicial Department
Law (General) Department
Revenue Department

BRITISH LIBRARY, ORIENTAL AND INDIA OFFICE COLLECTIONS, LONDON

Bengal Native Newspaper Reports
Bombay Native Newspaper Reports
Madras Native Newspaper Reports
Rulings of the Court of Sudder Udalat, 1858
Selections from the Government of India in the Home Department, no. 223. Home Department Serial No. 3. *Papers Relating to Infant Marriage and Enforced Widowhood in India.* Calcutta: 1886. Extract from the *Proceedings of the Government of India in the Home Department (Public)*, no. 35—1616.26 under date Simla, 8 October 1886.
Legal Advisor's Records (Class L/L, India Office Records)

Published Books, Documents, and Articles

Agarwal, Bina. *A Field of One's Own: Gender and Land Rights in South Asia.* Cambridge: Cambridge University Press, 1994.

Agarwala, S. N. *Age at Marriage in India.* Allahabad: Kitab Mahal, 1962.

Ahluwalia, Sanjam. "Demographic Rhetoric and Sexual Surveillance: Indian Middle-Class Advocates of Birth Control, 1920s–1940s." In *Confronting the Body: The Politics of Physicality in Colonial and Post-Colonial India,* ed. James H. Mills and Satadru Sen. London: Anthem, 2004.

Anaimuthu, Ve, ed. *Ī. Vē. Rā. Cintaṉaikaḷ* (The thoughts of Periyar E.V.R.). 3 vols. Tiruchirapalli: Cintanaiyalar Kazhakam, 1974.

Anandhi, S. "Reproductive Bodies and Regulated Sexuality: Birth Control Debates in Early Twentieth Century Tamilnadu." In *A Question of Silence? The Sexual Economies of Modern India,* ed. Mary E. John and Janaki Nair. New Delhi: Kali for Women, 1998.

———. "Women's Question in the Dravidian Movement." *Social Scientist* 19, nos. 5–6 (May–June 1991): 24–41.

Anderson, Benedict. *Imagined Communities: Reflections on the Origin and Spread of Nationalism.* London: Verso, 1983, rev. 1991.

Anderson, Michael. *Approaches to the History of the Western Family, 1500–1914*. Cambridge: Cambridge University Press, 1980, rev. 1995.

Appadurai, Arjun. *Worship and Conflict under Colonial Rule: A South Indian Case*. Cambridge: Cambridge University Press, 1981.

Armstrong, Nancy. *Desire and Domestic Fiction: A Political History of the Novel*. New York: Oxford University Press, 1987.

Arooran, K. Nambi. *Tamil Renaissance and Dravidian Nationalism, 1905–1944*. Madurai: Koodal, 1980.

Arumukam, Cuppu. *Tirumaṇa Nāl* (Wedding day). Madras: Minnoli, 1958.

Arunima, G. *There Comes Papa: Colonialism and the Transformation of Matriliny in Kerala, Malabar c. 1850–1940*. Delhi: Orient Longman, 2003.

Ayyamuthu, Kovai A. "Mayo's Charges: True or False." In *Selections from Mother India*, ed. Mrinalini Sinha. Ann Arbor: University of Michigan Press, 2000.

Baker, C. J. *The Politics of South India, 1920–1937*. Cambridge: Cambridge University Press, 1976.

Bannerjee, Himani. "Fashioning a Self: Education Proposals for and by Women in Popular Magazines in Colonial Bengal." *Economic and Political Weekly* 26, no. 43 (26 October 1991): WS50–WS60.

Barnett, Marguerite. *The Politics of Cultural Nationalism in South India*. Princeton, N.J.: Princeton University Press, 1976.

Basu, Srimati. "The Personal and the Political: Indian Women and Inheritance Law." In *Religion and Personal Law in Secular India: A Call to Judgment*, ed. Gerald James Larson. Bloomington: Indiana University Press, 2001.

Bayly, C. A. *Indian Society and the Making of the British Empire*. Cambridge: Cambridge University Press, 1988.

Bayly, Susan. *Caste, Society and Politics in India from the 18th Century to the Modern Age*. Cambridge: Cambridge University Press, 1999.

Bharati, Subrahmanya. *Makākāvi Pāratiyar Kataikaḷ* (Stories by the great poet Bharatiyar). 2nd ed. Madurai: Aruna, 1964.

———. *Peṇ Viṭutalai* (Women's freedom). Erode: Gnanabharati, 1981.

Bhattacharya, Nandini. "From Putrika to Nirindriya: A Study of Early Colonial Attitudes towards Women's Rights to Property and Inheritance in Bengal, 1765–1800." *Calcutta Historical Journal* 18, no. 2 (1996): 43–66.

Burton, Antoinette. *Dwelling in the Archive: Women Writing House, Home and History in Late Colonial India*. Oxford: Oxford University Press, 2003.

Cacireka, Civa. *Tamiḻ Itaḻkaḷ Kāṭṭum Makaḷir Nilai* (Status of women as shown in Tamil periodicals). Madurai: Parttipan Pattipakam, 1988.

Campantan, Ma Cu. *Tamiḻ Itaḻiyaḷ Kalañciyam* (Storehouse of Tamil periodicals). Madras: Tamil Publishing House, 1990.

———. *Tamiḻ Itaḻiyaḷ Varalāṟu* (History of Tamil periodicals). Madras: Tamil Publishing House, 1987.

Carroll, Lucy. "Daughter's Right of Inheritance in India: A Perspective on the Problem of Dowry." *Modern Asian Studies* 25, no. 4 (1991): 791–809.

———. "Law, Custom, and Statutory Social Reform: The Hindu Widows' Remarriage Act of 1856." *Indian Economic and Social History Review* 20, no. 4 (1983): 363–388.

Chakrabarty, Dipesh. "The Difference-Deferral of a Colonial Modernity: Public Debates on Domesticity in British Bengal." In *Tensions of Empire: Colonial Cultures in a Bourgeois World*, ed. Frederick Cooper and Ann Laura Stoler. Berkeley: University of California Press, 1997.

———. *Provincializing Europe: Postcolonial Thought and Historical Difference*. Princeton, N.J.: Princeton University Press, 2000.

Chakravarti, Uma. "Whatever Happened to the Vedic Dasi? Orientalism, Nationalism and a Script for the Past." In *Recasting Women: Essays in Indian Colonial History*, ed. Kumkum Sangari and Sudesh Vaid. New Brunswick, N.J.: Rutgers University Press, 1990.

Chandra, Sudhir. *Enslaved Daughters: Colonialism, Law and Women's Rights*. Delhi: Oxford University Press, 1998.

Chatterjee, Indrani. *Gender, Slavery and Law in Colonial India*. New Delhi: Oxford University Press, 1999.

———, ed. *Unfamiliar Relations: Family and History in South Asia*. Delhi: Permanent Black, 2004.

Chatterjee, Kumkum. *Merchants, Politics, and Society in Early Modern India: Bihar 1733–1820*. Leiden: E. J. Brill, 1996.

Chatterjee, Partha. *The Nation and Its Fragments: Colonial and Postcolonial Histories*. Princeton, N.J.: Princeton University Press, 1993.

———. "The Nationalist Resolution of the Women's Question." In *Recasting Women: Essays in Indian Colonial History*, ed. Kumkum Sangari and Sudesh Vaid. New Brunswick, N.J.: Rutgers University Press, 1990.

———. *Nationalist Thought and the Colonial World: A Derivative Discourse*. Minneapolis: University of Minnesota Press, 1986.

Clancy-Smith, Julia, and Frances Gouda, eds. *Domesticating the Empire: Race, Gender and Family Life in French and Dutch Colonialism*. Charlottesville: University Press of Virginia, 1998.

Cohn, Bernard S. "The Census, Social Structure, and Objectification in South Asia." In *An Anthropologist among the Historians and Other Essays*. Delhi: Oxford University Press, 1987.

———. *Colonialism and Its Forms of Knowledge: The British in India*. Princeton, N.J.: Princeton University Press, 1996.

———. "Recruitment of Elites in India under British Rule." In *Essays in Comparative Social Stratification*, ed. Leonard Plotnicov and Arthur Tuden. Pittsburgh: University of Pittsburgh Press, 1970.

Colebrooke, H. T. *Dayabhaga and Mitaksara: Two Treatises on the Hindu Law of Inheritance*. Reprint. Delhi: Parimal, 1984.

Comaroff, Jean, and John L. Comaroff. "Home-Made Hegemony: Modernity, Domesticity and Colonialism in South Africa." In *African Encounters with Domesticity*, ed. Karen Tranberg Hansen. New Brunswick, N.J.: Rutgers University Press, 1992.

Coontz, Stephanie. *The Social Origins of Private Life: A History of American Families, 1600–1900*. London: Oxford University Press, 1988.

Cooper, Frederick. *Colonialism in Question: Theory, Knowledge, History*. Berkeley: University of California Press, 2005.

Cooper, Frederick, and Ann Laura Stoler. "Between Metropole and Colony: Rethinking a Research Agenda." In *Tensions of Empire: Colonial Cultures in a Bourgeois World*, ed. Frederick Cooper and Ann Laura Stoler. Berkeley: University of California Press, 1997.

Cott, Nancy. *Public Vows: A History of Marriage and the Nation*. Cambridge, Mass.: Harvard University Press, 2000.

Dalrymple, William. "White Mughals: The Case of James Archilles Kirkpatrick and Khair un-Nissa." In *Unfamiliar Relations: Family and History in South Asia*, ed. Indrani Chatterjee. Delhi: Permanent Black, 2004.

Davidoff, Leonore, and Catherine Hall. *Family Fortunes: Men and Women of the English Middle Class, 1780–1850*. Chicago: University of Chicago Press, 1987.

Davin, Anna. "Imperialism and Motherhood." In *Tensions of Empire: Colonial Cultures in a Bourgeois World*, ed. Frederick Cooper and Ann Laura Stoler. Berkeley: University of California, 1997.

Debnath, Sailen. "Cultural Imperialism in British India: A Case Study of Cooch Behar Marriage in 1878." In *The Kingdom of Kamata Koch Behar in Historical Perspective*, ed. P. K. Bhattacharya. Calcutta: Ratna Prakashan, 2000.

Derrett, Duncan M. *Religion, Law and the State in India*. New York: Free Press, 1968.

Dirks, Nicholas. "Castes of Mind." *Representations*, no. 37 (Special Issue): *Imperial Fantasies and Postcolonial Histories* (Winter 1992): 56–78.

———. "From Little King to Landlord: Colonial Discourse and Colonial Rule." In *Colonialism and Culture,* ed. Nicholas Dirks. Ann Arbor: University of Michigan Press, 1992.

———. *The Hollow Crown: Ethnohistory of an Indian Kingdom.* Cambridge: Cambridge University Press, 1987.

Dube, Leela. *Women and Kinship: Comparative Perspectives in South and South-East Asia.* Tokyo, New York, and Paris: United Nations University Press, 1997.

Dumont, Louis. *Affinity as a Value: Marriage Alliance in South India, with Comparative Essays on Australia.* Chicago: University of Chicago Press, 1993.

Eley, Geoff. "Nations, Publics and Political Cultures: Placing Habermas in the Nineteenth Century." In *Habermas and the Public Sphere,* ed. Craig Calhoun. Cambridge, Mass.: MIT Press, 1992.

Engels, Dagmar. *Beyond Purdah? Women in Bengal, 1890–1930.* Delhi: Oxford University Press, 1999.

Engelstein, Laura. *The Keys to Happiness: Sex and the Search for Modernity in Fin-de-Siècle Russia.* Ithaca, N.Y.: Cornell University Press, 1992.

Fisher, Michael H. "Becoming and Making 'Family' in Hindustan." In *Unfamiliar Relations: Family and History in South Asia,* ed. Indrani Chatterjee. Delhi: Permanent Black, 2004.

Forbes, Geraldine. "Women and Modernity: The Issue of Child Marriage in India." *Women's Studies International Quarterly* 2, no. 4 (1979): 407–419.

———. *Women in Modern India.* Cambridge: Cambridge University Press, 1998.

Foucault, Michel. *The History of Sexuality.* Vol. 1. Trans. Robert Hurley. New York: Vintage Books, 1978.

Francis, W. *Madura.* Vol. 1, *Madras District Gazetteers.* Madras: Government Press, 1914.

Fraser, Nancy. "Rethinking the Public Sphere: A Contribution to the Critique of Actually Existing Democracy." In *Between Borders: Pedagogy and the Politics of Cultural Studies,* ed. Henry A. Giroux and Peter McLaren. New York: Routledge, 1994.

Galanter, Marc. *Law and Society in Modern India.* Delhi: Oxford University Press, 1989.

Gaunt, David. "Kinship: Thin Red Lines or Thick Blue Blood." In *Family Life in Early Modern Times, 1500–1789,* ed. David I. Kertzer and Marzio Barbagli. New Haven, Conn.: Yale University Press, 2001.

Geetha, V. "Periyar, Women and an Ethic of Citizenship." *Economic and Political Weekly* 33, no. 17 (25 April 1998): WS9–WS15.

Ghosh, Durba. *Sex and the Family in Colonial India: The Making of Empire.* Cambridge: Cambridge University Press, 2006.

Gillis, John R. "From Ritual to Romance: Toward an Alternative History of Love." In *Emotion and Social Change: Toward a New Psychohistory,* ed. Carol Z. Stearns and Peter N. Stearns. New York: Holmes and Meier, 1988.

Glosser, Susan L. *Chinese Visions of Family and State, 1915–1953.* Berkeley: University of California Press, 2003.

Gnanambal, K. *Religious Institutions and Caste Panchayats in South India.* Delhi: Government of India Press, 1966.

Goody, Jack, and S. J. Tambiah. *Bridewealth and Dowry.* Cambridge: Cambridge University Press, 1973.

Government of India. *Legislative Assembly Debates (Official Report).* Vol. 5, part 3 (7 March to 24 March 1925). Delhi: Government of India Press, 1925.

———. *The Legislative Assembly Debates (Official Report).* Vol. 6 (3 September 1925). Delhi: Government of India Press, 1925.

———. *The Legislative Assembly Debates (Official Report).* Vol. 6 (15 September 1927). Delhi: Government of India Press, 1927.

———. *The Legislative Assembly Debates (Official Report).* Vol. 1 (28 January to 23 February 1929). Delhi: Government of India Press, 1929.

———. *The Legislative Assembly Debates (Official Report).* Vol. 5 (19 September 1929). Delhi: Government of India Press, 1929.

———. *The Legislative Assembly Debates (Official Report).* Vol. 5 (23 September 1929). Delhi: Government of India Press, 1929.

———. *Report of the Age of Consent Committee, 1928–1929.* Calcutta: Government of India Central Publication Branch, 1929.

Government of Madras. *Madras Legislative Council Debates (Official Report)* 42, no. 1 (27 March 1929).

Gramsci, Antonio. *The Antonio Gramsci Reader: Selected Writings, 1916–1935*, ed. David Forgacs and Eric Hobsbawm. New York: New York University Press, 2000.

Guha, Ranajit. "Chandra's Death." In *Subaltern Studies V: Writings on South Asian History and Society*, ed. Ranajit Guha. Delhi: Oxford University Press, 1987.

———. *Dominance without Hegemony: History and Power in Colonial India.* Cambridge, Mass.: Harvard University Press, 1997.

Guha, Sumit. "The Family Feud as a Political Resource in Eighteenth-century India." *In Unfamiliar Relations: Family and History in South Asia*, ed. Indrani Chatterjee. Delhi: Permanent Black, 2004.

Haney, Lynne, and Lisa Pollard. "In a Family Way: Theorizing State and Familial Relations." In *Families of a New World: Gender, Politics and State Development in a Global Context*, ed. Lynne Haney and Lisa Pollard. New York: Routledge, 2003.

Hansen, Karen Tranberg, ed. *African Encounters with Domesticity.* New Brunswick, N.J.: Rutgers University Press, 1992.

Hardgrave, Robert L., Jr. *The Nadars of Tamilnad: The Political Culture of a Community in Change.* Berkeley: University of California Press, 1969.

Hareven, Tamara K. "The History of the Family and the Complexity of Social Change." *The American Historical Review* 96, no. 1 (February 1991): 95–124.

Helly, Dorothy, and Susan Reverby, eds. *Gendered Domains: Rethinking Public and Private in Women's History.* Ithaca, N.Y.: Cornell University Press, 1992.

Hershatter, Gail. "State of the Field: Women in China's Long 20th Century." *Journal of Asian Studies* 63, no. 4 (November 2004): 994–1016.

Hunt, Lynn. *The Family Romance of the French Revolution.* Berkeley: University of California Press, 1992.

Hunt, Nancy Rose. "'Le bébé en brousse': European Women, African Birth Spacing, and Colonial Intervention in Breast Feeding in the Belgian Congo." In *Tensions of Empire: Colonial Cultures in a Bourgeois World*, ed. Frederick Cooper and Ann Laura Stoler. Berkeley: University of California Press, 1997.

Ilango, Adigal. *Shilappadikaram* (The ankle bracelet). Trans. Alain Daniélou. New York: New Directions, 1965.

Iramanatan, R. *Kāntimati, allatu Kalappu Maṇam* (Kantimati, or mixed marriage). Kuala Lumpur, 1934.

Irschick, Eugene. *Politics and Social Conflict in South India: The Non-Brahman Movement and Tamil Separatism, 1916–1929.* Berkeley: University of California Press, 1969.

Iyengar, Bhashyam. "The Law of Hindu Gains of Learning." *Madras Law Journal* 10 (1900).

Jaising, Indira, ed. *Justice for Women: Personal Laws, Women's Rights and Law Reform.* Mapusa, Goa: The Other India Press, 1996.

Jayawardena, Kumari. *Feminism and Nationalism in the Third World.* London: Zed Books, 1986.

———. *The White Woman's Other Burden: Western Women and South Asia during British Colonial Rule.* New York: Routledge, 1995.

Jolly, Martha, and Martha Macintyre. *Family and Gender in the Pacific: Domestic Contradictions and Colonial Impact.* Cambridge: Cambridge University Press, 1989.

Kapur, Ratna. *Feminist Terrains in Legal Domains: Interdisciplinary Essays on Women and Law in India*. New Delhi: Kali for Women, 1996.

Kasturi, Malavika. *Embattled Identities: Rajput Lineages and the Colonial State in Nineteenth-Century North India*. New Delhi: Oxford University Press, 2002.

Keating, Christine. "Framing the Postcolonial Sexual Contract: Democracy, Fraternalism, and State Authority in India." *Hypatia* 22, no. 4 (Fall 2007): forthcoming.

Kent, Eliza. *Converting Women: Gender and Protestant Christianity in Colonial South India*. New York: Oxford University Press, 2004.

Kosambi, Meera. "Girl Brides and Socio-legal Change: Age of Consent Bill (1891) Controversy." *Economic and Political Weekly* 36, nos. 31–32 (3–10 August 1991): WS1851–WS1868.

Lakshmi, C. S. *The Face behind the Mask: Women in Tamil Literature*. Delhi: Vikas, 1984.

———. "Mother, Mother-Community, and Mother Politics in Tamil Nadu." *Economic and Political Weekly* (20–29 October 1990): WS72–WS83.

Lal, Ruby. *Domesticity and Power in the Early Mughal World*. Cambridge: Cambridge University Press, 2005.

Landes, Joan. *Women and the Public Sphere in the Age of the French Revolution*. Ithaca, N.Y.: Cornell University Press, 1988.

Lewis, Jan. "The Republican Wife: Virtue and Seduction in the Early Republic." *William and Mary Quarterly* 44, no. 4 (1987): 689–721.

Lewis, Jan, and P. N. Stearns, eds. *An Emotional History of the United States*. New York: New York University Press, 1998.

Ludden, David. "Anglo-Indian Empire." In *The Making of Agrarian Policy in British India, 1770–1900*, ed. Burton Stein. Delhi: Oxford University Press, 1992.

———. "Patriarchy and History in South Asia: Interpretive Experiments." *Calcutta Historical Journal* 17, no. 2 (1995): 1–18.

———. *Peasant History in South India*. Princeton, N.J.: Princeton University Press, 1985.

Lynch, Katherine A. "The Family and the History of Public Life." *Journal of Interdisciplinary History* 24, no. 4 (Spring 1994): 665–684.

MacPherson, C. B. *The Political Theory of Possessive Individualism: Hobbes to Locke*. Oxford: Clarendon, 1962.

Madan, T. N. "The Hindu Family and Development." In *Family, Kinship and Marriage in India*, ed. Patricia Uberoi. Delhi, Oxford University Press, 1993.

Mangalamurugesan, N. K. *Self-Respect Movement in Tamil Nadu*. Madurai: Koodal, 1979.

Mann, Kristin. "Marriage Choices among the Educated African Elite in Lagos Colony, 1880–1915." *International Journal of African Historical Studies* 12, no. 2 (1981): 201–228.

———. *Marrying Well: Marriage, Status and Social Change among the Educated Elite in Colonial Lagos*. Cambridge: Cambridge University Press, 1985.

Mayne, John D. *Mayne's Treatise on Hindu Law and Usage*. 13th ed. Revised by Alladi Kuppuswami. New Delhi: Bharat Law House, 1993.

Mayo, Katherine. *Mother India*. London: Jonathan Cape, 1927.

Minault, Gail. "Urdu Women's Magazines in the Early Twentieth Century." *Manushi*, no. 48 (September–October 1988): 2–9.

Mitter, Dwarka Nath. *The Position of Women in Hindu Law*. New Delhi: Inter-India Publications, 1913.

Moore, Erin. *Gender, Law and Resistance in India*. Tucson: University of Arizona Press, 1998.

Mukund, Kanakalatha. "Turmeric Land: Women's Property Rights in South India: A Review." *Economic and Political Weekly* 27, no. 17 (25 April 1992): WS2–WS6.

———. "Women's Property Rights in South India: A Review." *Economic and Political Weekly* 34, no. 22 (29 May 1999): 1352–1358.

Mulla, Dinshah Fardunji. *Principles of Hindu Law*. 8th ed. Revised by Vepa Ramesam. Calcutta: Eastern Law House, 1936.

Nair, Janaki. *Women and the Law in Colonial India: A Social History.* New Delhi: Kali for Women, 1996.

Natarajan, K. *Miss Mayo's Mother India: A Rejoinder.* Madras: G.A. Natesan, n.d.

Nishimura, Yuko. *Gender, Kinship and Property Rights: Nagarattar Womanhood in South India.* Delhi: Oxford University Press, 1998.

Oldenburg, Veena Talwar. *Dowry Murder: The Imperial Origins of a Cultural Crime.* Oxford: Oxford University Press, 2002.

Orr, Leslie. *Donors, Devotees, and Daughters of God: Temple Women in Medieval Tamilnadu.* New York: Oxford University Press, 2000.

Orsini, Francesca. "Domesticity and Beyond: Hindi Women's Journals in the Early Twentieth Century." *South Asia Research* 19, no. 2 (1999): 137–160.

Pandian, M. S. S. "Beyond Colonial Crumbs: Cambridge School, Identity Politics and Dravidian Movement(s)." *Economic and Political Weekly* (18–25 February 1995): 385–391.

Parashar, Archana. *Women and Family Law Reform in India.* New Delhi: Sage, 1989.

Pate, H. R. *Tinnevelly.* Vol. 1, *Madras District Gazetteers.* Madras: Government Press, 1917.

Price, Pamela. "Honor, Disgrace and the Formal Depoliticization of Women in South India: Changing Structures of the State under British Colonial Rule." *Gender & History* 6, no. 2 (August 1994): 246–264.

———. "Ideology and Ethnicity under British Imperial Rule: 'Brahmans,' Lawyers and Kin-Caste Rules in Madras Presidency." *Modern Asian Studies* 23, no. 1 (1989): 151–177.

———. "Kin, Clan, and Power in Colonial South India." In *Unfamiliar Relations: Family and History in South Asia,* ed. Indrani Chatterjee. Delhi: Permanent Black, 2004.

———. *Kingship and Political Practice in Colonial India.* Cambridge: Cambridge University Press, 1996.

Raman, Sita Anantha. "Crossing Cultural Boundaries: Indian Matriarchs and Sisters in Service." *Journal of Third World Studies* 18, no. 2 (Fall 2001): 131–148.

———. *Getting Girls to School: Social Reform in the Tamil Districts, 1870–1939.* Calcutta: Stree, 1996.

———. "Old Norms in New Bottles: Constructions of Gender and Ethnicity in the Early Tamil Novel." *Journal of Women's History* 12, no. 3 (Fall 2000): 93–119.

Ramanujan, A. K., trans. *The Interior Landscape: Love Poems from a Classical Tamil Anthology.* Bloomington: Indiana University Press, 1967.

Ramasami, E. V. *Periyar on Women's Rights.* Ed. K. Veeramani. Trans. R. Sundara Raju. Madras: Emerald, 1992.

Ramaswamy, Sumathi. *Passions of the Tongue: Language Devotion in Tamil India, 1891–1970.* Berkeley: University of California Press, 1997.

———. "Virgin Mother, Beloved Other: the Erotics of Tamil Nationalism in Colonial and Post-Colonial India." *Thamyris* 4, no. 1 (Spring 1997): 9–39.

Ramusack, Barbara. "Women's Organizations and Social Change: The Age-of-Marriage Issue in India." In *Women and World Change: Equity Issues in Development,* ed. Naomi Black and Ann Baker Cottrell. London: Sage, 1981.

Rangachari, K., and Edgar Thurston. *Castes and Tribes of Southern India.* Vol. 7 (T to Z). New Delhi: Asian Education Services, 1987.

Roy, Kumkum. "Unraveling the Kamasutra." In *A Question of Silence? The Sexual Economies of Modern India,* ed. Mary John and Janaki Nair. New Delhi: Kali for Women, 1998.

Rudner, David. *Caste and Capitalism in Colonial India: The Nattukottai Chettiars.* Berkeley: University of California Press, 1994.

Ryan, Mary. *Cradle of the Middle Class: The Family in Oneida County New York, 1790–1865.* Cambridge: Cambridge University Press, 1983.

Sangari, Kumkum, and Sudesh Vaid, eds. *Recasting Women: Essays in Indian Colonial History.* New Brunswick, N.J.: Rutgers University Press, 1990.

Sarda, Har Bilas. *Speeches and Writings.* Ajmer: Vedic Yantralaya, 1935.

Sarkar, Tanika. *Hindu Wife, Hindu Nation: Community, Religion, and Cultural Nationalism.* Bloomington: Indiana University Press, 2001.

Sen, Samita. "Offenses against Marriage: Negotiating Custom in Colonial Bengal." In *A Question of Silence? The Sexual Economies of Modern India,* ed. Mary E. John and Janaki Nair. New Delhi: Kali for Women, 1998.

Sen, Satadru. "Domesticated Convicts: Producing Families in the Andaman Islands." In *Unfamiliar Relations: Family and History in South Asia,* ed. Indrani Chatterjee. Delhi: Permanent Black, 2004.

Shah, A. M. *The Family in India: Critical Essays.* New Delhi: Orient Longman, 1998.

Shukla, Sonal. "Cultivating Minds: 19th Century Gujarati Women's Journals." *Economic and Political Weekly* 26, no. 43 (26 October 1991): WS63–WS66.

Sinha, Mrinalini. "Gender in the Critiques of Colonialism and Nationalism: Locating the 'Indian Woman.'" In *Feminism and History,* ed. Joan Wallach Scott. Oxford: Oxford University Press, 1996.

———. "The Lineage of the 'Indian' Modern: Rhetoric, Agency and the Sarda Act in Late Colonial India." In *Gender, Sexuality and Colonial Modernities,* ed. Antoinette Burton. London: Routledge, 1999.

———, ed. *Mother India: Selections from the Controversial 1927 Text.* Ann Arbor: University of Michigan Press, 2000.

———. *Specters of Mother India: The Global Restructuring of an Empire.* Durham, N.C.: Duke University Press, 2006.

Southall, Aidan. *Alur Society.* Cambridge: W. Heffer, 1956.

Spivak, Gayatri. "The Rani of Sirmur: An Essay in Reading the Archives." *History and Theory: Studies in the Philosophy of History* 24, no. 3 (1985): 247–272.

Sreenivas, Mytheli. "Conjugality and Capital: Gender, Families and Property under Colonial Law in India." *Journal of Asian Studies* 65, no. 4 (November 2004): 937–960.

———. "Emotion, Identity and the Female Subject: Tamil Women's Magazines in Colonial India." *Journal of Women's History* 14, no. 4 (Winter 2003): 59–82.

———. "Nationalizing Marriage in Tamil India, 1890s–1940s." Ph.D. diss., University of Pennsylvania, 2001.

Sreenivasan, Ramya. "Honoring the Family: Narratives and Politics of Kinship in Pre-colonial Rajasthan." In *Unfamiliar Relations: Family and History in South Asia,* ed. Indrani Chatterjee. Delhi: Permanent Black, 2004.

Stein, Burton. "Eighteenth Century India: Another View." *Studies in History* 5, no. 1 (1989): 1–26.

———, ed. *The Making of Agrarian Policy in British India, 1770–1900.* Delhi: Oxford University Press, 1992.

———. *Peasant State and Society in Medieval South India.* Delhi: Oxford University Press, 1994.

———. *Thomas Munro: The Origins of the Colonial State and His Vision of Empire.* Delhi: Oxford University Press, 1989.

Stoler, Ann Laura. *Carnal Knowledge and Imperial Power: Race and the Intimate in Colonial Rule.* Berkeley: University of California Press, 2002.

———. *Race and the Education of Desire: Foucault's History of Sexuality and the Colonial Order of Things.* Durham, N.C.: Duke University Press, 1995.

Stone, Lawrence. *The Family, Sex, and Marriage in England, 1500–1800.* New York: Harper and Row, 1997.

Subrahmanyam, Sanjay. *Penumbral Visions: Making Polities in Early Modern South India.* Ann Arbor: University of Michigan Press, 2001.

———. *The Political Economy of Commerce: Southern India, 1500–2002.* Cambridge: Cambridge University Press, 2002.

Subrahmanyam, Sanjay, and David Shulman. "The Men Who Would Be King? The Politics

of Expansion in Early 17th century Northern Tamilnadu." *Modern Asian Studies* 24, no. 2 (1990): 225–248.
Subramaniam, Lakshmi. *Indigenous Capital and Imperial Expansion: Bombay, Surat, and the West Coast.* Delhi: Oxford University Press, 1996.
Suntharalingam, R. *Politics and Nationalist Awakening in South India, 1852–1891.* Tucson: Arizona University Press, 1974.
Togo, S. A. Ramachandra. *Nāṭār Tirumaṇac Catañkukaḷ* (Nadar wedding customs). n.p., n.d.
Trawick, Margaret. *Notes on Love in a Tamil Family.* Berkeley: University of California Press, 1992.
Uberoi, Patricia, ed. *Family, Kinship and Marriage in India.* Delhi: Oxford University Press, 1993.
———, ed. *Social Reform, Sexuality and the State.* New Delhi: Sage, 1996.
Veeramani, K., ed. *Periyar on Women's Rights.* Madras: Emerald, 1992.
Venkatachalapathy, A. R. "Domesticating the Novel: Society and Culture in Inter-war Tamil Nadu." *Indian Economic and Social History Review* 34, no. 1 (1997): 53–67.
Viswanathan, Gauri. *Outside the Fold: Conversion, Modernity, and Belief.* Princeton, N.J.: Princeton University Press, 1998.
Walsh, Judith. *Domesticity in Colonial India: What Women Learned when Men Gave Them Advice.* Lanham, Md.: Rowan and Littlefield, 2004.
Washbrook, D. A. *The Emergence of Provincial Politics: The Madras Presidency, 1870–1920.* Cambridge: Cambridge University Press, 1976.
———. "Law, State, and Agrarian Society in Colonial India." *Modern Asian Studies* 15, no. 3 (1981): 649–721.
———. "Progress and Problems: South Asian Economic and Social History, c. 1720–1860." *Modern Asian Studies* 22, no. 1 (1988): 57–96.
Whitehead, Judy. "Modernizing the Motherhood Archetype: Public Health Models and the Child Marriage Restraint Act of 1929." In *Social Reform, Sexuality and the State,* ed. Patricia Uberoi. New Delhi: Sage, 1996.
Wink, Andre. *Land and Sovereignty in India: Agrarian Society and Politics under the 18th century Maratha Svarajya.* Cambridge: Cambridge University Press, 1986.

Newspapers and Journals

All-India Reporter, 1914–1965
Indian Ladies Magazine, 1903–1908, 1912–1913, 1918–1919, 1929–1932
Indian Law Reports, 1876–1878, 1889–1894, 1907–1964
Kalai Makaḷ, 1932–1935
Grihalakshmi, 1937–1940
Kuṭi Aracu, 1925, 1928–1933, 1935–1940, 1946–1948
Madras High Court Reports, 1870
Madras Law Journal, 1907–1963
Maṅkai, 1945–1946
Mātar Maṉōrañjini, 1905, 1916–1917
Mātar Maṟumaṇam, 1936–1939
Pakuttaṟivu, 1934–1935
Peṇ Kalvi, 1913–1916
Peṇmati Pōtini, 1892–1893
Puratci, 1934
Revolt, 1928
Stri Dharma, 1925–1935
Tirāviṭa Nāṭu, 1944–1962

Index

Italicized page numbers indicate illustrations.

Contemporary Indian Studies

Published in association with the
American Institute of Indian Studies

THE EDWARD CAMERON DIMOCK, JR. PRIZE
IN THE INDIAN HUMANITIES

Temple to Love: Architecture and Devotion in Seventeenth-Century Bengal
Pika Ghosh

Art of the Court of Bijapur
Deborah Hutton

THE JOSEPH W. ELDER PRIZE IN THE INDIAN SOCIAL SCIENCES

The Regional Roots of Developmental Politics in India: A Divided Leviathan
Aseema Sinha

Wandering with Sadhus: Ascetics in the Hindu Himalayas
Sondra L. Hausner

Wives, Widows, and Concubines: The Conjugal Family Ideal in Colonial India
Mytheli Sreenivas

Mytheli Sreenivas is Assistant Professor of History and Women's Studies at The Ohio State University.